ECONOMETRICS OF INVESTMENT

WILEY MONOGRAPHS IN APPLIED ECONOMETRICS

Editor

A. A. Walters, *Department of Economics, London School of Economics*

Commercial Bank Loan and Investment Behaviour
J. H. Wood,
University of Birmingham

Econometrics of Investment
J. C. R. Rowley,
Economic Council of Canada
and
P. K. Trivedi,
Australian National University

Further volumes in preparation

ECONOMETRICS OF INVESTMENT

J. C. R. ROWLEY
Economic Council of Canada
and
P. K. TRIVEDI
Australian National University

JOHN WILEY & SONS
London · New York · Sydney · Toronto

Library of Congress Cataloging in Publication Data:

Rowley, J.C.R.
    Econometrics of investment.
  Includes bibliographical references.
  1. Saving and investment. 2. Inventories.
  3. Econometrics. I. Trivedi, P.K., joint author.
  II. Title.
HB501.R77   332.6'01'82   74–32176

ISBN 0 471 74361 5

Photosetting by Thomson Press (India) Limited, New Delhi and printed in Great Britain by The Pitman Press, Bath, Avon.

EDITOR'S FOREWORD

Economics is a body of principles and a way of thinking that enables the professional economist to unravel practical problems and to make predictions of the consequences of specified actions. Many of these statements are scientific in the sense that one can examine the consequences of such actions in the real world to see if the theory predicted correctly. Such tests are the essence of scientific credibility. Any theory that fails to predict correctly should be rejected and one should retain propositions and pursue research programmes that have not been clearly discredited by their failure to forecast the essential or key events of the real world.

The economist can rarely resort to the dramatic evidence derived from contrived experiment. Like the astrophysicist he must be content with observations of natural or market phenomena. Although such observed data are the product of market and social processes and so do not possess the cloistered purity of experimental evidence, they are at least real-life events and are free from the antiseptic, artificial and often misleading environment of the laboratory. Analysis of the workings of the markets of the real world is, however, difficult and elusive. Econometrics was developed in order to enable one to sift the evidence of market observations into a form such that the propositions of economics can be tested. Considerable strides have been made in applying such techniques to various economies and there are many hard lessons that have been learned.

In this Series the authors attempt to give an account of the best econometric techniques now available in the context of some set of applied problems. The main focus is always on *practical* techniques that can be applied by virtually anyone with suitable computer access. In many problems, of course, it is still best to use simple methods of analysis; but it is one of the recurring themes of modern econometrics that however frequently simple methods may be usefully applied, in order to understand their subtleties one must be aware of the more complex and general methodology that underlies them.

The Series is devised for the practioner of econometrics—be he final year undergraduate, post-graduate student, thesis writer, civil servant, economic advisor, or any one of the many economists working in business and industry. We hope that the Series will have some effect in raising the standards of applied econometrics.

November 11, 1974   Alan A. Walters

PREFACE

We intend that this book, which contains a survey of critical issues and potential approaches, should be a contribution to 'applied econometrics'—a frontier zone of knowledge identified with the interactions of economic theory, statistical estimation of known structures, exploratory modelling of imprecise structures, statistical inference and the tentative use of empirical evidence. All of these components find some expression here. Undoubtedly some readers may be dissatisfied with our personal selection of material because we fail to 'do justice' to particular models or attitudes. Given the youth and vigour of applied econometrics, conflicting views as to appropriate emphases and topics seem to be inevitable. We hope that our ensemble will clearly illustrate the current state of affairs and provide some elements of a framework for future developments.

We also hope that our survey will prove a useful complement to the many works on applied econometrics which place greater emphasis on actual numerical results and their plausibility. We ourselves stress much more the wider issues such as the limitations inherent in current econometric practice, drawing our illustrations from the work on fixed and inventory investment. By escaping the morass of numerical detail, but using the concrete illustrations of general and local difficulties, we hope to stimulate the reader to think about those aspects of the econometric modelling process that interest him.

The book has six chapters, each of which is arranged in numbered sections. Asterisks are used to identify sections containing more difficult material. The first two chapter describe economic theories associated with empirical studies of real fixed capital formation and inventories. The final chapter presents some econometric evidence on inventories and contains a brief conclusion for the whole text. We feel that it is unnecessary to provide a detailed account of similar evidence for real fixed capital formation because several excellent surveys are readily available. Avoidance of this duplication enabled us to keep the size of this book manageable. In particular to overcome our omission, we recommend the surveys presented by Eisner and Strotz (1963), Meyer and Kuh (1957) and Jorgenson (1971) in addition to other comparative studies cited in the fourth chapter, one of our three short chapters describing more technical aspects of estimation. Some compensation for this asymmetry is reflected in the large number of references cited in the first chapter and in a bias toward illustrations drawn from empirical studies of fixed capital formation elsewhere.

Four important omissions must be acknowledged. First, we say little about the applicability of either bayesian or spectral approaches to estimation. Other researchers will later overcome this omission. Second, we generally restrict attention to single-equation problems in our technical chapters since to have adequately done otherwise would double the length of the book. Third, problems of measurement are seldom raised even though most contributors to our subject-matter are persistently confronted by them and several have initiated controversial debates concerning the measurement of particular aggregates. Our generation of econometricians became aware of difficulties through contact with the pessimism expressed by Morgenstern (1963). Readers might also follow the successive stages in the debate between Denison, Jorgenson and others cited in Section 1.1. Appropriate chapters in the official guide to British statistics, edited by Maurice (1968), are especially disturbing in view of their explicit statements on the reliability of data. Finally we do not explicitly deal with investment in residential construction whose importance in aggregate demand is considerable. The justification for this is simply the lack of space to deal satisfactorily with various aspects of this topic.

We have attempted to avoid mismatching of material wherever possible but some heterogeneity remains. Partly this is a consequence of geographical separation which we found to be a difficulty in coordinating our project. But partly this is attributable both to the nature of the subject matter and to the distinctive interests of the two authors.

In the preparation of the text, extensive prior discussions were made possible in the summer of 1972 by financial assistance from the Institute for Economic Research at Queen's University. We express our gratitude to the Economic Council of Canada, Queen's University, Statistics Canada and the Universities of British Columbia and Southampton for supporting this work at various stages. Many individual researchers have provided assistance beyond that to be expected from friendship. In particular, Carlton Braithwaite read several chapters and substantially improved their 'readability'. Grayham Mizon made some important suggestions and contributed two brief sections to Chapter Five. John Helliwell and Robert McRae helped with the illustrative dynamic simulations reported in Chapter Six. We also thank numerous colleagues who have taken the time and trouble to discuss individual sections of various chapters.

Economic Council of Canada   J. C. R. R.
University of Southampton   P. K. T.
October 1974

ACKNOWLEDGEMENTS

The authors wish to acknowledge the co-operation of the following for granting permission to reproduce passages of text from their publications.

Academic Press, Inc.
Page 24 (Treadway, 'Adjustment Costs and Variable Inputs in the Theory of the Competitive Firm', *Journal of Economic Theory*, 1970, **2**, 4, pp. 329–347)

American Economic Association
Page 20 (Eisner, 'Investment and the Frustrations of Econometricians' *American Economic Review*, May 1969)
Page 23 (Crain, 'Optimal Distributed Lag Responses and Expectations', *American Economic Review*, December 1971)
Page 43 (Georgescu-Roegen, 'The Economics of Production', *American Economic Review*, May 1970)

American Statistical Association
Page 83 (Merriwether, 'Small Sample Properties of Distributed Lag Estimators with Mis-specified Lag Structures', *Journal of the American Statistical Association*, **68**, 343, pp. 568–574).
Page 110 (Lovell and Prescott, 'Multiple Regression with Inequality Constraints: Pretesting Bias, Hypothesis Testing and Efficiency', *Journal of the American Statistical Association*, 1970, **65**, 330, pp. 913–925).
Pages 118 and 119 (Kruskal, 'Some Remarks on Wild Observations', *Technometrics*, 1960, 2, **1**, pp. 1–3).

American Telephone and Telegraph Company
Page 115 (Jorgenson, 'Investment Behavior', *The Bell Journal of Economics and Management Science*, 1972, **3**, 1, pp. 220–251).

Bureau of Economic and Business Research, University of Illinois
Page 28 (Modigliani and Cohen, *The Role of Anticipations and Plans in Economic Behaviour and Their Use in Economic Analysis and Forecasting*. Bureau of Economic and Business Research, University of Illinois, 1961).

Harvard Business School (Division of Research)
Page 120 (Meyer and Glauber, *Investment Decisions, Economic Forecasting, and Public Policy*, 1964).

Harvard University Press
Pages 30 and 116 (Meyer and Kuh, *The Investment Decision: An Empirical Inquiry*, 1957).

International Association for Research in Income and Wealth
Page 119 (Gordon, 'Measurement Bias in Price Indexes for Capital Goods', *Review of Income and Wealth*, 1971, Series 17, No. 2).

Iowa State University Press
Page 110 (Bancroft, *Statistical Papers in Honour of George W. Snedecor*, 1972).

James Nisbet & Co. Limited
Page 19 (Matthews, *The Trade Cycle*, 1959).

Macmillan
Pages 73 and 74 (Pearce, *International Trade*, 1970).

Mathematical Association of America
Page 2 (Evans 'The Dynamics of Monopoly' *The American Mathematical Monthly*, 1924, **31**, pp. 77–83).

National Bureau of Economic Research, Inc.
Page 27 (Hart 'Quantitative Evidence for the Interwar Period on the Course of Business Expectations: A Revaluation of the Shippers' Forecasts', in Hart, Modigliani and Orcutt, *The Quality and Economic Significance of Anticipations Data*, National Bureau of Economic Research, 1960).
Page 35 (Dhyrymes and Kurz, 'Investment, Dividend, and External Finance Behavior of Firms', in Ferber, *Determinants of Investment Behavior*, Colombia University Press, 1967).
Page 52 (Modigliani 'Business Reasons for Holding Inventories and Their Macro-economic Implications' in *Problems of Capital Formation: Concepts, Measurement and Controlling Factors*, National Bureau of Economic Research, 1957).

North Holland Publishing Company
Page 33 (Hochman, Hochman and Razin, 'Demand for Investment in Productive and Financial Capital' *European Economic Review*, 1973, **4**, 1, pp. 67–83).
Page 56 (Childs, *Inventories and Unfilled Orders*, 1967).
Pages 116 and 117 (Kuh, *Capital Stock Growth: A Micro-Econometric Approach*, 1963).
Page 117 (Fisher, *A Priori Information and Time Series Analysis*, 1962).
Page 155 (Balsey, *Industry Production Behaviour: The Order–Stock Distinction*, 1969).
Pages 165 and 166 (Lovell, 'Department Store Inventory, Sales, Order Relationships' in Duesenberry *et al. The Brookings Model: Some Further Results*, 1968).

Prentice-Hall Inc.
Page 4 (Hirshleifer, *Investment, Interest and Capital*, 1970).

Royal Statistical Society
Page 106 (Anscombe, 'Topics in the Investigation of Linear Relations Fitted by the Method of Least Squares' *Journal of the Royal Statistical Society*, Series B, 1967, **29**, pp. 1–59).

Society for Economic Analysis Limited
Page 23 (Gould, 'Adjustment Costs in the Theory of Investment in the Firm', *Review of Economic Studies*, 1968, **35(1)**, 101, pp. 47–55).
Page 47 (Kaldor, 'Speculation and Economic Stability' *Review of Economic Studies*, 1939, **7(1)**, pp. 1–27).
Page 90 (Schramm, 'The Influence of Relative Prices, Production Conditions and Adjustment Costs of Investment Behaviour', *Review of Economic Studies*, 37(3), 111, pp. 361–376).

The Brookings Institution
Page 118 (Bischoff, 'Business Investment in the 1970's: A Comparison of Models', *Brookings Papers on Economic Activity—1*, 1971).
Page 148 (Hickman, *Investment Demand and U.S. Economic Growth*, 1965).

University of Chicago Press
Page 9 (Jorgenson and Siebert, 'Optimal Capital Accumulation and Corporate Investment Behavior', *Journal of Political Economy*, 1968, **76**, no. 6).

CONTENTS

CHAPTER 1

Economic Theory (I): Fixed Capital Formation

Since the revival of interest in the dynamic behaviour of economic units, special attention has been given to fixed capital formation and its distribution. The acquisition and use of fixed real capital assets significantly affects the temporal stability and growth of these units' activities. During the last few decades, we have witnessed substantial efforts to establish the determinants of investment rates. However, these efforts have not yielded a stable image for determination. No single view, or even collection of views, can be said to have attained acceptance by a consensus of economists. To some extent, this failure may be due to the complexity of actual behavioural patterns in contrast to the explicit simplicity of most economic models for investment. Additional factors could include the inadequacies of available mathematical tools and, perhaps, a paucity of data in appropriate form or at appropriate levels of activity. We may, for example, have given insufficient attention to behaviour at the individual corporate level, to the institutional constraints reflecting rules of conduct within corporate bodies and to interfaces with financial markets, informational mechanisms and political forces.

The following outline of economic theories of investment does not provide a post-mortem for past failures. Instead it reflects qualified optimism, hopefully warranted, that many of the attitudes and issues that have emerged in the last three decades are appropriate bases for future progress. There is an emphasis on the need for eclecticism and flexibility. Some aspects of current debates are given more attention than they may deserve due to personal predilections, almost always unconscious, and other aspects are sometimes omitted even though they may prove to be significant. Thus a definitive account with comprehensive coverage must be sought elsewhere.

Our patchwork also omits many of the finer mathematical points but these may be pursued in the texts by Arrow and Kurz (1970), Intriligator (1971), Hadley and Kemp (1971) and in our particular citations. Note that a full understanding of contemporary contributions to economic literature is impossible without some familiarity with the calculus of variations and optimal control theory, albeit at an elementary level. This requirement is deliberately understated in the account provided here and, perhaps, overstated in some parts of the literature cited. Contributors frequently ignore a warning repeated by Evans (1924), who was one of the earliest users of these mathematical tools in this context, that the fascination of the calculus of variations 'is so great that neophytes seek to introduce it into problems which would otherwise be perfectly simple'!

Since many economic models of investment behaviour have continuous form whereas only discrete data are available, the relationships between models and their empirical approximations should be considered. There are some surprising difficulties of which an excellent account is provided by Telser and Graves (1972). Some econometric consequences are also discussed in a later chapter.

For convenience, the outline is arranged in six distinct sections. In view of the current inadequacies of our knowledge and the marked shifts in emphases which have been frequently experienced in the past, it would be foolish to assert that any particular approach is necessarily more appropriate than all others, or that any approach is wholly rejected as a basis for future developments. Also it should be remembered that distinct bipolarization of attitudes, which has been called the 'gladiatorial approach to economic theory', is a convenient but, sometimes, unfortunate fiction adopted by controversialists in academic debates. Thus an incomplete reading of economic literature with respect to investment might give the misleading impression that much of the recent theoretical work is devoted to the provision of support for either a 'position' which has been identified with Jorgenson or an alternative view associated with Eisner (or, in an earlier era, that it was preoccupied with the choice between the acceleration principle and an emphasis upon the restricted supply of residual funds available to firms). These conflicting choices represent only the more visible contributions in a heterogeneous process of development.

1.1 SIMPLE NEOCLASSICAL MODELS

Many distinct neoclassical models of investment behaviour have been put forward and certain of them continue to arouse considerable attention despite sustained criticisms of their primitive elements. Since adequate coverage is beyond the scope of the outline that is provided below, severe restrictions on inclusion are evident. Particular omissions of significance include the important contributions of Gordon (1962) and Modigliani and Miller (1958). These indicate a neglect of financial and valuation aspects. Fortunately Archer and D'Ambrosio (1967) have collected the views of many participants in the controversy initiated by Modigliani and Miller.

This portion of our brief outline has several parts. We begin with an account of myopic programmes for optimal capital accumulation when investment is reversible. Representative analyses have been provided in this context by Arrow (1964) and Jorgenson (1967, 1969). This account is followed by an indication of possible adjustments to acknowledge disequilibrium and variations in capacity-utilization. Finally, we cite some innovative studies concerning possible effects of uncertainty upon rates of investment and levels of capacity-utilization. Clearly, this is an area for important developments in the future. The increased complexity of stochastic models and availability of computational facilities will, perhaps, lead to a shift of emphasis from the recent search for analytical expressions, associating investment with its determinants, to an alternative search for iterative procedures as are usually involved in dynamic programming, 'learning-by-doing' and 'rules-of-thumb'. These procedures recognize the informational decision inherent in most decision situations and may be especially associated with 'fixity' characteristics of real assets and asymmetric relationships between the acquisition of these assets, their use and their disposal.

Basic reversible model

An essential feature of simple models for optimal capital accumulation is the assumption of a single active participant or a committee, a group of participants with a unified goal and identity, for each basic unit of choice. For example, we might envisage a single decision-maker who seeks to maximize the 'net worth' of the unit (that is, the present value of the stream of its net earnings over its temporal horizon plus the terminal valuation). To avoid complications associated with terminal valuation, it is convenient to assume that the decision-maker projects developments beyond his own lifetime and uses an infinite horizon for his plans. This simplification is, however, contrary to evidence provided by direct enquiries into the actual practices of decision-makers where short and variable horizons are usually indicated. Constraints are also imposed on productive activities and the discounting factor for future earnings so that the net worth is finite. In addition, within neoclassical frameworks, earnings are assumed to arise from the production and sale of outputs which have been transformed from a small collection of inputs by a smooth process without any period of gestation.

In this characterization, variable inputs are distinguished from capital inputs although paths for both types of inputs are chosen by the decision-maker to attain his objective. In some models, each capital input is affected by a constant rate of physical deterioration which causes the stream of capital services from a unit of capital stock to decline at an exponential rate as the age of the stock increases (or, alternatively for a large number of capital items of a given type, a constant rate of outright discards). Let this deterioration (or shrinkage) be termed capital consuption. In the absence of governmental intervention with respect to the taxation of earnings and restrictions on capital allowances, a continuous representation for this model with a single output may be expressed in the following algebraic forms:

$$\Phi(s) \equiv \int_{t=s}^{\infty} \mu(t,s) \left[p(t)Q(t) - \sum_{i=1}^{n} w_i(t)L_i(t) - \sum_{j=1}^{m} q_j(t)I_j(t) \right] dt, \qquad (1)$$

$$Q(t) = F(L_1(t),\ldots,L_n(t),K_1(t),\ldots,K_m(t);t) \quad \text{for all } t, \qquad (2)$$

$$\dot{K}_j(t) = I_j(t) - \delta_j K_j(t) \quad \text{for } j = 1,2,\ldots,m; \text{ all } t. \qquad (3)$$

In these specifications, p, w_i and q_j are the prices of output, the ith variable input and the jth capital input, respectively, whereas Q, L_i and I_j are the associated physical magnitudes. K_j is the net stock of the jth capital input when replacement investment in this input is assumed to equal its capital consumption. δ_j is the rate of physical deterioration or capital consumption of the jth capital input. For any arbitrary variable x, $\dot{x}$ is its rate of change dx/dt. The decision-maker attempts, at some fixed point in time s, to maximize $\Phi(s)$ subject to the constraints imposed by the production function (2) and the capital-consumption assumption (3). The function $\mu(t,s)$ is the discount factor at point of time s as it applies to net income occuring in the tth-period. Since a zero value for s does not cause any loss of generality, $\mu(t,0)$ may be replaced by $\mu(t)$ and the objective function treated as $\Phi(0)$. For convenience, the decision-maker is assumed to be a price-taker in all markets and to be free from other constraints affecting his activities.

If production possibilities are stable through time so that t can be removed as an explicit argument in (2), the objective of maximizing net worth can be identified with individual preferences under further restrictive conditions. Thus '... given perfect and complete markets, the productive decision is to be governed solely by the objective market criterion represented by attained wealth—without regard to the individuals' subjective preferences that enter into their consumptive decisions' (Hirshleifer, 1970, p. 63). Clearly this Separation Theorem indicates a very fragile basis for an assertion that the net worth criterion is necessarily superior to other criteria, although this fragility has not prevented such an assertion being made.

This model does not bound possible investment, which is then said to be 'reversible'. Arrow (1964) indicates two situations in which irreversibility, in the sense that gross investment must be non-negative, might not affect the conclusions based solely on (1), (2) and (3). For example, no explicit bound is needed if the non-negativity inequality is always satisfied by an optimal capital programme (for the equality-constrained model) or if the second-hand market for capital inputs is sufficiently efficient so that unnecessary capital stock can be sold at a price compatible with the price of new investment goods. The principal advantages of assuming complete reversibility arise, firstly, from the possibility of using the classical calculus of variations rather than more advanced techniques and, secondly, from the simplicity of the myopic rules established with reversibility. Unfortunately constraints on the rate of investment might be relevant for realistic models of actual investment behaviour; that is, the omission of these constraints may lead to predictive statements which are misleading and, perhaps, harmful if they form the bases for governmental actions. An excellent account of the implicit severity of constraints on reversibility is provided by Takayama (1972). He uses optimal control theory to investigate the essentially 'bang-bang' nature of optimal capital programme under such constraints. This is strictly analogous to the older discussions of ceilings and floors for economic activities.

In the simple reversible model, necessary conditions for optimality are provided by the Euler extremal conditions based on the augmented Lagrange functional,

$$
\begin{aligned}
\Phi^*(0) = \int_0^\infty \{ \mu(t)[p(t)Q(t) - \sum_{i=1}^n w_i(t)L_i(t) - \sum_{j=1}^m q_j(t)I_j(t)] \\
+ \lambda_0(t)[Q(t) - F(L_1(t),\dots,L_n(t),K_1(t),\dots,K_m(t))] \\
+ \sum_{j=1}^m \lambda_j(t)[\dot{K}_j(t) - I_j(t) + \delta_j K_j(t)] \} \, dt \\
= \int_0^\infty f(t)dt,
\end{aligned}
\tag{4}
$$

say, with $f(t)$ defined implicitly by comparison with (4). $\lambda_0(t), \lambda_1(t),\dots,\lambda_m(t)$ are Lagrange multipliers.

For notational simplicity, the subscript t may be omitted from the Euler conditions under the conventions that each symbol refers to a value at time t and each equation applies at each instance in the indefinite future. The optimality conditions are (2), (3),

$$
\frac{\partial f}{\partial Q} = \mu p + \lambda_0 = 0,
\tag{5}
$$

$$
\frac{\partial f}{\partial L_i} = -\mu w_i - \lambda_0 \frac{\partial F}{\partial L_i} = 0 \quad \text{for all } i,
\tag{6}
$$

$$
\frac{\partial f}{\partial I_j} = -\mu q_j - \lambda_j = 0 \quad \text{for all } j
\tag{7}
$$

and

$$
\frac{d(\partial f/\partial \dot{K}_j)}{dt} - \frac{\partial f}{\partial K_j} = \dot{\lambda}_j + \lambda_0 \frac{\partial F}{\partial K_j} - \lambda_j \delta_j = 0 \quad \text{for all } j.
\tag{8}
$$

Thus, for optimal input programmes,

$$
\frac{\partial F}{\partial L_i} = \frac{w_i}{p} \quad \text{for all } i,
\tag{9}
$$

from (5) and (6); and

$$
\frac{\partial F}{\partial K_j} = \frac{q_j(\delta_j - \dot{\mu}/\mu - \dot{q}_j/q_j)}{p} \quad \text{for all } j,
\tag{10}
$$

from (5), (7) and (8). These conditions are also sufficient for optimality under appropriate restrictions upon the production function.

Jorgenson describes $q_j(\delta_j - \dot{\mu}/\mu - \dot{q}_j/q_j)$, which we denote c_j, as 'the user cost of the jth capital input'. If the variable c_j is treated as a shadow price of the capital input, equations (9) and (10) resemble familiar conditions for static neoclassical models except that these equations hold for each instance. A relationship between the net-worth criterion and repetitive static profit-maximization is established by respecifying profit for the latter as $(pQ - \Sigma w_i L_i - \Sigma c_j K_j)$.

The conditions for optimality are myopic in the sense that, at any instance, the future path of net profits does not affect the conditions that represent the current decision. This myopia persists when more complicated specifications are made for capital consumption so that the instantaneous rate of discount $(-\dot{\mu}/\mu)$ and the deduction for capital gains $(\dot{q}_j/q_j)$ must be augmented in c_j by a weighted average of rates for capital consumption, which depends upon all future values of $\mu(t)$, instead of the single parameter δ_j associated with exponential deterioration.

Two frequent specifications for the production function (2) in empirical work based on this model are the Cobb–Douglas and Constant-Elasticity-of-Substitution (CES) characterizations. In these specific cases, optimal capital programmes have relatively simple expressions. Let asterisks identify optimal trajectories and suppose that the unidentified symbols which are used below represent fixed parameters. Then,

$$K_j^* \simeq \left(\frac{p}{c_j} Q^{\gamma-1}\right)^{\sigma} \tag{11}$$

if

$$Q^{\gamma} = \sum_{i=1}^{n} \alpha_i L_i^{\rho} + \sum_{j=1}^{m} \beta_j K_j^{\rho}$$

in (2) and $\sigma = 1/(\rho - 1)$;

$$K_j^* \simeq \frac{p}{c_j} Q \tag{12}$$

if

$$Q = \gamma \left(\prod_{i=1}^{n} L_i^{\alpha_i}\right)\left(\prod_{j=1}^{m} K_j^{\beta_j}\right)$$

in (2). These simple feedback rules are not found whenever these two popular specifications are replaced by any of the Variable-Elasticity-of-Substitution (VES) forms, which are being increasingly discussed in other contexts. Notice that, with the two popular forms and constant returns to scale, the optimal capital-output ratio depends only on the price ratio (p/c_j). Jorgenson (1972, pp. 245–8) provides a spirited defence for these restrictive assumptions with empirical evidence for the economy of the United States.

Variable utilization rates

Taubman and Wilkinson (1970a,b) indicate some 'realistic' modifications to the production function and the specifications for capital consumption which might be adopted in the model presented above. In particular, they suggest that the decision-maker has additional choices in the form of utilization rates for each of the stocks of capital inputs. Let H_j represent an index of utilization for the jth capital stock; that is, the rate at which a flow of capital services is obtained from this stock. Then the collection of these indices, which Jorgenson explicitly fixes at normalized unit values in his exposition of our preliminary model, may be introduced both as additional control arguments in the production function and as influences upon the rates of capital consumption $\delta_j(H_j)$. The instability of these indices leads to unanswered theoretical questions with respect to the determination of the prices for used capital inputs in the resale market. These prices would seem to depend upon the consumption rates $\delta_j(H_j)$ throughout the anticipated life of each unit of capital input and upon the rates at which future income is discounted. This dependence is extremely difficult to specify in a tractable mathematical model. For their dynamic model, Taubman and Wilkinson ignore this problem and treat all expected prices of inputs as proportional to the expected price of output, which is assumed to be generated by the familiar adaptive-expectations mechanism. (They modify the objective function by replacing all prices with expected prices, where expectations are formed at the point of decision.) These expectational assumptions are very restrictive and it is not clear that the Taubman–Wilkinson analyses add much to our understanding of investment behaviour as they present them. However, their suggestions with respect to rates of utilization are potentially very significant.

Since the inclusion of variable rates for utilization of capital stocks leads to unresolved theoretical problems, many empirical studies have adopted alternative schemes based upon 'reference' series for utilization. Thus data for output, unemployment, utilization of electrical power sources and several other variables have been used to derive indices of utilization. These indices are usually introduced as simple multiplicative adjustment factors associated with stocks of inputs in the production function. The influences on capital consumption and prices of variations in utilization rates are ignored and reference series are often presented without acknowledgement of the added dimensions of the choice of utilization rates by the decision-maker. For example, Okun and Solow have popularized the use of data for unemployment to form indices of utilization which apply equally to all inputs. The Wharton Index is based on an alternative approach. It represents a comparison of the level of output with the value provided by a trend through peaks in the series for output. (See Klein and Preston, (1967).) Following earlier work by Foss (1963), Jorgenson and Griliches (1967) derive a reference series for the relative utilization of electric motors in the U.S. manufacturing sector. They assume that the relative utilization of capital inputs is the same for all inputs and for all sectors. Further, they assume that their reference series for electric power is an appropriate proxy for this uniform rate of utilization. After valid criticism by Denison (1969), who asserts that the imposition of a uniform rate will introduce errors of measurement, this technique has been modified and some of the earlier conclusions revised by Christensen and Jorgenson (1969). A survey of these developments is provided by Nadiri (1970) and the principal contributions to the debate between Denison and Jorgenson and Griliches are reproduced in the *Survey of Current Business* (May 1972).

Two-step adjustment mechanism

Further modifications to the simple neoclassical model may be found in our later discussions of costs for installation and adjustment of capital inputs and policies for fiscal and monetary controls as assessed within this theoretical framework. Attention is directed here at the significant difficulty in using the model as a basis for empirical assessments. This difficulty is persistent and later modifications will not eliminate it. In many fits for the U.S. economy, Jorgenson and his associates interpret K_j^* as a moving target value so that investment behaviour follows the discrete adjustment path

$$I_j(t) = \frac{B^h a(B)(1-B)}{b(B)} K_j^*(t) + \delta_j K_j(t), \tag{13}$$

where $a(B)$ and $b(B)$ are polynomials in the lag operator B, which is defined for arbitrary variable $x(t)$ by the equality of $x(t-1)$ and $Bx(t)$. h is a positive integer which indicates an important delay of response. It is frequently chosen by reference to existing direct evidence on lead times as presented, for example, by Mayer (1960). Notice that the transfer function of dependence between K_j^* and I_j in (13), $[B^h a(B)(1-B)/b(B)]$, is identical for each determinant of K_j^*. This specification may be excessively restrictive and would introduce errors of measurement if applied when incorrect. The consequences for estimation and use of fitted relations are discussed later in Chapter Three. Suppose $b(B)$ is $[1-Bg(B)]$ where $g(B)$ is another polynomial in the lag operator, then (13) may be arranged as

$$I_j^n(t) = g(B)I_j^n(t-1) + a(B)[K_j^*(t-h) - K_j^*(t-h-1)], \tag{14}$$

where

$$I_j^n(t) \equiv I_j(t) - \delta_j K_j(t). \tag{15}$$

A stochastic error is usually added to this form and the parameters of $g(B)$ and $a(B)$ estimated by the least-squares technique. The sequence of additional errors for any sample are usually assumed to be independently and identically distributed with finite variances. Clearly, if these errors are more appropriately added to (13), then least-squares estimates based on (14) will be affected by the contemporaneous occurrence of a moving-average generating process for the errors and lagged dependent variables. Use of the popular autoregressive transformation or the Hildreth–Lu approach would not eliminate the auto-correlation which results for (14).

The discrete adjustment path (13) is an addendum to the simple neoclassical model, which ignores the constraint imposed upon optimal programmes for inputs by the existence of delays in response. There seems to be an intrinsic contradiction in this procedure. Why should the decision-maker adjust to a moving target path which ignores an important constraint on his actions? This important question remains unanswered. Instead, numerous rationalizations for the two-step procedure have been propounded. For example, Jorgenson and Siebert (1968a, p. 1124) assert 'By permitting discrepancies between desired and actual levels of capital, the model can incorporate the effects of gestation lags in investment and lags between actual and expected values of the determinants of investment. With perfect foresight, the actual and expected values of these determinants would be identical and the actual level of capital would always equal the desired level. Thus, we relax the assumption of perfect foresight that underlies conventional treatments of the neoclassical theory of optimal capital accumulation.' Persistent use of the two-step procedure should probably be attributed to mathematical difficulties in the derivation of tractable forms for empirical studies from models which explicitly acknowledge constraints on adjustment. An additional problem arises from the procedure when a choice is to be made between different theoretical models on the basis of empirical results. This choice is invariably confounded by additional post-model speci-fications as represented by the adjustment path in (13).

When the Cobb–Douglas form of the production function is chosen, the least-squares fit for (14) is straightforward and yields an estimate of β_j, as well as estimates for the parameters previously cited. However, if the CES form is chosen, the method of estimation must be modified unless both γ and α are known. Rowley (1970) indicates an approximation which permits the least-squares technique to be used even when these parameters are unknown. This approximation requires the inclusion of additional linear adjustment factors and is discussed in Chapter Four.

Introduction of the discrete adjustment path is an explicit recognition of disequilibrium as the assertion by Jorgenson and Siebert rightly suggests. Whether it is an appropriate recognition depends upon the response to the question posed above. Thurow (1969) has produced estimates based upon an alternative characterization of disequilibrium. Suppose we represent the earlier expression for c_j as c_j^* (the user cost of the jth capital input in equilibrium) and use $\bar{c}_j$ to denote the current rate of return on capital. In the absence of governmental intervention, this is given by

$$\bar{c}_j(t) \equiv \frac{p(t)Q(t) - \sum_i w_i(t)L_i(t) - \sum_j q_j(t)I_j(t)}{K_j(t-1)} \tag{16}$$

Thurow suggests an alternative discrete adjustment path of the form

$$I_j(t) = \frac{B^h a(B)(1-B)}{b(B)} \bar{K}_j(t) + \delta K_j(t-1), \tag{17}$$

where

$$\frac{\bar{K}_j(t)}{K_j(t-1)} \equiv \frac{\bar{c}_j(t) - c_j^*(t)}{\bar{c}_j(t)}$$

This specification is based on the Cobb–Douglas production function with constant returns to scale.

Thurow's estimates are especially significant. As he suggests, if they are contrasted with the results of Jorgenson and his associates, they reveal the importance of post-model specifications. Very different pictures of the investment process emerge from the two choices of adjustment mechanisms. Since this simple choice does not exhaust the list of potential mechanisms and the differences are so marked, economists must exercise sufficient self-restraint before using the results from a single specification as the basis for advice sought by governmental decision-makers. Future theoretical developments may eliminate the problem of sensitivity by making the two-step procedure redundant.

Uncertainty

Only deterministic models have been cited above. In most practical situations, decision-makers are subject to uncertainties arising in a number of different ways. First, they may be uncertain about the output which will be obtainable from given levels of factor inputs due perhaps to imprecise knowledge of the productive processes. Then they may be uncertain about the prices which their outputs will obtain or about the prices facing them in factor markets. Part of the problem could stem from the need to predict how other market-participants will act. It has also been pointed out that, in conflict situations, rational behaviour by individual decision-makers could involve deliberate acts creating further uncertainties to mislead or to increase the informational costs of competitors. In addition, decision-makers may be faced with uncertainties about the supply of investment goods or those of other inputs in present and future periods.

Recognition of uncertainty in economics has a long history but its integration into mathematical models of economic behaviour for investment is of relatively recent vintage. Borch (1973) describes the attitudes of the early Austrian School to uncertainties affecting knowledge of the productive processes while the work by Tintner (1941) may signal the onset of more formal approaches. Tintner pointed out that, if output from given levels of factor inputs is uncertain, then so is profit. The proposition can be extended to involve other sources of uncertainties and it is now generally accepted that profit-maximization is a vacuous criterion for optimality in the presence of uncertainty.

We can distinguish two broad streams in recent theoretical attempts to modify standard models and predictions by the explicit introduction of uncertain elements. One concerns analyses of individual decision-makers attempting to maximize expected profits. Three representative examples are given below. The other stream emphasizes wider considerations such as incomplete markets and the impact of diverse ownership in money capital markets.

As our first illustration of the more narrow stream, Hartman (1972) examines the effects on investment of increased uncertainty in wage-rates and the future prices of investment goods and output. Smith (1969, 1970) chooses an alternative approach. He considers the role of demand uncertainties in the decisions of a monopolistic firm as they affect the price of output, utilization of capital stock, and investment in real fixed assets. Finally, Kamien and Schwartz (1972) investigate the optimal capital stock for a firm which is uncertain as to the time of a rival's entry into its market.

In a neoclassical model with constant returns to scale in production, Hartman restricts investment by installation costs (as discussed in a later section) and the prices of output by a stationary subjective distribution. In this framework, he suggests that increased uncertainty in either the price of output or wage-rates will lead to a non-negative change in current investment. Further, more uncertainty in the installation or adjustment costs for investment leaves current investment unaffected. Clearly these optimal strategies are dependent upon the restrictive characteristics of Hartman's model.

The acute sensitivity of theoretical results to prior model specification is also demonstrated by Smith. His neoclassical model includes a utilization factor which is multiplicative with capital stock as an argument for a linear homogeneous production function. This factor affects the depreciation-in-use of capital stock. In Smith's models, output is determined by the level of demand which is either exogenous or dependent upon both exogenous stochastic factors and the price of output. The relationship between optimal capital stock and uncertainty appears to depend critically upon particular specifications for the form of the production function and the determination of demand. For example, if price is fixed and demand exogenous, the optimal capital stock will be larger as the variance of demand increases provided the elasticity of substitution does not exceed unity. With alternative specifications where demand depends upon endogenous price, a contrary prediction is indicated. Utilization of capital declines as uncertainty of demand increases for both specifications.

The work by Kamien and Schwartz opens a wide area for study. They suggest that optimal capital stock will depend upon the discount rate for future income and on the anticipated delay for entry of a competitor. The recognition that alternative market structures must be considered is clearly significant. It is also an important consideration in studies within the wider stream to which we turn briefly. A useful introduction to these studies is provided by Leland (1974).

The existence of money capital markets suggests another area where uncertainty might occur. It could affect the behaviour of owners of firms as well as the (managerial) decision-makers considered above, where the latter are assumed to act in the interests of the former. Then the principle of maximizing expected profits may be difficult to reconcile with financial equilibrium as multiple owners, with different expectations of yields and different attitudes to risk, adjust their individual portfolios of finanacial assets. Many contributors to the second stream have sought to establish whether some form of unanimity might arise here with respect to managerial decisions, affecting production and the choice of input levels. Leland shows that such unanimity of stock-holders can occur in many uncertain situations. He also concludes that, in a stochastic environment, production and financial variables are inextricably interrelated. This is a more complex view of behaviour than is presented in the simple neoclassical models cited earlier. It may serve as a bridge to the eclectic models described in Section 1.5.

1.2 REPLACEMENT INVESTMENT*

Many recent empirical investigations of fixed capital formation have partitioned gross investment expenditures into two broad categories which have been labelled 'net investment' and 'replacement investment'. The former is usually explained in terms of the levels and changes in the levels of other economic variables and it may be further partitioned into other categories such as 'induced' and 'autonomous' (see, for example, Youngson (1956) and Horvat (1958)), whereas the latter is frequently treated as independent of such influences. In particular, there has been a growth in the practice of assuming that replacement investment is mechanistic and that it may be eliminated from the analysis by subtraction of some proportion of estimated capital stock from gross investment as in equations (13)–(15), (17) above. An account of an asymptotic result that has been used to justify this practice is given below. The practice is non-trivial since the proportion of gross investment expenditures assessed as replacement (and capital consumption) usually falls in the range from 50 to 80 per cent depending upon the measures of capital stock used and the economies covered. Since this proportion is assumed to be independent of the direct influences of governmental instruments, governmental control of investment expenditures is inevitably affected by long adjustment lags.

The proportionality hypothesis

Symbols introduced above are maintained. $R_j(t)$ and $I_j^n(t)$ represent replacement and net investment in the jth fixed input respectively within the tth time period. Initially, only one fixed input is used so the j-subscript is suppressed. The basic model is represented by two equations in discrete form:

$$K(t + 1) = K(t) + I(t) - R(t), \tag{18}$$

$$R(t) = \sum_{i=0}^{\infty} m(i,t) I(t - i - b), \tag{19}$$

with weights $m(i,t)$ to be specified. b is a positive integral lag between the purchase of fixed inputs and the onset of capital consumption. These equations are non-contentious in the absence of technical progress. (18) is simply a definition of changes in capital stock, whereas (19) is an amalgam of the proposition that capital consumption is immediately replaced by new purchases with an accounting list for capital consumption. Thus $m(i,t)$ is the proportion of gross investment in the $(t - i - b)$th period that is consumed and replaced in the tth period.

The proportionality hypothesis is derived by imposition of the following set of sufficient conditions upon the basic model (18) and (19) and an approximation.

(A1) The weights $\{m(i,t)$ for $i = 0, 1, 2,...$ and all $t\}$ are constant over time. They can therefore be individually represented as $m(i)$ and collectively characterized by the coefficients of a stationary generating function $M(\cdot)$. (See Rowley (1973, Ch. 3).) To conserve notation, B is used as a symbol for the lag operator and, also, for an arbitrary complex variable in the generating function.

$$
\begin{aligned}
R(t) &= \sum_{i=0}^{\infty} m(i) I(t - i - b) \\
&= \sum_{i=0}^{\infty} m(i) B^{i+b} I(t) \\
&= B^b [m(0) + m(1)B + m(2)B^2 + ...] I(t) \\
&= B^b M(B) I(t),
\end{aligned}
\tag{20}
$$

where $M(B) \equiv \sum_{i=0}^{\infty} m(i) B^i$ is the generating function of the weights.

(A2) $M(B)$ is a rational function; that is, we can find finite polynomials $U(B)$ and $V(B)$, without common zeros, such that $M(B)$ is the ratio $U(B)/V(B)$. (A constant c is a zero of $M(B)$ if $M(c)$ is zero.)

(A3) $V(B)$ is a polynomial of order s, which is at least unity.

(A4) $U(B)$ has lower order than $V(B)$.

(A5) The zeros of $V(B)$ are both distinct and real. Let these zeros be represented by $B_1, B_2,..., B_s$. Then, $V(B)$ can be represented as

$$
V(B) = \alpha \prod_{h=1}^{s} (B - B_h),
$$

where α is a scale factor.

(A6) The absolute value of B_1 is lower than the absolute value of any other zero of $V(B)$.

Suppose these assumptions are acceptable, then

$$M(B) = \frac{U(B)}{V(B)}$$

$$= \frac{U(B)}{\alpha \prod\limits_{h=1}^{s} (B - B_h)}$$

$$= \sum_{h=1}^{s} n_h (B_h - B)^{-1} \text{ for a collection of constants } \{n_h\}$$

$$= \sum_{h=1}^{s} \frac{n_h}{B_h} \left(1 - \frac{B}{B_h}\right)^{-1}$$

$$= \sum_{h=1}^{s} \frac{n_h}{B_h} \sum_{j=0}^{\infty} \left(\frac{B}{B_h}\right)^{j}$$

where B is constrained so that the additional expansion converges.

$$M(B) = \sum_{j=0}^{\infty} \left[\sum_{h=1}^{s} \frac{n_h}{B_h^{j+1}}\right] B^{j}.$$

Thus, by comparison with the definition of $M(B)$, the initial weights $m(i)$ can be identified with sums of s quotients involving n_h and B_h;

$$m(i) = \sum_{h=1}^{s} \frac{n_h}{B_h^{i+1}} \qquad \text{for } i = 0, 1, 2,\dots.$$

For large i, (A6) implies that we can approximate $m(i)$ by the geometric progression

$$\hat{m}(i) = \frac{n_1}{B_1^{i+1}} \qquad \text{for } i = 0, 1, 2,\dots.$$

Let $\hat{M}(B)$ represent the generating function of these approximate weights.

$$\hat{M}(B) \equiv \sum_{i=0}^{\infty} \hat{m}(i) B^{i}$$

$$= \sum_{i=0}^{\infty} \frac{n_1}{B_1^{i+1}} B^{i}$$

$$= \frac{n_1}{B_1} \sum_{i=0}^{\infty} \left(\frac{B}{B_1}\right)^{i}$$

$$= \frac{n_1}{B_1 - B}.$$

For further accounts of this approximation, its mathematical basis in partial-fraction expansions, and definitional expressions for the weights $\{n_h\}$ see Feller (1965). Suppose we approximate $M(B)$ by $\hat{M}(B)$ in (20) so that approximate replacement investment, $\hat{R}(t)$, is given by

$$\hat{R}(B) \equiv \frac{B^b n_1}{B_1 - B} I(t)$$

or

$$B_1 \hat{R}(t+b) = \hat{R}(t+b-1) + n_1 I(t). \tag{21}$$

Substitute $I(t)$ from this equation in (18) and we obtain an approximation, $\tilde{R}(t)$ say, in terms of capital stock:

$$K(t+1) = K(t) + \frac{1}{n_1}[B_1 \tilde{R}(t+b) - \tilde{R}(t+b-1)] - \tilde{R}(t)$$

or

$$\tilde{R}(t+b) = \frac{n_1(1-B)}{B_1 - B - n_1 B^b} K(t+1). \tag{22}$$

(A7) The weights of the approximation for $M(B)$ should be normalized so that they sum to unity on the grounds that all investments in real fixed assets are eventually replaced. That is, $\hat{M}(1)$ is unity or n_1 is equal to $(B_1 - 1)$.

This normalization constraint is used to simplify (21) by eliminating B_1.

$$\tilde{R}(t+b) = \frac{n_1(1-B)}{n_1 + 1 - B - n_1 B^b} K(t+1). \tag{23}$$

Clearly, the relationship between capital stock and the approximation for replacement investment is a simple constant if b has a unit value. In that case $\tilde{R}(t)$ is equal to $\delta K(t)$ where δ is $n_1/(n_1 + 1)$. This is the proportionality hypothesis.
For $b \geq 2$,

$$\tilde{R}(t+b) = \frac{n_1}{n_1 + 1 + n_1 \sum\limits_{j=1}^{b-1} B^j} K(t+1).$$

$$= \frac{\delta}{1 + \delta \sum\limits_{j=1}^{b-1} B^j} K(t+1),$$

so that we have

$$\tilde{R}(t+b) = \delta[K(t+1) - \sum_{j=1}^{b-1} \tilde{R}(t+b-j)]. \tag{24}$$

If the proportionality hypothesis is accepted as a sufficiently close approximation so that its error can be ignored, then it also provides a method of measurement for capital. Thus, if $K(0)$ and $K(T)$ are two bench-marks for capital stock,

$$K(T) = (1 - \delta)^T K(0) + \sum_{j=0}^{T-1} (1 - \delta)^j I(T - j - 1) \tag{25}$$

from the hypothesis and repeated use of (18). Knowledge of these bench-marks and the stream of gross investment expenditures can be the basis for a polynomial equation in δ with known coefficients. Solution of this equation yields an estimate of δ. (See Jorgenson and Stephenson (1967a, p. 218).) Unfortunately the data for bench-marks need to be justified. The use of book values for these data requires special pleading as provided, for example, in the discussion of duality between replacement and depreciation by Jorgenson (1974). This theoretical pleading should be contrasted with empirical evidence to the extent that the latter is available. As early as 1947, Leontief asserted that use of depreciated coefficients implies that capital stocks decrease in efficiency in exact relation to the depreciation charge. Most available evidence indicates that this is not a reasonable assumption. Recent evidence and commentaries may be found in contributions to the dispute between Denison and Jorgenson and Griliches, which were cited above, and in Jorgenson (1974).

Empirical background

The scarcity of data for replacement investment and the convenience of the proportionality hypothesis are two well-established justifications for its use. However, as appropriate data become available, they provide some new bases for tests of the approximation. Eisner (1972), Feldstein and Foot (1971), Feldstein (1974) and Foot (1970) cite empirical results based on new American data. Their estimated coefficients and test statistics suggest rejection of the hypothesis. Clearly many different fits might be considered. A simple one which could be based on equation (21) is

$$\tilde{R}(t + b) = (1 - \delta)\tilde{R}(t + b - 1) + \delta I(t) \qquad \text{for any } b \geq 0. \tag{26}$$

For the special case of the proportionality hypothesis (with a value of unity for b), this becomes

$$\tilde{R}(t + 1) - \tilde{R}(t) = \delta I^n(t), \quad I^n(t) \equiv I(t) - \tilde{R}(t). \tag{27}$$

This particular specification is investigated by Feldstein who introduces an additive normal error and constant. He tests the linear hypotheses that δ and the coefficient for the constant are zero. An alternative test may be based on (14). Jorgenson (1965) adds replacement investment to both sides of this equation so that the dependent variable becomes gross investment whilst $K(t)$ is an additional explanatory term. The least-squares estimate of δ from this specification is compared with the value calculated from the polynomial equation described above. Since the latter value has been used to calculate both net investment and user-cost, its mis-specification must affect the power of this test. (See Griliches (1968, p. 217).)

If the proportionality hypothesis is rejected, some alternative approach must be adopted. Feldstein and Rothschild (1974) have attempted to develop an economic model of replacement as a feasible alternative. A number of other economists reject empirical attempts to partition gross investment expenditures. They treat them all as determined by the same collection of economic influences. Interviews conducted for the Illinois project, which are reported in Eisner (1956), and elsewhere give partial support to this approach.

The assumptions which form the basis for the proportionality hypothesis are extremely restrictive. Suppose we reject (A2)–(A5) on the grounds that all fixed inputs provide services for only a finite number of time periods. Thus, there exists a positive integer ξ such that the weights $m(i)$ in (A1) are zero for i greater than this integer. Then (20) can be written as

$$R(t) - \sum_{i=0}^{\xi} m(i)R(t-i-b) = \sum_{i=0}^{\xi} I^n(t-i-b). \tag{28}$$

This equation can be interpreted as a non-homogeneous difference equation in replacement investment. Its general solution is the sum of a particular solution for (28) and a general solution for the homogeneous equation

$$[1 - \sum_{i=0}^{\xi} m(i)B^{i+b}]R(t) = 0. \tag{29}$$

The latter is the source of 'pure replacement cycles' whereas the former is the source of 'derived cycles' (in the terminology introduced by Einarsen (1938)). Necessary and sufficient conditions for the pure cycles to be damped are given by Howrey (1965) in terms of the primitivity of the companion matrix of the coefficients $m(i)$.

Jorgenson (1965) suggests that the earlier study by Meyer and Kuh (1957) failed to reveal the 'echo effect' of bunched replacement investments identified with pure cycles. He interprets this as an indirect test of the proportionality hypothesis. Clearly there are no pure cycles generated by the homogeneous part of (27). In fact, the data of Meyer and Kuh may not provide an appropriate framework for distinguishing between pure and derived cycles. They found a 'senility effect' whereby financially conservative managements tended to retain stocks of capital inputs for longer periods than those used by other managements. This appears to be contrary to any mechanistic interpretation of replacement and, in their subsequent investigations in this field, both Meyer and Kuh have separately treated gross investment expenditures as if there were no adequate empirical foundation for explicitly partitioning them.

Two other areas of concern may be associated with the proportionality hypothesis. First, although its bases are more easily imposed upon individual capital inputs, the hypothesis has been used at many different levels of aggregation. Often several levels are used by researchers in empirical work without any assessment of the difficulties that arise in attempts to reconcile distinct approximations at different levels. Second, the hypothesis involves an assumption of separability whereby the rate of physical deterioration for any given capital input is wholly independent of all uses of other inputs. The neglect of potential interactions between capital inputs should be contrasted with the very detailed treatments of tax practice which are provided in the same studies

1.3   COSTS OF ADJUSTMENT AND THE FLEXIBLE ACCELERATOR

The 'acceleration principle' has a long history of use in economics. In the original formulation by Clark (1917), changes in the stock of real fixed assets were assumed to be proportional to positive rates of change in output over appropriate intervals. (Its applicability has also been extended to changes in inventories as Chapter Two makes clear.) Thus, in the notation of earlier sections, the simplest representations of the 'accelerator' are

$$(I - R)_t = \beta(Q_t - Q_{t-1}),\tag{30}$$

where β is a positive 'accelerator coefficient' with a time dimension, and

$$(I - R)_t = \beta(Q_{t-s} - Q_{t-s-1})\tag{31}$$

with a discrete lagged effect over s time-periods. Clearly these representations have to be qualified. The principle is not as rigid as they suggest. In a more recent expression, it asserts the readily acceptable proposition that fixed investment will tend to be positively related to increases in output which are considered to be 'permanent' by the decision-maker. This might be represented by

$$(I - R)_t = \sum_{j=1}^{n} \beta_j(Q_{t-s-j} - Q_{t-s-j-1})\tag{32}$$

$$= b(B)B^s(1 - B)Q_t,$$

where B is the lag operator and $b(B)$ is the polynomial

$$b(B) = \beta_1 B + \beta_2 B^2 + \ldots + \beta_n B^n.$$

Here the distributed lag of changes in output is being used as an indicator of the permanence of these changes, s time periods is an appropriate interval for gestation as before and n is the duration time for the formation of expectations on the basis of available evidence.

Additional flexibility in formal specifications was introduced by Goodwin (1948) and Chenery (1952) with use of the concept of 'desired' stock or 'equilibrium' stock of real fixed assets, represented here by K^*. This flexible accelerator might be written in the form

$$(I - R)_t = \beta(K_t^* - K_{t-1}),\tag{33}$$

or, with a distributed effect, as

$$(I - R)_t = b(B)(K_t^* - K_{t-1}).\tag{34}$$

Desired capital stock might depend upon output and, perhaps, upon other economic influences. For example, in a discrete representation of Goodwin's specification, K^* is the linear function of output $(\alpha_0 + \alpha_1 Q_t)$, where α_0 and α_1 are unknown parameters. On substitution in (33), this implies

$$(I - R)_t = \beta(\alpha_0 + \alpha_1 Q_t - K_{t-1}).\tag{35}$$

A simple comparison of either (33) or (34) with the earlier emphasis on the change in output does not explicitly make clear why these equations are associated with acceleration. However this association can readily be established with simple manipulation. Since net investment may be written as $(1 - B)K_t$, we have

$$(1 - B)K_t = b(B)(K_t^* - K_{t-1})$$

from (34), so

$$[1 - B + Bb(B)]K_t = b(B)K_t^*.$$

Thus, subject to qualifications on the form of $b(B)$,

$$(1 - B)K_t = W(B)(1 - B)K_t^*, \tag{36}$$

where

$$W(B) \equiv \frac{b(B)}{1 - B + Bb(B)}.$$

Thus

$$(I - R)_t = W(B)(K_t^* - K_{t-1}^*) \tag{37}$$

and

$$(I - R)_t = \alpha_1 W(B)(Q_t - Q_{t-1}), \tag{38}$$

using Goodwin's specification. The distributed lag in this form has infinite length

$$W(B) = W_0 + W_1 B + W_2 B^2 + \dots$$

with individual weights $\{W_j\}$ depending only on the parameters of $b(B)$. For example, when $b(B)$ is a simple scalar β,

$$W(B) = \frac{\beta}{1 - (1 - \beta)B}$$
$$= \beta[1 + (1 - \beta)B + (1 - \beta)^2 B^2 + \dots].$$

Equation (35) has been termed the 'stock adjustment principle' but its basis in acceleration has almost always been explicitly recognized as, for example, by Matthews (1959) who indicated that 'investment decisions will vary directly with the level of national income and inversely with the stock of capital in existence. This incorporates the basic idea of the acceleration principle, that investment will be directed towards bringing the stock of capital into alignment with the level of income recently prevailing, without attempting any undue precision.'

The outstanding exponent of the acceleration principle in recent empirical work is Eisner, who in a lengthy series of papers (1960, 1963, 1964, 1967 and 1969) explored its explanatory power for the U.S. economy, sometimes by contrast with alternative approaches emphasizing profits or the residual funds of purchasing corporations. Eisner's formulations, however, are markedly different from the simple distributed lag in form (32), which provided his starting point. For example, Eisner often uses gross investment expenditures divided by the value of gross fixed assets in some initial or reference period as his dependent variable. (This 'deflation' of variables is motivated by the desire to avoid heteroscedastic error terms.) These expenditures are explained by a long sequence of changes in sales, divided by the average level of sales in a number of observational periods, and by depreciation changes and post-tax profits, again divided by the value of gross fixed assets in the initial period. Notice that no distinction is made here between investment for expansion and investment for replacement of existing assets. Substantial experience with interviews and questionnaires failed to reveal to Eisner any acceptable basis in actual behaviour for partitioning gross investment expenditures into these two categories. This contrasts with the wide-spread adoption of the simple proportionality hypothesis for replacement expenditures, and is an addendum to the acceleration principle.

For one particular specification, Eisner (1969) found that the elimination of growth in sales would, on average, reduce gross investment expenditures by about a quarter. The supplementary (to acceleration) variables and constant term affect the remaining three-quarters of expenditures. Here the principal determinant appeared to be depreciation charges although the size of the constant term indicated that twenty per cent of investment was independent of variables explicitly introduced in the model. Although Eisner found 'differences in results from the various groupings of individual firm, industry and aggregate cross-sections, time-series and overall regressions', these empirical results clearly indicate both a role for the acceleration principle and a substantial need for the recognition of other factors in the determination of investment expenditures.

Many other researchers have adopted the alternative flexible accelerator, (33) and (34), often expressing desired capital stock as the linear functions of variables indicated by a variety of prior notions. These functions vary considerably although they usually contain real output amongst their explanatory variables. However, the market value of the firm has been substituted on some rare occasions. Two important adjustments should be especially noted. First, Chenery introduced an additional parameter in (33) to yield

$$(I - R)_t = \beta(K_t^* - \lambda K_{t-1}).$$ (39)

This modification is designed to reflect excess capacity made desirable by economies of scale. Thus, if demand for his output is expected to increase at a constant relative rate, the decision-maker's optimum degree of overcapacity will be a constant proportion $(1 - \lambda)$ of total capacity. This 'capacity form' was found by Kisselgoff and Modigliani (1957) to provide the prime explanation for investment in the U.S. electric power industry. This was possibly due to strong institutional and legal pressures upon the firms in this industry to meet demand and, also, to the support of capitalization by regulatory bodies.

Second, Koyck (1954) initiated a series of attempts to approximate the polynomial $b(B)$, possibly of infinite length, by a generating formula which depends upon a few parameters. In particular, he suggested the use of the sum of a geometric series $(1 + \rho B + \rho^2 B^2 + \ldots)$ where the parameter ρ is less than unity in absolute size. This sum is the inverse of $(1 - \rho B)$ so that Koyck's approximation for (34) is

$$(1 - \rho B)(I - R)_t = \mu(K_t^* - K_{t-1})$$ (40)

or

$$(I - R)_t = \rho(I - R)_{t-1} + \mu(K_t^* - K_{t-1}) + u_t - \rho u_{t-1} \tag{41}$$

if the initial specification (34) contains a random error term u_t. An obvious generalization of Koyck's approximation, illustrated by the investment study of Griliches and Wallace (1965), is

$$(1 - \rho_1 B - \rho_2 B^2)(I - R)_t = \mu(K_t^* - K_{t-1}), \tag{42}$$

where ρ_1 and ρ_2 are parameters constrained so that the inverse of this quadratic operator $(1 - \rho_1 B - \rho_2 B^2)$ can be written as a polynomial of infinite length. Many alternative schemes for such approximation of distributed lags have been suggested. These and their attendant problems of estimation are extensively discussed in Chapter 3 and will not be pursued here.

Costs of adjustment

All of the preceding discussion illustrates that, for much of its historical use, the basis for the acceleration principle in both theoretical and empirical studies of investment has been somewhat imprecise. This basis was clarified by Eisner and Strotz (1963) and the extensions which stemmed from their seminal contribution. Essentially Eisner and Strotz sought to investigate whether the acceleration principle could be derived from a model involving optimization by decision-makers. Their success hinged upon the introduction of 'costs of adjustment' for investment in real fixed capital inputs in contrast with the relatively cost-free changes in the use of variable inputs. Thus the 'fixity' of any particular type of input in the production process might be classified according to the costs involved in the adjustment of its level rather than in terms of the temporal scheme traditionally used. The level of a fixed input can, accordingly, be adjusted reasonably quickly but the cost of this adjustment will be relatively high as compared with the cost of adjusting a so-called variable input. These two definitions of fixity may not be as distinct as they appear. Rothschild (1971) was able to show that, under somewhat restrictive conditions, optimal behaviour may be consistent with the traditional definition even when it is derived from a model of investment behaviour where costs of adjustment are present. His result depends critically upon the form taken by these costs.

Eisner and Strotz outlined two potential sources of adjustment costs: one of which is internal to the activities of any particular firm and another which is either partially or wholly external to such activities. The first source stems from the problems associated with the installation of new capital equipment, its dislocation of ongoing productive activities, and the stresses imposed upon the managerial and administrative capabilities of existing planning staff. The second source is the marketing practices of capital-supplying industries, which could involve a short-run supply price for new capital assets.

With respect to internal costs of adjustments, Penrose (1966) has provided the most extensive discussion of the role of managerial limits to the growth of particular firms. She asserted that certain managerial and administrative abilities which are required in the process of expansion are basically different from those which are needed in on-going management of existing administrative structures and current levels of productive activities. Further, these expansionary abilities are not readily acquired from outside the firm and absorbed with full efficiency into its existing stock of managerial resources. Uzawa (1968, 1969) termed such restrictions 'the Penrose Effect' and, in his papers, represented them by a simple constraint and by the inclusion of managerial and administrative abilities amongst capital assets. Since these abilities are not readily measured, empirical studies giving primary emphasis to these restrictions have been rare.

With respect to external costs of adjustment, discussions have extended from the wholly external specification of given supply schedules for capital assets to more complex optimization models involving delivery lags, the delays between the placements of orders for new equipment and their deliveries. In a recent contribution, Maccini (1973a, b) considered such lags from both sides of the market. Optimal lengths can be established for the delivery lags of suppliers of real capital assets when these suppliers produce only to order. Of more significance for the current context, Maccini illustrates how the purchasing firm can affect the actual price of its new acquisitions when suppliers make prices depend upon the lead time of orders.

Earlier contributors seldom considered adjustment costs in this minute detail. They usually amended the specified form of the production function or explicitly introduced simple forms to represent a 'cost-of-adjustment function', separate from production. Eisner and Strotz introduced a quadratic function of net investment to represent these costs. For a single capital input, they restricted attention to behaviour in the neighbourhood of a long-run stationarity and obtained an optimal relationship that resembled Koyck's specification for the flexible accelerator. This result was extended to a vector of capital assets by Lucas (1967a), who maintained the Eisner–Strotz 'static-expectations' assumptions that, apart from the costs indicated by the adjustment constraint, all prices are assumed to be beyond the decision-maker's control and that he behaves as though current price levels will persist throughout all future periods. These latter assumptions were maintained by Gould (1968) and Lucas (1967b), who introduced constraints on production. Both used a linear and homogeneous production function; however, Lucas explicitly introduced gross investment as an additional argument in his production specification so that it did not exhibit constant returns to scale in the usual sense, and Gould made adjustment costs depend upon a quadratic function of gross rather than net investment. They indicated that, with these restrictions, optimal investment is uniquely determined and constant over time so that actual capital stock monotonically approaches its long-run desired level. In continuous form, this optimal behaviour can be represented by

$$\dot{K} = \delta(\bar{K} - K_t), \tag{43}$$

where $\bar{K}$ is the constant level of optimal gross investment divided by δ, the constant rate of depreciation assumed to affect the capital stock. (The constancy of optimal investment depends crucially upon the assumption of a linear homogeneous production function.)

Gould also indicated the severity of the static-expectations assumptions. In their absence, the optimal rate of investment 'will depend on the entire path of prices so that, even in the case where, say, two alternative time-paths of of prices ultimately lead to the same long-run level of capital stock, the firm's adjustment to that long-run level will be affected by differences which may occur at any point along the price paths'. His results encouraged a number of researchers to investigate possible alternative specifications for the prices anticipated by decision-makers. For example, Taylor (1970) made use of Kalman filtering theory and a simple Markov process for prices, Tinsley (1969, 1970) used a more general model which contained both Gould's and Taylor's specifications as special cases, Craine (1971) used the same model and Nerlove (1972) considered the use of Muth's concept of 'rational expectations'. See also Ando et al. (1974). These approaches do permit the expression of optimal adjustment equations in partial adjustment formats similar to (43) but with the symbol $\bar{K}$ now interpreted as a non-stationary 'target' trajectory. Craine illustrated the extreme sensitivity of this target to different assumptions concerning the generation of forecasts by decision-makers. His assertions that 'optimal-adjustment models depend in a fundamental way on future values' and that 'the dependence should be explicitly recognized and not cavalierly dismissed with the assumption of static expectations' seem to be appropriate conclusions emerging from this collection of studies.

Recognition of non-static expectations has a two-fold significance for applied research. First, theoretical investigations suggest severe interpretative difficulties for many existing empirical studies including both those overtly rationalized in terms of the flexible accelerator with costs of adjustment and static expectations and those based on the neoclassical models cited in Section 1.1. Second, these investigations establish a critical need for the derivation of simple forms that are consistent with acceptable price hypotheses and that are amenable to estimation.

Another important line of development stemming from the Eisner–Strotz paper has been taken by Treadway (1969, 1970, 1971). In his initial contribution, he used the separability assumption of a dynamic production function in the form

$$Q = f(K, L) - C(\dot{K}) \tag{44}$$

to acknowledge installation costs. $C(\dot{K})$ represented the functional dependence of losses in output associated with capital expansion. Alternative separable forms for this function had earlier been specified by Gould (1968) and Lucas (1967a). In subsequent contributions, Treadway rejected separability and illustrated that, contrary to restrictive models with separable technical processes, long-run demand or target trajectories for desired capital stock, K^* or $\bar{K}$, derived from dynamic models of net-worth optimization are not necessarily equivalent to those conventionally derived from static profit maximization. In particular, 'when we formulate an adjustment cost model to yield not only comparative static theorems but also the lag process itself, we find that possible *a priori* conditions exist under which the standard comparative statics theorems themselves are not valid. This stems from the fact that there is no necessity for a static production function constraint in a dynamic optimization theory'. Thus the optimal investment trajectory may not even be stable. Again this leaves many existing empirical regression results difficult to interpret and indicates the need for further research.

Despite these two important sources of qualifications to models using the flexible-accelerator framework and, also, the problem that prices may adjust to output and input disequilibria in addition to the input adjustments described above (Hamermesh, 1973), some recent empirical studies are worth reading if only to gain awareness of current practice. For example, the three studies by Coen and Hickman (1970), Nadiri and Rosen (1969) and Schramm (1970) illustrate some of the results obtained when the flexible accelerator is extended to include interrelated factor demands. A more extensive account is provided in the recent book by Brechling (1973).

1.4 FORWARD-LOOKING INDICATORS AND REALIZATION FUNCTIONS

Studies of investment are diverse both in their forms and in the intentions of their authors. Earlier sections have focused attention on models which seek to clarify structures of behavioural patterns affecting fixed capital formation and related expenditures, although most of these models are also used to predict future levels of investment. In particular circumstances where researchers are primarily concerned with forecasting levels of expenditures for some specific future period, why should they not simply ask decision-makers what are their anticipations, intentions or plans for these periods of interest? Alternatively, why should they not ask the decision-makers what funds have been appropriated for future use? Such questions are clearly predicated on adequate communication between researchers and decision-makers and on the availability of financial support to the former.

Direct approaches (questionnaires and interviews) have been used for some narrowly defined projects but proportions of responses received from firms have been typically and understandably small. This causes an important shift of resources into analyses of 'non-responses' in order to interpret available data. Fortunately individual deficiencies have often been overcome by the activities of larger agencies (especially employers' federations, governmental departments and publishing houses) although the gains in responses and general accuracy are obtained at the expense of some restrictions on the types of data collected. Thus questions which an individual researcher might want to pose may not be answered but questions of general interest would be both posed and answered by a large number of respondents, often with great care.

Data on anticipations, plans and appropriations have been systematically collected in the United States for over two decades, often on a quarterly basis. For example, the Office of Business Economics in the U.S. Department of Commerce and the Securities and Exchange Commission have jointly produced data on anticipated investment expenditures (by industry division) since 1947. These are regularly recorded with supporting commentaries in the *Survey of Current Business*. In addition, the McGraw-Hill Publishing Company has completed surveys of business plans for a similar period of time. (See Keezer *et al.* (1960) for a concise account of these surveys and their origin.) Both of these sets of data have enjoyed widespread use. On the supply side of the market, *Fortune* undertook surveys of producers concerning expected deliveries of new capital equipment. The outstanding sources of information for appropriations on a continuing basis are the series assembled by the (National Industrial) Conference Board and issued in their monthly statistical bulletin. (Cohen (1960) provides an assessment of this data in a 'foreshadowing' role.)

Data on forward-looking indicators are not restricted to the United States. Statistics Canada and the Federal Department of Industry, Trade and Commerce jointly prepare an annual outlook for investment by both private and public sectors of the Canadian economy. This outlook has a forward horizon of up to a year and was supplemented in past years by annual surveys (1968–1971) of investment intentions over five-year horizons by the Economic Council of Canada. Similarly, there are data readily available in Great Britain on such indicators. Since 1955, larger companies in the manufacturing industry, the distributive and the service trades and the shipping industry have been asked to provide returns on their investment intentions. Responsibility for the collection and presentation of these returns has been shared between the Board of Trade, Ministry of Technology and, more recently, the Department of Trade and Industry. An account of these inquiries, conducted three times a year, is presented in *Economic Trends* (Sept. 1970). The Confederation of British Industries regularly completes surveys of industrial trends over a wide area of activity. (Glynn (1969) gives a description of these surveys.) Again, on the supply side, evidence on both deliveries and orders in British engineering industries is published regularly by the Department of Trade and Industry. (See, for example, *Economic Trends* (April 1972).)

Anticipations, intentions and plans

Two collections of paper assembled for the National Bureau of Economic Research, *Short-Term Economic Forecasting* (1955) and *The Quality and Economic Significance of Anticipations Data* (1960), are basic references for all interested in the use of forward-looking indicators. They provide accounts of alternative theoretical constructs, explanations of U.S. practice in the compilation of data, and empirical evidence with appropriate attempts at interpretation. In many respects, these papers have not been surpassed and later research has essentially supplemented them. Historically they illustrate the transitional period between two different stages in the use of anticipatory data. Discussions of the 'deficiencies' in anticipations (in the sense that they were inaccurate as exact forecasts) characterized the first stage whereas the second stage can be characterized by systematic adjustments to anticipations in simple forms, 'realization functions', and by the introduction of more complicated distributed lags between anticipations and realized levels of investment.

As representatives of the first stage, Foss and Natrella (1957) outlined the following possible explanations for a tendency of OBE–SEC anticipations to understate actual expenditures.

(i) Anticipations are given in value terms. The assumption that firms neglect future price changes may have some basis in fact but it is far from being generally true.

(ii) Data on expenditures reveal distinctive seasonal patterns with approximate weights of $\{91, 102, 100, 107\}$ for the four quarters. The largest weight for the fourth quarter's outlays may be attributed to firms' accounting practices whereby books are sometimes held open longer at the end of accounting years or include some accruals. These patterns may differ between industries and, hence, lead to understatements even though some adjustments have been made to OBE–SEC data on these grounds since mid-1952.

(iii) Cyclical fluctuations may be incorrectly anticipated.

(iv) There are substantial dispersions of inaccuracies between industries so the understatement may be due to aggregation.

(v) Larger firms generally predict more accurately so smaller firms' errors might be responsible for the understatement of actual expenditures. In particular, smaller firms may frequently choose to record 'no change' in their levels of activities.

(vi) Anticipations are more accurate when the scale of investments are high relative to existing capital stocks, due to longer periods of both commitments of funds and planning and, perhaps, due to the need for external funding.

This list does not exhaust the list of potential explanations. Further, both overstatements and understatements are encountered when other series for anticipatory data are considered. (See Gort (1962) for a wider survey.) Perhaps as a consequence, researchers shifted their emphasis to more mechanistic adjustments to anticipatory data. For example, given any particular source for anticipations, an obvious first step was to specify

$$I_t = \beta_0 + \beta_1 I_t^a, \tag{45}$$

where I_t denotes realized investment expenditures, I_t^a represents anticipated investment in the tth period with anticipations formed some periods in advance, and the other symbols are unknown parameters to be estimated. (Note the change in notation from earlier sections.) Usually β_0 and β_1 are found to be significantly different from zero and unity, respectively. Similarly in the alternative first-difference form

$$I_t - I_{t-1} = \gamma_0 + \gamma_1(I_t^a - I_{t-1}^a), \tag{46}$$

where γ_0 and γ_1 are unknown parameters and I_{t-1}^a represents anticipated investment in the $(t-1)$th period with anticipations formed with the same horizon as for I_t^a, γ_1 is usually significantly different from unity.

With the deficiencies of particular anticipatory series in mind, Hart (1960) asserted that 'confronted with such a systematic bias, the natural response of the analyst who wants to forecast is to counter it by a systematic correction'. Thus he reconstitutes the series using a non-linear function of both anticipations and earlier realizations. Other researchers (Evans and Green (1966), Ball and Drake (1964), for example) have found that either better statistical fits for existing data or better predictive performances are obtainable when raw anticipatory data (or plans) have been supplemented with a linear function $f(\cdot)$ of other variables (X). They specify

$$I_t = f(X_t) + \beta I_t^a, \tag{47}$$

where the parameters of $f(X_t)$ and β are to be estimated. These adjustments are essentially *ad hoc* in nature.

In his contribution to this area, Jorgenson (1965) has indicated how anticipations might be both explained and then used to explain expenditures. He argues that the formation of anticipations or plans are an intermediate stage in the investment process, and that they are distributed through time. Systematic understatement may then be interpreted as due to a truncation of a distributed-lag response. Unfortunately, in order to formalize his image of the investment process and, hence, to use it in econometric modelling, Jorgenson is compelled to introduce severe constraints on the process. In particular, the proportions of transitions between any two successive stages in this process are assumed to depend only on the time elapsed since the first of these stages began, and they are assumed to be independent of transitions between earlier stages. Then actual net expenditures on expansion (after replacement needs) I_t are determined by anticipated levels I_t^a with a distributed lag. Further, anticipations are determined by desired capital services K^* (as indicated by the neoclassical model outlined in Section 1.1) again with a distributed lag. Recalling the notation B for the lag operator, his model becomes

$$I_t^a = m(B)(1-B)K^* \tag{48}$$

and

$$I_t = n(B)I_t^a, \tag{49}$$

where $m(B)$ and $n(B)$ are rational functions of the lag operator. Thus

$$I_t = n(B)m(B)(1 - B)K^*. \tag{50}$$

Whether (49) or (50) is used to forecast expenditures becomes a choice for the individual researcher.

Realization functions

A more complex treatment of anticipations is associated with the use of 'realization functions'. In essence, these are relations between errors of anticipations for several variables and divergences of planned and realized investment expenditures. Thus anticipated levels of investment may not be realized because the decision-makers' environment has changed, new information has become available to him concerning the paths of uncontrolled variables, or objectives have been revised. If anticipations are formed in the $(t - \alpha)$th period with respect to the level of investment expenditures in the tth period, the decision-makers must have projected values for both supply and demand factors over the interval between the two periods. Hence, the discrepancy between anticipations and realizations may be attributed to unforeseen changes in these factors. For example, Eisner (1962, 1965) put forward realization functions in the form

$$\frac{I_t - I_t^a}{I_t^a} = a(B)\frac{I_{t-1} - I_{t-1}^a}{I_{t-1}^a} \tag{51}$$

$$+ b(B)\frac{S_t - S_t^a}{S_t^a}$$

$$+ c(B)\frac{\pi_t - \pi_{t-1}}{\pi_{t-1}}$$

$$+ d(B)\frac{O_t - O_{t-\alpha}}{I_{t-1}^a} \, ,$$

where all anticipations, indicated by a superscript (^{a}), have a 'forward horizon' of α periods. S, π and O denote levels of sales, post-tax profits and unfilled orders, respectively. $a(B)$, $b(B)$, $c(B)$ and $d(B)$ are polynomials in the lag operator. The most extensive account of the theoretical underpinnings for this realization-function approach is provided by Modigliani and Cohen (1961). They suggest that the systematic exploitation of interrelated anticipations and plans in this form 'might simplify considerably the task of deriving specific behaviour functions of the type required in the simultaneous equation approach to forecasting. It would enable us to bypass the problem of estimating general behaviour functions, replacing it with the presumably much easier task of estimating realization functions, that is, determining the extent to which errors to anticipations cause the actual course of action to deviate from decisions and plans.' This reduced-form approach acknowledges our imprecise knowledge of basic structural relations in investment behaviour and wholly concentrates on simple forecasts. A concise account, which avoids the mathematical sophistication required to read the previous reference, is provided by Modigliani and Weingartner (1958). Methods of interpolation adopted when anticipations are not collected with sufficient frequency are indicated in Eisner (1965) and Agarwala, Burns and Duffy (1969).

Finally, although most of these approaches are concerned with systematic discrepancies between anticipations and realizations as if these indicated deficiencies in the data, an alternative view has been advanced by Bossons and Modigliani (1960) that these discrepancies are quite 'reasonable'. This view is explained in Section 4.7 rather than here because of its potentially wide area of relevance for inventory investment.

Appropriations and commitments

The Conference Board's series for appropriations have been used to explain levels of investment expenditures (as, for example, by Hart (1965) using 'hybrid' realization functions), but emphases in recent studies have shifted so that appropriations are usually specified as dependent variables. Thus Almon (1965, 1968), Campagna (1968), Greenberg (1965), Hart (1965) and Sachs and Hart (1967) use explanatory variables suggested by the theories outlined in other sections of this chapter as the bases for empirical equations explaining appropriations rather than equations explaining investment expenditures. These particular studies illustrate a wide variety of research interests. For example, Almon uses the distributed-lag technique which bears her name (see Chapter Three) to assess the responses of appropriations to their determinants, Campagna concentrates on the instability over time of the parameters associated with these determinants, whereas Greenberg uses Zellner's model of 'seemingly unrelated' equations to associate appropriations in several industries.

Campagna repeats an important point made earlier by Burns, that there are at least two distinct decisions in the investment process; namely, the choice between investing and not investing and the choice of when to invest. Appropriations usually do not have any specific relationship with the timing of expenditures. The latter will depend upon supply factors, unanticipated price changes and technical problems so that both postponements and outright cancellations are common. Thus, given the general empirical difficulty of taking account of a sufficient number of influences, regression coefficients may be temporally unstable. Appropriations data suffer from a number of other deficiencies. They may not be as precise as their users' needs. Further they may reflect only major projects. (A more complete list of qualifications are provided in the review by Cohen, cited above.)

Despite these shortcomings, appropriations appear to be both useful forward-looking indicators and structural components in the investment process. Unfortunately the Conference Board's series have not been replicated elsewhere and researchers have been compelled to search for alternative indicators provided by suppliers of capital-equipment. See, for example, Tanner (1972) and Hodgins and Tanner (1973) for some indications of the potentialities and problems associated with the use of building permits and contractual commitments in forecasting investment in non-residential construction.

1.5   ECLECTIC FRAMEWORK AND MONEY CAPITAL

Some researchers use the adjective 'eclectic' to describe their images of the behavioural patterns for investment in fixed real capital assets. They 'place the business investment decision in a context of many very different constraints, motives, and reasons for desiring new productive equipment and they are not certain that they completely understand all the mechanisms by which these forces work.' Clearly, this is an intermediate attitude which conveniently falls between the reduced-form approach of realization functions and the structural specificity of neoclassical approaches. Outstanding illustrations of this attitude are provided by Meyer and Kuh (1957, 1963), Kuh (1963) and Meyer and Glauber (1964). These studies also provide fine examples of current econometric practice and will be cited again in several sections of later technical chapters.

In these particular eclectic studies, there are two important characteristics which markedly differ from those of models cited earlier. First, both the demand and supply of investable funds are given central significance. Second, behavioural relationships are treated as non-stationary representing, in part, mechanistic procedures 'often attributable to administrative rules used for simplifying the internal control of business operations'. To acknowledge these and other characteristics, Meyer and Kuh identified the 'Accelerator-Residual Funds' (ARF) theory of investment, which combines a long-run target for the ratio of dividends to net profits with short-run financing rules and a basic productive relationship between average output and capacity.

Neoclassical model again

Before considering the ARF theory in greater detail, there are some advantages in clarifying the treatment of money capital in Jorgenson's neoclassical model (which is partially described in Section 1.1) since this treatment provides a suitable basis for comparison. In the original formulation of Jorgenson's model, the rate of interest on long-term bonds was used both to discount net income from future periods to the date of decision-making and to represent payments for borrowed funds. This usage is consistent with the three assumptions that all investment expenditures are wholly financed by funds from sources external to the firm, only expenditures on real fixed capital assets are associated with changes in money-capital requirements (unless, say, inventories, trade credit and other possible uses of funds are treated as inputs in the productive process) and debt is redeemed so as to always keep the value of stocks of such assets proportional to the firm's level of indebtedness.

In a later formulation of Jorgenson and Stephenson (1967a), the rate at which future net income is discounted is given by the ratio of a firm's current net income to the 'market valuation' of its assets. Let net income at time t be denoted $\pi(t)$. Then, its net worth is given by

$$\Phi(0) = \int_0^\infty \mu(t)\pi(t)dt, \tag{52}$$

where $\mu(t)$ is exp $(-rt)$ and r is a constant discount factor defined implicitly by (52) when $\Phi(0)$ is identified with the Stock-Market valuations of the firm's existing stock of outstanding shares and fixed indebtedness. For a constant stream of net income, $\Phi(0)$ is $(1/r)\pi(0)$ which permits the discount rate to be calculated from current financial accounts and market quotations. This modification to acknowledge the existence of money capital is very convenient in empirical work but introduces distortion of uncertain effect. In particular, one might doubt the wisdom in applied work of using the two restrictive assumptions of a constant level of net income (especially when the purpose of the model is to explain net investment expenditures over a substantial period of time, replacement expenditures having already been explained by a mechanistic proportionality rule) and of the equality of internal and external valuations of the firm. Further, since the holders of ordinary shares might be considered 'owners' of the firm, the objective of the decision-maker might need to be redefined in terms of their incomes. The net worth of the firm to its owners will be the sum of a stream of dividends and the capital gain or loss on sale of ownership. Finally, once financial characteristics of a firm are introduced, the dimensions of decision-making are increased. The decision-maker is confronted with an important choice between dilution of ownership, increased fixed indebtedness, and use of retained earnings whenever investment expenditures are to be undertaken.

Survey evidence

In addition to the complications indicated in our clarification of Jorgenson's model, there are others associated with the usual funding practices of firms. Harkins and Walsh (1968) undertook a survey of over 300 U.S. firms, of which four-fifths had incurred long-term debt in the preceding five years. They found that borrowed funds were often used for working capital (both to finance more inventories and to carry larger balances for accounts receivable), acquisitions of other firms, and the refinancing or retirement of short-term debt quite apart from their use in acquiring real fixed capital assets. Similar findings have been reported for British firms by Barna (1962) and in the *Quarterly Bulletin of the Bank of England* (1967). With respect to sources of funds, Harkins and Walsh found that 30 percent of the loans reported in their sample took the form of leases. Many of these leases have short durations or involve small amounts of money but over a quarter of the firms in their sample undertook substantial commitments in the form of leases for municipally owned manufacturing plants and other facilities. These were financed by the issue of industrial revenue bonds and, therefore, add a locational dimension to investment decisions. Since these figures are fair representations of those presented in a host of other direct enquiries, some of their implications are worth making explicit. Four are given here.

(i) There are many sources and uses of investable funds available and adopted by firms.

(ii) The rate at which future net income is discounted has been called the 'cost of capital' to signify its dependence upon the nature of funding. (See Solomon (1963) for an introduction to the theoretical literature concerned with the cost of capital, as seen from a financial viewpoint.) Clearly there exists no simple relationship between the subjective cost of capital for the decision-maker and the temporally variable financial data on funding and valuation which are available for empirical research.

(iii) There is no simple relationship between the level of indebtedness (or its structure) and the value of stocks of real fixed capital assets.

(iv) Methods of funding change over time. Regional incentive programmes, the development of better informational systems and new techniques of financial management, and changes in the relative profitability of funding methods due to both fiscal and monetary measures have all contributed to substantial variability in corporate practice.

Most of these implications support eclecticism although not necessarily in the particular forms associated with the ARF theory. They suggest that a model with mathematical elegance and simple analytical properties, such as some of the models cited in Sections 1.1 and 1.3, must omit many well-established features of actual behaviour. These omissions also provide important qualifications to the predictive uses of econometric models, some of which are indicated in the next section.

The accelerator–residual funds theory

Money capital enters into the ARF theory in two distinct ways. First, earlier investigations by Lintner persuaded Meyer and Kuh that many firms appear to use a long-run target level for the ratio of dividends to net profits. Second, there is a 'crucial' asymmetry in short-run relationships of financial considerations and investment, which depend upon the general state of expansion. Thus, in expansionary periods, investment is determined by the acceleration element; namely, the growth in demand for the firm's output relative to its capacity. Funding is then usually arranged as conservatively as possible. Investment may be constrained by the availability of funds at appropriate levels of managerial risk but 'such occurrences would seem to be rare in true growth situations'. However, in cyclical downturns in activity, investment expenditures are usually confined to a level that can be funded from previously retained earnings. These expenditures will often be concerned with objectives not necessarily associated with increased capacity alone. For example, Meyer and Glauber cite mergers that are motivated by product-diversification, defensive holdings of liquid assets, and cost-reducing investments. Notice that, in the ARF theory, debt is dependent on investment and available internal funds during expansionary periods but the direction of causation runs from the availability of internal funds to investment when existing assets are underutilized.

At least six important differences can be distinguished between the characteristics of the ARF theory and Jorgenson's neoclassical (JN) theory. In the ARF theory, firms are reluctant to use external funds. They are conscious of the need to maintain long-term stability in the stream of dividends. Their outputs' markets are affected by oligopolistic structures. The decision-makers have imprecise estimates of future developments and, hence, adopt short horizons and, frequently, defensive behaviour with respect to both liquidity and flexibility. Cyclical variations and the attendant variable utilization of capital stocks regularly affect the investment decision and its constituent collection of determining influences. Finally the ARF theory does not indicate specific expressions, of similar form to (11) and (12), for the level of 'desired' capital stocks.

In contrast, the JN theory posits, initially, that firms always use funds from external sources and that dividends have no role in their investment decisions. This role was partially acknowledged by a later modification to the 'cost of capital' without making other suitable adjustments to the specification of net worth, such as replacing net profits by the stream of dividends. Hochman et al. (1973) suggest that, when these adjustments are made in an alternative neoclassical model, the pressure of 'imperfections' in capital markets implies that 'investment in productive capital is a substitute to investment in financial assets at some phases and is complementary to it in some other places'. Thus neoclassical formulations can acquire some eclectic features. In the JN theory, the decision-maker is confronted by competitive markets and enjoys both perfect foresight and reversibility in his capital assets so that there is no need for him to be concerned about cyclical downturns in activity. He maintains a vision of perpetual equilibrium in all markets to guide his actions. Further, his awareness of structural relationships permits the derivation of explicit expressions associating desired capital stock and its determinants.

The concurrent use of these divergent theories indicates both the current pragmatism of economic research and the failure of past empirical research to discriminate between the theories and enable the elimination of one or the other (or both) from our collection of non-discarded approaches.

Our account of the ARF theory has not explained why firms may markedly discriminate between funds from internal and external sources. This proposition has a long history with the articles by Hart (1942) and Kalecki (1937) amongst the earliest expositions. The former gave substance to the concepts of 'capital rationing', where investible funds are limited by considerations other than profitability, and 'stepped capital markets', whereby interest rates for additional indebtedness depend upon the size of existing debt relative to equity. Both concepts were based upon assumptions of imprecise knowledge, the positive costs and limitations of acquiring information to reduce areas of uncertainty, and the use of short-run flexible programmes to permit newly acquired information to be acted upon. Kalecki developed the well-known 'principle of increasing risk' for which Penrose (1966, pp. 57–64) and Quirk (1961) have provided more recent accounts.

Differences in a decision-maker's attitudes to external and internal funds can be represented by a discontinuity in the supply schedule for investible funds. This discontinuity occurs at a point fixed in any given period by the sum of depreciation expenses, excess cash assets and retained earnings. The acceleration element in ARF theory arises in the (partial) synchronization of shifts in both demand and supply schedules due to the joint dependence of desired capacity and retained earnings upon the general level of economic activity in the economy. More complete accounts of this interdependence are provided in the references cited earlier for eclectic approaches.

Other approaches

Among the many other attempts to introduce money capital, we can distinguish at least three broad streams of thought. One stream treats money as a form of producers' capital such that production requires (in addition to variable labour inputs) both capital in the forms of equipment and structures and capital in the form of inventories of various goods. A short list of contributors to this stream with real money balances as productive inputs is given by Sinai and Stokes (1972), who also provide parametric estimates for a suitably amended production function. As they suggest, it is one thing to assert real balances belong in the production function and another to formalize a theory. Moroney (1972) makes a similar comment and adds, justifiably, that existing analyses within this stream stimulate more questions than they answer. Clearly, this is a sceptical challenge to some aspects of recent research rather than a complete dismissal of the approach.

The second stream develops money-capital requirements from a basis provided by the Wicksellian or Austrian theory of capital as clarified, in part, by Smithies (1935) and Lange (1936) but extended beyond its original preoccupation with replacement or 'circulatory' investment. An important illustrative approach within this stream is given by Gabor and Pearce (1952, 1958). They suggest that firms operate in the interests of their owners so that they should be considered as financial investments. Decision-makers within firms are assumed to receive contractual rewards and expected to seek a maximal rate of return on the invested money capital of the owners. Money is the 'controlling factor' in the operations of firms, it acts as a catalyst for production and enters analyses as a constraint rather than as an input in a production function. The approach can usefully be extended to include many popular images of financial markets as illustrated in the excellent study by Vickers (1968).

The third stream contains a miscellany of *ad hoc* specifications representing various prior notions about the roles of financial factors in real capital formation. The *ad hoc* nature is usually clearly stated as, for example, by Dhrymes and Kurz (1967) '... we shall not explicitly consider the technological constraint on the firm's activities in the form of a production function, nor the institutional characteristics of the factor and product market in which it operates'. This particular study stresses stable interdependencies between dividends, external finance and investment, in contrast with the non-stationarity assumed in the ARF theory, and argues that 'single-equation' approaches obscure the character of decision processes. Other illustrations of this heterogeneous stream are provided by Anderson (1964, 1967) and Resek (1966).

1.6 POLICY

Researchers often complain about a lack of variability in their data since this affects their abilities to discriminate between the alternative influences upon investment decisions. However, in the context of policies concerning both tax rates and capital allowances, such complaints seem ill-placed. In fact, one commentator felt compelled to describe the sequence of shifts between initial allowances and investment allowances in British governmental policies as analogous to the rapidity of oar strokes at a Henley regatta! Nevertheless, we have not yet succeeded in adequately determining the effects of changes in either tax rates or capital allowances upon investment expenditures, at least to the extent that past econometric results could serve as a reliable basis for governmental actions. Even qualitative predictions are often severely qualified. To illustrate the present state of knowledge, some areas of controversy and potential directions of future research, we shall use Jorgenson's neoclassical model of net-worth maximization, as represented by Hall and Jorgenson (1967, 1969, 1971) and their critics. This illustration is followed below by discussion of a number of other issues associated with either the use or interpretation of past studies.

Capital allowances and static expectations

Jorgenson's model was introduced in Section 1.1 but the earlier formulation ignored both corporate taxation and equity financing. A modification to take partial account of the latter problem was mentioned in the last section and will be discussed again below. First, consider a decision-maker who seeks to maximize the net worth of an enterprise (henceforth assumed to have corporate form), where net worth $\Phi(0)$ is defined as the present value of the stream of post-tax profits over an infinite horizon. Elemental net worth, the contribution to this stream at time t, is

$$\pi = \left(pQ - \sum_{i=1}^{n} w_i L_i - \sum_{j=1}^{m} q_j I_j\right) - u\left(pQ - \sum_{i=1}^{n} w_i L_i - A\right), \tag{53}$$

where the dependence upon t is suppressed for notational simplicity, and net worth is

$$\Phi(0) = \int_{t=0}^{\infty} \mu(t)\pi(t)dt. \tag{54}$$

In these specifications, the notation of Section 1.1 is repeated. Thus p, w_i and q_j are prices of output, the ith variable input and the jth capital input, respectively, whereas Q, L_i and I_j are the associated physical magnitudes. $\mu(t)$ is the discount factor applied to elemental net worth, u is the effective rate of corporate income tax and A is the sum of capital cost allowances and deductions permitted (and claimed) for income-tax purposes.

In his early papers, Jorgenson restricted analysis to the case of a single variable input, a single capital input and an exponential specification for $\mu(t)$; namely, $\exp(-rt)$ with a constant 'cost of capital' r. He suggests that by ignoring the problem of accelerated depreciation, A might be represented by

$$A = v_1 qR + v_2 rqK + v_3 \dot{q}K, \tag{55}$$

where qR, rqK and $\dot{q}K$ signify current replacement cost, total cost of money capital, and capital gains accruing to the owners of the physical capital stock K. v_1, v_2 and v_3 are the proportions of these items that are allowable against income for tax purposes in the United States. Clearly, with an obvious extension in notation, the corresponding multiple-input specification for A is

$$A = \sum_{j=1}^{m} v_{1j} q_j R_j + r \sum_{j=1}^{m} v_{2j} q_j K_j + \sum_{j=1}^{m} v_{3j} \dot{q}_j K_j. \tag{56}$$

In Jorgenson's case, if net worth is maximized subject to the proportionality hypothesis for replacement (3) and a neoclassical production constraint for output (2), optimal trajectories for inputs must satisfy (9) and

$$\frac{\partial F}{\partial K_j} = \frac{c_j}{p}, \tag{57}$$

where the 'user costs' c_j of the capital inputs are defined by

$$c_j = q_j \frac{\delta_j(1 - uv_{1j}) + r(1 - uv_{2j}) - \dot{q}_j(1 - uv_{3j})/q_j}{(1 - u)}. \tag{58}$$

The presence of capital gains in these expressions indicates one major deficiency of this specification. Capital allowances are based upon the historical costs of capital assets and not upon replacement costs. Thus the parameters $\{v_{1j}\}$ are unlikely to be stable. In fact, it is difficult to believe that any simple expression can provide an adequate representation for depreciation charges when the time paths of both input prices and investment expenditures are irregular. The problem is exacerbated when allowable rates of capital allowances for individual assets have varied in the past.

Similar criticisms can be made with respect to the second collection of terms representing the total costs of money capital. Jorgenson's earliest model was based upon pure debt financing of the enterprise's investment activities. It made no provisions for either stock equity or retention of earnings. Thus, with stationary prices and bond rates, the cost of money capital (debt) could be made proportional to the sum of market valuations of the stocks of capital assets by appropriate policies for refunding and retirement of debt. In contrast with the direct evidence cited in Section 1.5, this presumes that funds are not borrowed for other purposes. In later models, other sources of funds have been introduced. We return to this area of difficulties later in this section with an account of adjustments to the cost of capital r.

It will be recalled that a relationship between the net-worth criterion and repetitive static profit-maximization may be established in this model when profit is respecified for the latter as $(pQ - \Sigma w_i L_i - \Sigma c_j K_j)$. This equivalence was used by Hall and Jorgenson in their three studies to make more 'realistic' choices for the allowances specification. It also has been used by their critics to show the severity of the static-expectations assumptions that underlie the equivalence. For the moment, it is convenient to ignore these criticisms and concentrate on the Hall–Jorgenson approach, which permits adjustment for accelerated depreciation of capital assets. Their approach is a simple two-step procedure. First, expressions for $\{c_j\}$ are derived from depreciation formulae and simplifying assumptions. These are then substituted in the simple feedback rule

$$K_j^* = \frac{p}{c_j} Q \tag{12}$$

associated with a Cobb–Douglas production function.

Instead of looking backwards at the historical pattern of acquisition and prices, Hall and Jorgenson derived $\{c_j\}$ by assuming that decision-makers look forward with static expectations. Past variability is ignored and all prices, rates of taxation and patterns of allowable capital allowances are expected to persist at the levels existing when each decision is made. No allowance is made for learning by experience; the decision-maker looks forward over an infinite horizon but looks backwards not at all. Then, for a single capital input, the user cost is

$$c = q(r + \delta)\frac{1 - v - uz + uzv_0}{1 - u}, \tag{59}$$

where v is the proportion of an investment expenditure which is allowable as a capital allowance for tax purposes at the time of purchase, v_0 is an appropriate adjustment for this allowance in the depreciation base and z is the present value of future capital allowances $A^*(s)$ over the tax lifetime T for the newly acquired asset,

$$z = \int_{s=0}^{T} A^*(s)\exp(-rs)ds. \tag{60}$$

Both v and v_0 may be established by tax rules when accelerated depreciation is permitted. For example, in the first two years of the U.S. investment tax credit 1962–3, the statutory rules for v and v_0 were seven per cent for certain capital assets. The effective rate was somewhat lower due to some exceptions in general availability. In later years, v_0 was set at zero when the depreciation base ceased to be reduced after repeal of the Long amendment to the 1962 tax bill. In Britain, these differences in treatment may be identified with initial allowances and investment allowances, the latter being associated with more favourable treatment. A history of the switches between these allowances and time-series for the attendent values of v are given in Rowley (1969). Their coverage affected about three-quarters of acquisitions of new capital assets and appropriate weighted averages of permissible rates of allowances range from five percent to twenty percent before the further drastic shift to another alternative, the investment grants system, at the beginning of 1966.

Particular expressions for both $A^*(s)$ and z have been presented by Hall and Jorgenson and, also, by Bischoff (1971a) for a number of alternative formulae. For example, the straightline depreciation and 'sum-of-years-digits' depreciation formulae indicate $1/T$ and $2(T-s)/T^2$ as appropriate specifications for $A^*(s)$ during the tax lifetimes. The former formula was generally used before 1954 in the United States whereas the latter was one of a number of methods of accelerated depreciation introduced to stimulate investment at this time. Eight years later, the investment tax credit was introduced and enjoyed a somewhat checkered career. In Britain, the accelerated investment allowances had been introduced for a short period beginning in 1954 and were reintroduced for a wide collection of assets in 1962, the less-favourable initial allowances being applicable in the intermediate period. Given additional adjustments to tax-lives and other components of the neoclassical model, Jorgenson and his associates have found very substantial effects of tax practice upon both investment levels and timing with specifications of this type. However, in assessing these results, our earlier criticisms should be recalled. The two assumptions of a constant utilization rate and the proportionality hypothesis for replacement investment also are relevant in assessments. With respect to the first assumption, the equilibrium basis of the basic neoclassical model (as outlined in Section 1.1) makes the reality of excess capacity difficult to reconcile with it. Thus the model and its associated empirical fits indicate investment expenditures adjusting to changes in both tax rates and depreciation rules but it is difficult to believe that such adjustments would occur when, say, only three-quarters of capacity is being utilized. With respect to the second assumption, several tax measures have explicitly sought to affect the lives of capital assets. For example, both American and British authorities have changed tax-lives in the hope of reducing actual lives either to increase average capital productivity or stimulate the industries supplying capital goods. A 'reserve ratio test' was even used in the United States for some years to encourage depreciation claims to be in line with actual replacement. Clearly, if fiscal measures do substantially effect replacement behaviour, the proportionality hypothesis is seriously jeopardized.

The cost of capital

Monetary and fiscal policies also affect the cost of capital which enters into this neoclassical model in two roles; namely, as a discount factor for future elements of income and in the deductions for the costs of money capital. It should be noted that many governments have been directly involved with controls in the market for investable funds. For example, capital issues were controlled in Britain until 1958 and French authorities have intervened with a variety of direct techniques to augment the flow of funds. Controls and interventions of these types are extremely difficult to introduce in models of investment. Perhaps the simplest approach is to ignore data from any time periods in which they enter with pronounced roles.

Specifications for the cost of capital in empirical fits for the U.S. economy have varied considerably. Jorgenson (1963, 1965) began with the long-term rate on government bonds. In his papers with Hall he used an after-tax rate of return in the form $(1 - u)\gamma$ with a constant value of 14 percent for the parameter γ, and later a value of 20 percent for this same parameter. Jorgenson and Stephenson (1967a, b) accepted more detailed financial specifications. In particular, they set the cost of capital equal to the ratio of post-tax profits and net monetary interest to the value of all outstanding securities, where the latter is the sum of the value of equity (measured as the ratio of post-tax profits to Standard and Poor's earnings price ratio for manufacturing corporations) and the value of debt (the ratio of net monetary interest to Standard and Poor's bond yield for the same corporations). This specification was linearly augmented by Jorgenson and Siebert (1968a, b) to include the relative change in the value of securities over time. Bischoff (1971a) used a weighted average of Moody's industrial bond yield, Moody's industrial dividend–price ratio, the corporate tax rate and a time trend. Since all of these choices have been identified with particular regression results that fulfilled a conventional list of criteria for satisfactory performance, the overall impression of this evidence is perplexing. The picture is not clarified by British results. Rowley (1969) considered many alternative choices for the cost of capital including both variable and fixed rates. He concluded that there was no possibility of discrimination amongst these choices on the basis of empirical fits for available data and existing criteria.

If attention is shifted to theoretical bases for choice, the situation is not markedly improved since each choice for the cost of capital is associated with a different choice for the income stream in net worth. Clearly if the appropriate model permits both equity and debt, the income stream should be based upon dividends and, perhaps, also upon the taxshelter effect of retained earnings. Its objective function would then depend upon both corporate and personal taxation as well as upon monetary phenomena.

Our space constraints preclude further discussion of the many contributions to problems associated with the cost of capital. Some impression of the wide-ranging discussions in both empirical and theoretical literature may be gleened from the representative studies of Brannon (1972), Feldstein (1973), Haley (1971), de Leeuw and Gramlich (1969) and the references they cite.

Further interpretative problems

In most applications of the non-eclectic models cited in this and earlier sections, researchers have assumed continuity in the response of investment to changes in its determining factors, including both fiscal and monetary instruments. Many empirical papers contain estimates for dynamic multipliers and comparative-static multipliers representing this temporal response. Implicitly (sometimes explicitly) we are led to believe that we can simply scale these multipliers by changes in the determinants to establish the resultant changes in investment. This procedure is too crude for practical use in directing governmental action at this time. We have already suggested that responses may depend critically upon the degree of excess capacity and, also, upon the existence of supply shortages.In addition, corporate decision-makers are unlikely to react favourably to policy changes that are expected to be of short duration, especially as major investment projects are frequently spread over considerable periods of time. This indicates one major deficiency of models based on static expectations—levels do not persist nor, frequently, are they expected to.

Three other problematic areas must also be recognized. First, recall the complexity of non-stationarities identified in the eclectic models of Section 1.5. These models indicate substantial variability in responses and their interaction with other factors due to imprecise market and administrative knowledge, multiple constraints upon actions and multiple (perhaps conflicting) objectives of decision-makers. Similar variability can be associated with the installation costs cited in Section 1.3 especially as formulated in the Penrose effect. Second, the stock of capital assets is rarely reduced even in severe recessions. Both machinery and structures often experience functional down-grading or standby status rather than outright scrapping or demolition. We should notice two distinct approaches to this asymptotic rigidity (or irreversability in Arrow's term); namely, those concerned with path-dependencies or 'hysteresis' effects and those with the so-called 'supply price' of capital. The former are represented by a clearly defined stream of economic literature, including the work of Clower (1954a,b), Smith (1961) and Witte (1963), and emphasize the stock-flow distinction associated with the rigidity. In this context the notion of 'capital services' is difficult to sustain since capital assets act as a catalyst in production rather than in the earlier role associated with factors in a neoclassical production function. On the other hand, the concept of the supply price of capital emphasizes the linkage between existing (rigid) stocks of capital assets and their absorption into the portfolios of wealth-owners. The influence of monetary policy here depends critically upon the differentials for investors between the prices of capital assets' admission to their portfolios, or retention in them, and the rates of return anticipated from ownership of newly produced capital assets. Perhaps the best introductions to this latter concept are provided by Tobin (1961, 1969).

The final problematic area is obscured by the demand-bias in economic models of investment. In almost all of the models outlined both here and in earlier sections (with a rare exception provided by Maccini in Section 1.3) there exists an emphasis upon the sources of demands for real fixed capital assets. Supplies of these assets are (often implicitly) assumed to be automatically available. However, in most of the developed countries for which investment equations have been fitted, supply constraints have been severe during particular periods. For example, the United States experienced a steel strike and related dislocations during 1955–1956. Further, in his study of the effects of direct controls in the post-war British economy, Dow (1964) was able to distinguish five major instruments of control—restrictions on investment, consumer rationing, import controls, allocation of materials and price controls—each of which may have a significant effect on the stream of investment expenditures. His survey contains a detailed chronology of variations in controls and there is no need to reproduce it here. Apart from this survey the Treasury *Bulletin for Industry* provides clear indications of the evolution of British governmental policy and of supply restrictions in the first post-war decade. For example, it reported that the government had direct control over 40 percent of the investment field in July 1950 and building controls provided the major instrument exercised over the remainder. In September 1952, it reported steel shortages. Finally, in May 1954, it acknowledged that investment in the previous five years had been severely curtailed by steel shortages, the defence programme and the need to increase engineering exports, although these restrictions were not operating continuously. Clearly constraints in this form do affect the efficacy of changes in other governmental instruments as they influence investment..

There are many other matters which affect the interpretation of empirical fits and their applicability as guides for governmental policies. Some are mentioned below. First, there are the immense difficulties in taking account of the existence and variability of payments' lags in the two-way flows of funds between firms and governments. This area, where interactions of fiscal and monetary policies are especially marked, has been surprisingly neglected. An earlier British debate distinguished between the liquidity and profitability aspects of alternative capital allowances but this distinction has tended to be overlooked in our current preooccupation with net-worth maximization. Thus, although modifications to the simplest models have introduced non-bond external funding and the influence of retained earnings upon growth, our treatment of short-term liquidity and trade credit remains inadequate. Clearly static-expectations models are a doubtful basis for considering the cyclical effects of liquidity upon investment behaviour. Some numerical evidence of related interest has been presented for Britain by Sayers (1967) using an explicitly cyclical framework to investigate the former preceding-year basis of corporate income tax. In addition, we should remember the deliberately accelerated collection of U.S. corporate tax in 1965–1966 as an anti-inflation measure. On the reverse flow from governments to firms, there have been substantial delays in the payments associated with the British investment grants and refunds for selective employment tax. Nor is the difficulty of reconciling the delays with payments for on-going investment programmes made any easier by the functional split in responsibilities of governmental departments. For example, the Board of Trade is charged with administration of the investment-grants system whereas the responsibilities for the SET refunds were shared by the Ministries of Labour, Social Security and Agriculture!

Second, in the use of particular regressions to assess potential policies, it is possible to forget the constraints imposed by the political process. Salutory reminders are provided by the failure of the Johnson administration to introduce a general U.S. tax increase in 1966 and, also, by the recent difficulties experienced by a minority Liberal government in Canada with the introduction of a proposed cut in corporate taxes. The political cycle in British economic activity is as relevant today as in period when it was first identified by Kalecki.

Third, as researchers, we frequently define 'rational' behaviour in terms of specific economic objectives only to find that actual decision-makers behave 'irrationally', at least in terms of these objectives. The extent of the non-adoption of accelerated-depreciation methods in both Britain and the United States provides a good illustration of this. In Britain, a major factor in the shift from an allowance system to a grant system was the doubts expressed concerning the efficacy of the former system in persuading firms to take account of accelerated depreciation in their investment planning. These doubts were demonstrated by responses of corporate decision-makers to questionnaires as reported by Neild (1964) and Corner and Williams (1965). More substantial reports on non-adoption are available for the United States. See especially the reports of Stevenson (1965a,b; 1966), Ture (1967) and Young (1968a,b) which all reveal significant levels of non-adoption of accelerated-depreciation methods even where this omission reduces profits. How should we react to such evidence? Clearly this depends upon individual researchers' attitudes. We could dismiss the evidence as based on either unscientific methods or poorly chosen samples. We could accept it and criticize corporate decision-makers as irrational, short-sighted or simply incompetent. Alternatively, we could reformulate our models so that they capture non-adoption phenomena within a determinate framework.

Finally, the many sources of international influences might be explored. The overwhelming influence of multinational corporations in some countries and in some industrial sectors is an important development too-often ignored in investment studies. Their transfer pricing provides a substantial area for affecting tax payments and their size may lead national governments to compete between themselves in order to attract branch plants. In addition, multinational corporations may enjoy preferential treatment during periods of monetary stringency due to the stability of their overall growth performance and their ability to draw funds not only from several national markets but also from global levels of retained earnings.

In order to stimulate domestic producers of capital assets, a national government might make the rates of capital allowances depend upon the origins of purchased assets as, for example, with the introduction of a 10 percent tax credit in the United States during August 1971. This credit was only available for defraying the costs of new equipment produced in the United States. International differences in capacity utilization of supplying industries may also be influential. For example, the *Monthly Report of the Deutsche Bundesbank* (February, 1973) suggests that the rapidly increasing output of the German machine-tools industry at the end of 1972 may partially be explained by its relatively low level of utilization as compared with its international competitors and by the generally high level of export demands within total demands for this output.

In the account presented above, we introduced symbols to represent 'capital stocks' and 'production functions' without qualification. However, it would be inappropriate to conclude our survey without expressing some concern with the too-ready acceptance and manipulation of such symbols by econometricians. In the last two decades we have seen an acrimonious debate as to whether bases can be established for this acceptance. The debate, identified in the literature associated with aggregation and the existence of capital aggregates or in the 'Cambridge controversy', has been highly public. Some other views should also be cited although they have not generated as much attention. Thus Lachman (1956) provides a 'morphological' approach to capital and a 'plan-period' method of error-correction which indicate some difficulties with contemporaneous aggregate approaches and a possible foreshadowing of future recursive models of investment. The former, with its emphasis on disequilibrium, should be read alongside the more recent statement in aggregation literature by Gorman (1968). Finally, we should avoid the negligence indicated by Georgescu–Roegen (1970): 'in our haste to mathematize economics we have often been carried away by mathematical formalism to the point of disregarding a basic requirement of science; namely, to have as clear an idea as possible about what corresponds in actuality to every piece of our symbolism.'

CHAPTER 2

Economic Theory (II): Inventories

This chapter provides a survey of those theoretical issues in inventory behaviour which have direct implications for empirical work. In this category we include both 'micro' and 'macro' analyses. Micro-analytical literature provides us with bases for establishing concepts and relationships which are the subject of empirical investigations. Many possible hypotheses concerning the determinants of inventory behaviour are examined for their relevance to empirical work. They include not only those aspects concerning the determinants of desired stock, for example, production-smoothing and the acceleration principle, but also others relating to the interrelationship between inventories on one hand and aggregate income, unfilled orders and prices on the other. The final section below considers the role of inventories with respect to the stability of the economy.

2.1 FACTORS INFLUENCING DESIRED INVENTORY

A central notion in analyses of aggregate inventory behaviour is the concept of desired inventory levels, to be determined for every point in time. In pursuit of specific goals, the 'rational' entrepreneur is assumed to seek a particular level of inventory affected by cost, revenue and technological factors in both production and distribution. For example, the decision-maker may attempt by his choice of inventory levels to minimize storage and handling costs, to maximize his profits constrained by these costs, or some other goal. This choice could occur once or, alternatively, it could be part of a sequential procedure.

A standard classification of motives for holding inventories is into transactions, precautionary and speculative types. The transactions motive is essentially concerned with the lack of synchronization between receipt and sale of goods or production and delivery of goods or (as in manufacturing) between receipt and usage of goods. This motive may be simply illustrated by the following model in which a decision-maker, faced by a known level of sales, X, evenly spread over a year, chooses his pattern of orders to minimize costs. Each order is assumed to be for the same amount and is instantly filled so that there is no problem of 'stock-outs' and the concomitant loss of sales. Essentially by fixing the level of his orders, S, the decision-maker establishes their frequency (X/S). Let c_1 represent the administrative cost of placing an order. (This is assumed to be independent of the size of the order.) Further, let c_2 and c_3 represent the unit costs of storage and orders, respectively. Then, since the average inventory is $S/2$, total costs are $(c_1 X/S + c_2 S/2 + c_3 X)$. These costs are minimized by the choice of $(2c_1 X/c_2)^{1/2}$ for the desired level of orders S^* which establish the desired levels of inventories. Clearly, only if c_1 is zero will the desired level of inventories be zero. In the above context, we note that the assumption of certain demand by itself does not preclude holding of inventories.

Closely associated with the transactions motive is the holding of stocks due to technological factors. Many manufacturing processes are time consuming so that at any moment a certain amount of 'work in progress' will be held. Similarly, for both retailers and wholesalers, stocks will be needed for sample, display and advertisement purposes and, analytically, this could be treated in the same way as manufacturers' work in process. A major problem here is to determine the nature of relationship between work in process and the rate of production.

The precautionary motive or buffer-stock motive lies at the heart of most econometric discussions of inventory behaviour. In its most basic form this motive is concerned with the role of inventories as a buffer against unforeseen and foreseen fluctuations in sales which is best treated as a random variable. Supply of goods may also be uncertain. Probability distributions of the relevant random variables could be such as to necessitate carrying buffer-stocks which bear the brunt of unforeseen or uncontrollable fluctuations. A buffer stock provides a service insofar as it cushions production against demand fluctuations, and reduces or eliminates the possibility of loss of profit or customer goodwill resulting from inability to meet existing demand. The first of these is closely allied to the concept of production-smoothing which is considered later in this chapter.

Our discussion of the transactions motive illustrates how cost and revenue considerations must be explicitly introduced in the model if we are to derive precise functional relationships linking inventories with other variables. The following one-period model of Carlson and O'Keefe (1969) takes account of the random nature of demand and also both the inventory carrying costs and the penalty costs of not carrying inventories (termed backlog costs).

Let X_t denote sales in period t, $f(X_t)$ the probability density function for X_t, I_t the net inventories at the end of period t, and Q_t the quantity produced in period t. The random variable X_t is assumed to have a uniform distribution,

$$f(X) = \frac{1}{\beta - \alpha}, \text{where } \alpha \leq X \leq \beta, \tag{1}$$

and zero otherwise. Then the mean of X is $\bar{X} = (\beta + \alpha)/2$. Assume that I_t may be negative or positive (negative inventories are termed 'backlogs'). Let c_1 represent the cost of carrying one unit of finished goods for one unit of time and c_2 represent the unit cost of backlogging. The actual cost of net inventories, c_I, per period is $c_1 I$ when I is positive and $(-c_2 I)$ otherwise. When demand (X) per period exceeds the supply $(I + Q)$ in that period, a backlog $(X - I - Q)$ accrues. The expected cost of this backlog is given by the product of $-c_2$ and the weighted density function of X, integrated over all possible values of the backlog, that is, over the interval $[I + Q, \beta]$, yielding

$$-c_2 \int_{I+Q}^{\beta} (X - I - Q).f(X)dX.$$

Similarly, the expected cost of carrying stocks is the product of c_1 and the mean value of the stock which has to be carried. The stock is $(I + Q - X)$ and its mean value is given by integrating the product of $(I + Q - X)$ and $f(X)$ over all possible values of X for which there is a stock. The expected carrying cost of inventories is therefore

$$c_1 \int_{\alpha}^{I+Q} (I + Q - X)f(X).dX.$$

Expected total costs are given by the sum of the two integrals:

$$E[c_I(Q^*)] = c_1 \int_{\alpha}^{Q*} (Q^* - X).f(X)dX - c_2 \int_{Q*}^{\beta} (X - Q^*)f(X)dX, \quad (2)$$

where Q^* is $I + Q$.
Substituting for $f(X)$ and integrating, the right-hand side of (2) becomes

$$\frac{c_1}{2(\beta - \alpha)} Q^{*2} - \frac{\alpha c_1}{(\beta - \alpha)} Q^* + \frac{\alpha^2 c_1}{2(\beta - \alpha)} + \frac{c_2}{2(\beta - \alpha)} Q^{*2}$$

$$- \frac{\beta c_2}{(\beta - \alpha)} Q^* + \frac{\beta^2 c_2}{2(\beta - \alpha)},$$

which is a quadratic function in Q^* with a minimum when

$$Q^* = \frac{\alpha c_1 + \beta c_2}{c_1 + c_2}. \quad (3)$$

Since the expected value of X_t is $(\alpha + \beta)/2$, the cost-minimizing level of production is $\bar{X}$, which when subtracted from the above equation yields the optimum inventory,

$$I^* = \frac{(c_2 - c_1)(\beta - \alpha)}{2(c_1 + c_2)}. \quad (4)$$

This will be positive if c_2 exceeds c_1 but negative when the cost of carrying inventories exceeds the cost of backlogs.

Equation (4) shows how cost considerations determine the precautionary demand for inventories. However, the problem considered ignores another essential feature of inventory holding; namely, the consideration of risk which arises in a multi-period analysis. As other authors have emphasized, the assumption of a single period planning horizon is rather restrictive. The decision taken in one period will frequently affect subsequent decisions since inventories will generally be carried over to the next period. Furthermore, the inventory policy of a rational firm may be based on minimization of expected costs not only in the current period but in several future periods too. For a lucid account of the nature of this problem, see Mills (1962, Ch. 6).

In general, although the inventory problem involves expectations of costs and sales in several future periods, only the optimal inventory policy for the first period need be determined initially. A decision taken will usually be a function of information available at a point in time and decisions will possess a recursive structure, each decision being a function of information available then, including previous decisions. This point will emerge clearly when we consider production planning and its relation to optimal inventory-holding policies — a topic to which we will turn after considering the speculative motive. The reason for doing so is that consideration of the speculative motive also involves issues of risk in multi-period planning which are essentially similar to those of production planning.

Stockholding and speculation

In the context of the speculative motive, Kaldor (1939) defines speculation as 'the purchase (or sale) of goods with a view to resale (repurchase) at a later date, where the motive behind such action is the expectation of a change in the relevant prices relative to the ruling price and not a gain accruing through their use, or any kind of transformation effected in them or their transfer between different markets'. The definition emphasizes that the only reason for purchase (or sale) is the expectation of an impending price change; therefore, the ordinary transactions of the dealers are explicitly excluded. Clearly speculative stocks are 'the difference between the amount actually held and the amount that would be held if, other things being the same, the price of that thing were expected to remain unchanged'. This difference can be negative or positive. The relevant expectations here are the expectations of the individual speculator which may or may not coincide with the 'general' expectations. Speculative stockholding would be significant in the aggregate when the 'general' expectations regarding prices depart considerably from the current price.

Inductive reasoning along lines of Kaldor (1939) suggests that not all goods are equally likely objects of price speculation. Indeed it is not hard to suggest several categories of manufacturing production where speculation can be ruled out by *a priori* reasoning. This has direct implications for econometric work with aggregate data.

Muth (1961) has considered the question of optimal speculation. Consider an individual who, in period t, has an opportunity of purchasing goods at a known price P_t for sale in period $(t + 1)$. Suppose costs of transactions are negligible.

Price in $(t+1)$ is unknown but he knows its probability distribution and uses its mean as the expected price P_{t+1}^e in that period. Let σ_{t+1}^2 be the variance of this distribution. Let I_t^s represent the speculative inventory at the end of period t. Then the expected profit $E(\pi_t)$, or expected speculative gain, is

$$E(\pi_t) = I_t^s(P_{t+1}^e - P_t). \tag{5}$$

How is the extent of an individual speculator's commitment determined? Let U denote his utility function and U', U'' its first and second derivatives respectively. For a small range of variations in profits, the utility function may be approximated by the first few terms of its Taylor series expansion around the origin. Thus,

$$U = U(\pi_t) = U(0) + U'(0)\pi_t + \tfrac{1}{2}U''(0)\pi_t^2 + \ldots \tag{6}$$

and, taking expectations,

$$E[U(\pi_t)] = U(0) + U'(0)E(\pi_t) + \tfrac{1}{2}U''(0)E(\pi_t^2) + \ldots. \tag{7}$$

From (5) and the definition of σ_{t+1}^2

$$E(\pi_t^2) = (I_t^s)^2(\sigma_{t+1}^2 + (P_{t+1}^e - P_t)^2]. \tag{8}$$

Substituting for $E(\pi_t)$ and $E(\pi_t^2)$ in the Taylor expansion, we obtain

$$E(U_t) = U(0) + U'(0)I_t^s(P_{t+1}^e - P_t) + \tfrac{1}{2}U''(0)(I_t^s)^2[\sigma_{t+1}^2 + (P_{t+1}^e - P_t)^2] + \ldots.$$

Differentiating with respect to I_t^s

$$\frac{\partial E(U_t)}{\partial I_t^s} = U'(0)(P_{t+1}^e - P_t) + U''(0)I_t^s[\sigma_{t+1}^2 + (P_{t+1}^e - P_t)^2] + \ldots$$

so that, to a first approximation, optimal inventory is given by

$$I_t^s = -\frac{U'(0)(P_{t+1}^e - P_t)}{U''(0)[\sigma_{t+1}^2 + (P_{t+1}^e - P_t)^2]}. \tag{9}$$

Suppose $U'(0)$ is positive and $U''(0)$ is negative, then speculative inventory is an increasing function of the expected change in price. What is the relation between this expression and the one conventionally adopted in empirical work,

$$I_t^s = \alpha(P_{t+1}^e - P_t), \tag{10}$$

where α is a constant? Note that the Taylor expansion is only valid for small changes. Suppose that $(P_{t+1}^e - P_t)^2$ is small enough to be neglected. Then, provided the mean P_{t+1}^e is independent of σ_{t+1}^2 we see that

$$\alpha = -\frac{U'(0)}{U''(0)\sigma_{t+1}^2}.$$

To take account of storage costs, interest costs, etc., it is only necessary to reinterpret the current price P_t. That is, the speculator's gain should be treated as proportional to the difference between P_{t+1}^e and P_t plus costs of carrying stocks.

In criticizing the work of Abramovitz (1939) and Shaw (1940), Arrow *et al.* (1958) observed that in their analyses of speculative inventories these writers had provided an inadequate treatment of non-negativity conditions. (Recall the discussion of irreversibility in Chapter One.) The analysis of Abramovitz and Shaw was more appropriate to the situation where prices were expected to rise through time. In the case where they were declining, the non-negativity constraint on inventories would operate so that no inventories would be held. In Muth's analysis which was discussed above, there was no explicit treatment of non-negativity conditions either.

A multiperiod model

It is important to grasp the nature of the link between production plans and inventories. This frequently brings into consideration the notion of production-smoothing which is important in the empirical literature. To illustrate, we shall draw upon the model of Modigliani and Hohn (1955).

Suppose that for a given commodity the decision-maker has estimates of demand for each of T future periods of equal length. Assume that the demand fluctuates. Given variations in costs of both production and storage, then the decision-maker will seek to schedule his production in such a way as to minimize these costs over the T periods. If the marginal cost of producing the commodity is constant and there are no capacity constraints, then total costs will be minimized by reducing the storage costs to the minimum. This can be achieved by producing in each period an amount just sufficient to cover the sales requirements of that period. When, however, the marginal cost of producing an extra unit is increasing, then the optimal schedule of production will not be arrived at by consideration of storage costs alone.

Let q_i and x_i ($i = 1, 2, ..., T$) denote, respectively, production and demand in the ith period, and let the initial inventory be zero. Inventory at the end of period τ, I_τ, is the accumulated difference between production and sales,

$$I_\tau = \sum_{i=1}^{\tau} q_i - \sum_{i=1}^{\tau} x_i = Q_\tau - X_\tau. \tag{11}$$

If $F(q_t)$ gives the variable cost (the fixed costs may be ignored without loss of generality) of producing q_t, the total variable cost for T periods is

$$C_p = \sum_{t=1}^{T} F(q_t). \tag{12}$$

The unit cost of storage is assumed proportional to the length of storage time. The cost of storing a unit for one period is h. If we further assume that, within a period, production and sales take place at an even rate, then the average inventory in period t will be $\frac{1}{2}(I_t + I_{t-1})$ and the storage costs will be

$$C_s = \frac{h}{2} \sum_{t=1}^{T} (I_t + I_{t-1}) \tag{13}$$

$$= h \sum_{t=1}^{T-1} I_t + \frac{h}{2} I_0 \qquad \text{if } I_T = 0.$$

The total variable cost of production and storage cost is

$$C = C_p + C_s = \sum_{t=1}^{T} F(q_t) + h \sum_{t=1}^{T-1} I_t + \frac{h}{2} I_0. \qquad (14)$$

The optimum production programme for T periods is one which satisfies the following conditions: total cost of the programme is minimum, $\{I_t\}$ is non-negative $(t = 1, 2, \ldots, T)$, $\{Q_t\}$ is non-negative $(t = 1, 2, \ldots, T)$, I_T is zero. In order to solve the problem it is necessary to take a specific cost-function. A quadratic function was considered by Modigliani and Hohn as a possibility.

Modigliani and Hohn consider the problem of minimizing (14) subject to these conditions. The solution to this constrained minimization problem is termed by them the 'fundamental solution' and they show that the optimal plan for a T-period problem is made up of a sequence of fundamental solutions over successive blocks of periods. The fundamental solution is obtained by setting up the Lagrangean function

$$C^* = \sum_{t=1}^{T} F(q_t) + h \sum_{t=1}^{T} [I_0 + Q_t - X_t] + \frac{hI_0}{2} + \lambda[I_0 + Q_T - X_T] \qquad (15)$$

and equating the derivatives with respect to each q_t to zero. Thus we obtain

$$\frac{\partial C^*}{\partial q_t} = \frac{dF(q_t)}{dq_t} + \lambda + (T - t)h = 0 \qquad (t = 1, \ldots, T)$$

which implies, for example,

$$\frac{dF(q_{t+j})}{dq_{t+j}} = \frac{dF(q_t)}{dq_t} + hj \qquad (2 \le t + j \le T). \qquad (16)$$

The left-hand side of (16) measures the marginal cost of making available, in period $(t + j)$, a unit produced in that period, whereas the right-hand side is the cost of making it available in period $(t + j)$ having produced it in period t and stored it for j periods. If, for any sequence $\{q_i\}$, the right-hand side of the above equation exceeds the left-hand side, then costs could be reduced by reducing q_t and increasing q_{t+j}. Thus the optimal plan is one for which the left-hand side is at the most equal to the right-hand side.

We shall not concern ourselves with the interesting and non-trivial question of the method of working out the fundamental solution or with the proof that a particular method yields an optimum. Here we are more concerned with the insight that this model gives into the way in which stocks may be used to act as a buffer between sales and production. Given increasing marginal costs production plans do not mirror the fluctuations in sales and inventories are used to smooth production. Thus production will be relatively stable in spite of fluctuations in sales. Stocks will be built up when demand is low and run down when it is high. The inventory at the termination of the plan period will be, however, zero.

One issue raised by the preceding discussion concerns how many periods ahead the firms look; that is, what is T? In the case considered above, it was assumed known, but in practice is a choice variable. Modigliani and Hohn (1955, pp. 64–65) argued that for goods with a seasonal pattern of demand the plan horizon would not extend beyond a 'full seasonal cycle (or shorter interval yet if storage costs are high) but is not likely to extend beyond this cycle except in the presence of a rapidly rising over-all trend. Furthermore, if the relevant horizon extends beyond the current cycle, this extension is likely to proceed by whole cycles. Finally, to the extent, that new information will make it necessary to replan in the course of a seasonal cycle, the revised plan itself will cover the balance of the given cycle, plus possibly one but seldom more than one, later cycle.' Econometrically, the size of T is not trivial since it determines, in an important way, the specification of behavioural equations describing planned production and inventory behaviour. Some authors have emphasized the increase in variances of forecast errors as T increases and the increased expense of additional computations as grounds for truncating the horizon. However, a rigorous argument showing the relative importance of different factors does not appear to be available.

2.2 THE ACCELERATION PRINCIPLE AND ITS RELATION TO MOTIVES FOR HOLDING INVENTORIES

In empirical work it is the acceleration principle which is invoked most often to explain the changes in the rate of inventory investment. This is in contrast to the approach adopted in theoretical models of inventories, for example, in the Carlson–O'Keefe one period model. In both empirical and theoretical work it is usual to relate the desired level of stocks at the end of period t to the expected level of sales or output in either that period or the next; that is

$$I_t^* = \alpha + \beta \hat{X}_t, \tag{17}$$

where the superscripts * and ^ distinguish between desired and expected quantities, or

$$I_t^* = \alpha + \beta \hat{X}_{t+1}. \tag{18}$$

Thus the desired investment in inventories is proportional to the expected rate of change of sales, β the positive accelerator coefficient. It is the acceleration in demand that determines the rate of inventory investment. This specification is consistent with the assumption of an optimum inventory-sales, or inventory-output ratio which decision-makers may strive to maintain or behave as if they try to maintain. Thus an increase in expected sales gives rise to a situation in which inventories would get 'out of line' with sales if the firms did not attempt to increase them. It is sometimes argued that there are some underlying factors which make it rational for a firm to want to do so. Notice that, apart perhaps for work in progress, no technical considerations govern the relation between inventories on one hand and output or sales on the other. Derivation of the accelerator hypothesis must come from elsewhere.

Modigliani (1957) has considered the particular question of the consistency between optimization of a well-defined objective function at a micro-level and the acceleration principle as applied to aggregate behaviour. He puts forward four micro-economic reasons justifying the assumption of a 'desired' sales–stock ratio. First, suppose it is the case that firms face different demand and cost conditions and consequently have different optimal ordering rules; such as, for example, the square-root rule. Despite such apparent diversity the hypothesis of a fixed desired stocks to sales ratio is reasonable since 'when dealing with a large number of firms (or products within a firm) whose cycles of order occur at random, a stable relationship between average stocks and sales for each individual over time will tend to generate, for any given (constant) rate of sales, a stable relation between aggregate stocks and aggregate sales at each point of time', (p. 500). Thus the relationship in question, though not a behavioural rule for each firm, may provide a reasonable hypothesis for the aggregate. Second, fluctuations in sales (especially seasonal fluctuations) are not reflected in coincidental fluctuations in production, since there are costs involved in changing the rate of production and, in attempting to minimize costs, firms will use inventories to smooth or stabilize production by building inventories up at times of low (including seasonally low) demand and running them down in periods of high demand. If the seasonal fluctuations are the only source of variations in sales, then stocks held at a point in time and average stocks held during the year will bear a definite and stable relation to the rate of sales.

The third reason stems from the possibility of making a speculative gain from rising prices. As we have already seen, provided the expected rise in inventory prices exceeds the carrying cost speculative considerations will operate even when there is no uncertainty regarding demand. The quantity that will be purchased will depend on storage costs and expected prices but will tend to equal a certain number of months' requirement.

Finally, an entirely separate reason for holding stocks is the possible inability to meet demand during the procurement lead time period. At the time of delivery of an order the stock will not be zero but some positive (buffer) quantity which will generally tend to increase with the rate of sales.

The essence of Modigliani's reasoning is that the desired stock is a quantity which takes account of a number of factors influencing stockholding. Although the desired stock–sales ratio may be any number within a certain band, the hypothesis of a stable stock-sales relation is a useful approximation in dealing with broad aggregates.

Flexible accelerator models

The acceleration principle relates desired inventory at end of period t to expected sales in period t (or $t + 1$). Additional flexibility is gained by relating planned inventory investment to desired inventory level and, thus, indirectly, to expected sales. The simplest version of the flexible accelerator model stresses that firms will not immediately adjust their actual levels of inventories to a new desired level. Rather, they will only aim at removing a fraction, say δ, of the discrepancy between the desired and actual stocks. Thus we have:

$$I_t - I_{t-1} = \delta(I_i^* - I_{t-1}), \qquad 0 < \delta \le 1. \tag{19}$$

Two main reasons why firms are supposed to adjust their stocks by only a fraction of the desired change are inertia on the part of firms and the cost of making the full adjustment when the future is uncertain. We have already seen that production smoothing is motivated by the desire to avoid rapid fluctuations. These fluctuations keep actual stock close to the desired level. Thus in trying to lower the cost of making changes firms will adjust their stocks only partially towards the desired level. Rearranging (19), it can be seen that the current level of stock is a geometrically weighted average of past desired levels of stocks,

$$I_t = \delta I_t^* + \delta(1 - \delta)I_{t-1}^* + \delta(1 - \delta)^2 I_{t-2}^* + \ldots$$
$$= \sum_{i=0}^{\infty} \delta(1 - \delta)^i I_{t-i}^*. \tag{20}$$

The assumption of partial adjustment leads naturally to a distinction between the short-term and the long-term accelerator effect.
Combining (17) and (19) we obtain

$$I_t = (1 - \delta)I_{t-1} + \delta\alpha + \delta\beta\hat{X}_t,$$

whence we see that a unit increase in $\hat{X}_t$ leads to increase in inventories of $\delta\beta$ in the period 0, $\delta(1 - \delta)\beta$ in period 1, $\delta(1 - \delta)^2\beta$ in period 2, and $\delta(1 - \delta)^j\beta$ in period j. In terminology introduced in Chapter Three, $\delta\beta$ is the impact effect and $\delta(1 - \delta)^j\beta$ is the jth period effect. The equilibrium or comparative static effect is given by

$$\delta\beta + \delta(1 - \delta)\beta + \ldots = \beta \sum_{j=0}^{\infty} \delta(1 - \delta)^j = \beta.$$

The impetus to study various technical and institutional factors contributing to slower adjustment came originally from the empirical work of Abramovitz (1950) which confirmed that changes in output and stocks did not coincide. Rather the changes in stocks tended to lag behind changes in output. Subsequently the flexible accelerator hypothesis which provides an explanation of this phenomenon was examined most closely in empirical work by Lovell (1961) and has been adopted as a basis in many studies since.

Arguments which lead one to take the partial adjustment hypothesis as a useful starting point do not of course imply that the assumption of geometrically declining weights is the most appropriate one, though it is doubtless one of the simplest. (This point is examined more thoroughly in Chapter Three.) At present we simply note that there are several families of adjustment processes which are all consistent with partial adjustment, and the problem of choosing the most appropriate amongst these raises a whole host of econometric specification and estimation problems.

While the acceleration principle may not do full justice to various relevant micro-economic considerations influencing stockholding behaviour, it is not basically in conflict with them. Its shortcomings as a hypothesis have been extensively discussed elsewhere. (See, for example, Knox (1952).) However, these criticisms are widely believed to be much less applicable to inventories than to fixed capital. Nevertheless there is a possibility that while the acceleration principle may provide a good description of the way stocks behave over long periods, it may still be quite inadequate in explaining the very short-term fluctuations resulting from factors which are not adequately represented either in the simple flexible accelerator model or in extensions of that model. Mack (1957, 1967) has made precisely this point.

She contends that the accelerator-type models are mechanical and pay too little attention to market conditions and their influence on purchasing decisions, the interaction between expectations, purchasing decisions and the resulting changes in market conditions. As a consequence the accelerator mechanism is incapable of explaining the observed facts of strongly cyclical shifts in orders for materials. In Mack (1967) she attempted to provide an alternative description and explanation of this phenomenon, but her image is complex and not amenable to a symbolic treatment. In her model, the main behavioural variable is 'market-oriented buying' through which the firms alter their 'ownership position'; that is, the sum of outstanding orders and stock of goods on hand. Market-oriented buying must be distinguished from buying merely for purposes of efficient servicing of sales, the former being determined primarily by expectations regarding future price, supply and demand conditions. The model is an attempt to explain how a wave of buying is initiated and terminated and to delineate the factors which determine the extent of participation by an individual firm in such a buying wave. One implication is that orders, being a part of ownership position, must not itself be used as an explanatory variable in an inventory model. Rather it should be explained within that model. Furthermore, the positive feedback relationship linking purchases, expectations and buying prices should be recognized and greater emphasis placed on the constraints operating on the buyers themselves.

Analytic treatment of orders

We have previously considered the possibility of a firm holding a negative inventory or backlog. A question which has been sharply raised in recent discussions concerns the analytical treatment of this variable; in particular, whether it is satisfactory to think of the variable as merely the negative of inventories. Another question concerns the empirical usefulness and relevance of the distinction.

The existence of unfilled orders is closely tied up with the operation of industries which produce largely or mainly to order. The reasons for this are to be found in the nature of the product which they manufacture. Industries which produce heavy durable capital equipment, often to particular specifications, are unlikely to hold stocks because storage is costly, demand uncertain and their product is capable of being rendered obsolete by technical advance or changes in fashion. Stocks of finished goods tend to be negligible in volume. The related pattern of production is one which is based on receipt of new orders which must take place in a queue before work on them is done. Since many of the characteristics of products which encourage production to order also imply that production is itself a time-consuming process, there exists at any time a backlog of partly or wholly uncompleted orders. Where production is mainly on the basis of 'first-come-first-served', the volume of the backlog represents the length of the queue in front of a newly received order. The backlog serves the same purpose as inventories. It is a buffer between demand and production, and the cost of holding a zero backlog in the presence of changing demand may be reflected in a fluctuating level of production.

Abramovitz (1950) appears to have been one of the earliest workers to stress the distinction between production to order (PTO) and production to stock (PTS), and point to the usefulness of this distinction for empirical analysis of inventories. Stanback (1962) extended this work in his analysis of post-war inventory cycles and Zarnowitz (1962) examined the relation between price changes and changes in unfilled orders to see whether backlogging was accompanied by price increases. These studies made a considerable impact on empirical research on inventory behaviour.

Two studies which may be particularly noted are those of Childs (1967) and Belsley (1969). The latter argues that unfilled orders and inventories are not simply the negatives of each other. On the contrary the reasons for holding a backlog as well as the costs of doing so are entirely different from inventory associated costs. First, a commitment to supply at an agreed price raises the possibility that the input prices may change between the receipt and completion of the order. Second, when the existing backlog is high, the firm may not profit from meeting new orders at a more favourable price in future, should such a possibility arise, in view of its existing commitments. There is also the possibility of lost sales resulting from quoting long delivery delays. The order–delivery lag is a significant dimension of competition and since, for a given rate of production, a firm with the larger backlog takes longer to get through it, the opportunity cost of such a large backlog will be the orders which the firm might otherwise have received. Of course, when backlogs are great and demand still rising, the firm may attempt to meet these conditions by an expansion of its productive capacity. But the effects of such an expansion will not be experienced in the short run. Thus the impact on the existing backlog may not be perceptible in the short run. Much will depend on the specific nature of market conditions with the consequence that the kind of generalizations offered above must be subject to qualifications.

A possibility exploited by both Childs and Belsley treats the decision-maker as having, in addition to a desired inventory level, a desired level of unfilled orders. The level of unfilled orders at the end of period t, U_t, is given by the identity

$$U_t = U_{t-1} + (N_t - D_t), \tag{21}$$

where the term in parentheses measures the excess of new orders received over the deliveries (shipments) made in that period. But, with U_{t-1} given, and N_t exogenously determined for a particular firm, having desired U_t simply amounts to having a target rate of deliveries. Put in this way the assumption seems quite appropriate.

On the question of determination of desired level of backlogs, Childs argues that it depends on the actual rate of production, Q_t. In particular he assumes that

$$U_t^* = a + bQ_t, \quad b > 0. \tag{22}$$

The logic of this seems to be that the higher the rate of production, the more rapidly can a given backlog be reduced to zero, and hence the higher is the optimal level of that backlog.

Diagrammatically, see Figure 1, we have curve (a) which reflects costs that are declining as the backlog gets larger. These are essentially those costs which

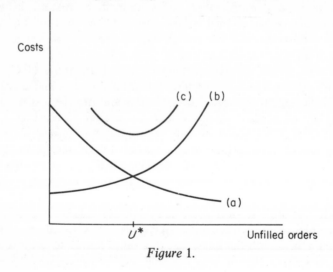

Figure 1.

are associated with bulk materials purchasing, flexibility in scheduling production, elimination of uncertainty given a large backlog. Curve (b) on the other hand reflects costs which increase with the size of the backlog. 'Penalty costs for cancellation of orders', writes Childs, 'for expediting particular orders in response to customer requests and the probility of loss of future sales all increase as the size of the backlog increases and the lead time lengthens.' Curve (c) is a vertical sum of curves (a) and (b); the minimum point on curve (c) then represents the optimal of desired level of unfilled orders, U^*. This reasoning does not justify a linear relationship between desired unfilled orders and production and is an approximation only.

The similarity of the unfilled-order variable to inventories raises the question of the way it has been treated in analytical and empirical work. Suppose for simplicity that when unfilled orders are positive, the stock of finished goods is zero. Then, if unfilled order merely indicate a commitment to deliver a certain amount in future, the primary use of unfilled orders would be in providing an explanation of the rate of production. But the cost considerations relating to unfilled orders indicate that the behaviour may be more complex than this since manufacturers may also wish to maintain unfilled orders at a certain desired level, say U_t^*. If production-smoothing considerations operate simultaneously, then the optimal level of production and unfilled orders must represent a compromise between the extreme of low unfilled orders and high variability in production on one hand and high unfilled orders and low variability in production on the other. If we allow firms with positive unfilled orders to hold stocks of finished goods also, the model becomes even more complex, for now there is the additional possibility of the firm wishing to control its stocks of finished goods too (an addition of a target with the number of instruments unchanged). In the next section, we shall formally consider the kind of decision rules that emerge when the problem is considered in the framework of quadratic cost functions and linear constraints.

2.3 A FRAMEWORK: QUADRATIC COSTS AND LINEAR CONSTRAINTS

A number of models of interdependence between pricing, output and inventory decisions are in the framework of quadratic cost functions and linear constraints. The standard references here are Holt *et al.* (1960), Holt and Modigliani (1961) and Theil (1964).

Consider a firm that has a planning horizon of T discrete periods of equal length. To simplify matters suppose that the firm produces for stocks only and has no order backlogs. The net inventory change is then given by

$$I_t - I_{t-1} = Q_t - X_t. \tag{23}$$

There are a number of costs associated with production and inventory holding and we shall assume that, in the neighbourhood of the point where the firm operates, these costs can be approximated by quadratic functions. For concreteness suppose there are only three elements in the cost: direct cost of production, inventory connected costs and costs of fluctuations in production. Introduction of fixed costs does not make any essential difference to the main argument and these are, therefore, omitted. Let C_t denote the total costs. Then, by assumption,

$$C_t = c_3 Q_t + c_4 (I_t - I_t^*)^2 + c_5 (Q_t - Q_{t-1})^2, \tag{24}$$

where the first term on the right-hand side of the equation represents the direct costs of production Q_t, the second term represents the costs of inventory at the end of period t deviating from the desired level I_t^* (thus c_4 reflects not only the financial costs but also the psychic costs of such an event) and the last term represents the costs of changing the level of production. The inclusion of direct costs needs no justification; the inclusion of inventory costs is based on the assumption that if inventories exceed a certain desired level then there will be costs of storage, insurance, deterioration and obsolescence, whereas if they fall below the desired level there will be costs arising from inability to service sales efficiently. Somewhat unrealistically these costs are assumed to be symmetrical about I_t^*.

I_t^* may be assumed to be linearly related to the expected level of sales in $t + 1$; thus

$$I_t^* = c_1 + c_2 \hat{X}_{t+1}, \tag{25}$$

where c_1 and c_2 are constants. Substituting for I_t^* in the cost function yields

$$C_t = c_3 Q_t + c_4 [I_t - (c_1 + c_2 \hat{X}_{t+1})]^2 + c_5 (Q_t - Q_{t-1})^2.$$

Costs associated with changing the level of production arise from the need to reorganize the workforce and machines which may arise when production levels are changed. It is not unusual, for example, for goods to be produced in runs keeping the rate of production constant, in order to minimize costs of reorganization, machine set-up costs and possible hiring or discharge of workers. The assumption that the relevant costs may be approximated by a quadratic function symmetric around the minimum is, of course, a simplification. Next assume that the cost parameters are known with complete certainty to the firm and that the only uncertainty lies in the firm not knowing its sales in any future period. We also impose the restriction that there is no outside buying which means that inventories are simply the difference between production and sales. Let C_T be the present value of total costs in T periods,

$$\sum_{t=1}^{T} \lambda^{t-1} C_t,$$

λ being the discount factor. For a given sequence $\{\hat{X}_t\}$, the decision-maker's problem is to choose a sequence $\{Q_t\}$ so as to minimize C_T subject to constraint (1). It is obvious that the solution to the constrained maximization problem involves a compromise between various categories of costs, a greater weight being attached to the relatively more important costs and lesser to the less important. Thus by keeping inventories at I_t^* in each t the inventory associated costs could be eliminated entirely, but only at the expense of increased costs of fluctuations in production. The problem of choosing the best sequence of production decisions is a difficult one for at least three major reasons. Firstly, decisions taken now will affect decisions taken in the future; secondly, not one but several decisions may be involved; thirdly, the decisions have to be taken in face of uncertainty and conditional on forecast values of variable—

forecasts which may be subject to substantial error. The problem is essentially dynamic since not all T decisions have to be taken all at once. The decision for t may be taken conditional upon the initial conditions for $t - 1$ and the best information (or guesses) that can be made for X_{t+1}. At the beginning of $t + 1$, the previous decision would have generated new initial conditions, and additional information would have accumulated regarding X. The next decision regarding production will be based therefore on these new initial conditions and on the best guess for $t + 1$ conditional on information available then, and so on. Thus only the first-period decision need to taken at any time. But note that future sales are not known with certainty. The available information on sales may take the form not of fixed values, but of a probability distribution. The problem is not of minimizing C_T but a reformulated one where, for example, its expected value is minimized. This is obtained by replacing the sequence $\{X_{t+1}, t = 1,..., T\}$ by a sequence of expected values. Does it matter if we work out the optimal strategy first and then replace the unknown values of future sales by expected values rather than replace the unknown values of future sales in the cost function first, and then work out the optimal strategy? If one had certain knowledge of future sales, then to work out the optimal strategy one differentiates the total cost function with respect to Q_t ($t = 1, 2,...,$ T) and solves the resulting equations. Is this approach any different when there is uncertainty? Here the assumptions of quadratic cost function and linear constraints come to the rescue. Mathematical expectations and differentiation are linear operations whose order may be reversed, differentiation being performed first. The resulting optimal decision sequence would be no different from that which would have been obtained had the future values of the exogenous variables been replaced by their mathematical expectations. This is the Simon–Theil certainty equivalence theorem. (See Simon (1956) and Theil (1957, 1964).) The first period solution gives the optimal decision value for that period and subsequent solutions are best estimates of what future values of decision variables will be. But only the decision for the first period is taken at any one time and as more information on the exogenous variables accumulates each succeeding decision is based on that information.

This brief account should make clear why in spite of the natural appeal of more general cost functions and/or non-linear constraints, successive investigators have chosen to stay within the framework. By so doing they have been able to invoke the certainty equivalence theorem which they would not otherwise be able to make—at least not without first extending the mathematical framework. Another issue which has not been mentioned so far concerns the explicit derivation of the decision rules. But, given the framework adopted, these decision rules will be linear in the initial conditions and all current and future exogenous variables whose values are not known at time t, thus

$$Q_t = A_0 + \sum_{i=1}^{T} B_i \hat{X}_{t+i} + A_1 Q_{t-1} + A_2 I_{t-1}, \tag{26}$$

where the coefficients A_i, B_i are computed from the parameters of the cost function. The decision rules are in fact linear difference equations with coefficients that remain the same for every period so long as the cost function is unchanged. The substitution of the linear decision rule for Q_t in the identity (23) yields a decision rule for inventories. This rule is not, of course, an independent decision rule. The precise manner of dependence can be shown in a proper derivation which involves use of z-transforms. (See Rowley (1973), Ch. 3.) But since our concern is much more with the implications of the approach for macro-econometric research, we shall not go into this. Detailed illustrations can be found in Holt and Modigliani (1961) and Childs (1967).

The linear decision rules derived in this framework have been used as approximations to inventory and/or output behavioural equations in a number of econometric studies at different levels of aggregation. (See Belsley (1969), Childs (1967), Hay (1970b) and Trivedi (1970c, 1973).) An important question from the viewpoint of econometric methodology concerns the benefit of doing so over the somewhat easier approach of stock-adjustment type models. More specifically, we may ask about the relevance of the approach at the level of aggregation at which econometric work has been done to date. First there is little doubt that with such highly aggregated data which obscures considerable heterogeneity in micro-behaviour, identification of cost parameters is not feasible. No investigator to date has set himself this task. Rather the approach has been to use the linear decision approach to seek more general guidance about specification. The clearest illustration of this is provided by the inventory/output behaviour in the group of industries which produce largely to order. As we shall see later there are good arguments suggesting differences in cost structures of this group of industries compared with those producing to order. The cost function framework explains clearly how the differences are translated into differences in behaviour and it also helps focus attention on the most relevant variables including the decision variables.

The approach has in our view several weaknesses, at least in the way it has been utilized to date. Firstly, insufficient attention is paid to the manner in which auxiliary relationships are incorporated into the cost function. The relationship $I_t^* = c_1 + c_2 \hat{X}_{t+1}$ is an example of an auxiliary relationship and it can be argued to result from some type of optimizing behaviour by the firm. Indeed we went into a lengthy discussion earlier in this chapter which dealt with Modigliani's justification of the acceleration principle based on optimizing behaviour at the micro-level. If the auxiliary relationship has already taken account of cost-minimizing considerations, what is the logic of including it yet again in the cost function together with those cost elements on which it is supposedly based? It is possible that either double-counting is present, suggesting a more elaborate cost function than is necessary, or the auxiliary relationship is based on cost considerations which are altogether separable from the others which enter the cost function directly. In the absence of some prior analysis of the auxiliary relationship, it will not be clear what is going on. Ideally one would like a model in which the auxiliary relationships are themselves derived from explicitly stated assumptions and not imposed upon (arbitrarily) the cost function.

The second drawback of the cost function approach as a basis for econometric

TABLE 2.1. Cost structures and associated decision rules

Authors	Cost structures	Decision rules
Metzler (1941)	$C = \sum\limits_{t=0}^{T} [c_5(I_t - c_1 - c_2 X_t)^2 + c_0 + c_3 Q_t]$	$Q_t = \hat{X} - (I_{t-1} - c_1 - c_2 \hat{X}_t)$
Whitin (1953)	$C = \sum\limits_{t=0}^{T} [c_5(I_t - c_4\sqrt{X_t})^2 + c_0 + c_3 Q_t]$	$Q_t = \hat{X}_t - (I_{t-1} - c_4 \hat{X}_t^{1/2})$
Modigliani and Sauerlander (1955)	$C = \sum\limits_{t=0}^{T} [c_5(I_t - c_1 - c_2 X_t)^2 + c_0 + c_3 Q_t$ $+ c_6 Q_t^2]$	$Q_t = \sum\limits_{i=0}^{T} w_i \hat{X}_{t+i} - c_{12}(I_{t-1} - c_1$ $- c_2 \sum\limits_{i=0}^{T} y_i \hat{X}_{t+i})$
Holt, Simon and Mills	$C = \sum\limits_{t=0}^{T} [c_5(I_t - c_1 - c_2 X_t)^2 + c_0 + c_3 Q_t$ $+ c_7(Q_t - Q_{t-1})^2]$	$Q_t = \sum\limits_{i=0}^{T} w_i \hat{X}_{t+i} - c_{12}(I_{t-1} - c_1$ $- c_2 \sum\limits_{i=0}^{T} y_i \hat{X}_{t+i}) + c_{14} Q_{t-1}$

C = total cost
I_t = finished goods inventory, end of period t
X_t = sales in period t

$\hat{X}_{t+i}$ = forecast made in period t of X_{t+i}
Q = production in t
c_i, w_i, y_i are constants.

work is that it is possible to specify an embarrassingly large number of cost structures which lead to a decision rule (and hence an estimating equation) of the same or very similar form. A frequently adopted objective of the investigator is to use the results of the empirical investigation to discriminate between alternative cost structures. But if the cost structures are observationally equivalent or almost so, then discrimination is not possible. The following table derived from Holt and Modigliani (1961) shows alternative cost structures and associated decision rules for output. It should be made clear that the cost structure given against the name of the author(s) is not the one explicitly given by him but rather one which can be said to be implied by the decision rules which the firms are assumed to follow. Thus, for instance, Metzler assumed that firms produce in any period an amount equal to expected sales plus the full discrepancy between their desired and actual sales. This interpreted as a decision rule is consistent with the cost structure given in Table 2.1. Note also that only the fourth cost structure introduces the penalties of unevenness in the rate of production and the optimal decision rule associated with this is one which gives some weight to Q_{t-1}. An interesting question one can ask in relation to all this is how great a difference must there be in the cost structures before the decision rules begin to 'look different'. A little thought reveals that in fact apparently rather different cost structures will yield similar looking decision rules (the coefficients in these may of course differ). An implication of this is that identifying the underlying cost structure using the decision rule as a guide is far from being a straightforward matter.

It is not possible to pursue in detail here the improved understanding of the dynamic responses of firms which can result from the Holt–Modigliani approach. They illustrate how the response of inventories and production is determined by the decision rule and the sales forecasting rule employed by decision makers.

The assumption of price rigidity adopted so far is unrealistic. We therefore consider models of Mills (1957, 1962) and Hay (1970b, 1972) where the interrelatedness of price and output decisions is considered in a profit-maximizing framework. The complexity of Mills' model prevents us from giving a detailed discussion on the available space so that the interested reader would find it useful to supplement this by Steuer and Budd (1968).

When, as here, it is assumed that prices are rigid, inventories or output bear the brunt of any adjustment that the firm may need to make. If the firm finds itself with excess inventories because of an error in forecasting sales, it must either vary selling expenditures, or revise production and/or inventory plans. However, given control over pricing decisions, a price may be set so as to eliminate desired or excess inventories without alterations in production plans. Alternatively, a combination of the two policies may be chosen, the precise course adopted depending on the goal of the desion-maker. Mills and, more recently, Hay considered this additional dimension of choice. Mills assumes that market demand has both deterministic and stochastic components. Further, the inventory associated cost function includes production smoothing and back-order costs. Having set up the cost and revenue functions, one may consider the problem of choosing the combination of output (Q) and output price (P) which maximize total profit. In Mills' case these decision rules are of the form

$$Q_t = A_0 + A_1 \hat{X}_t + A_2 I_{t-1} + A_3 Q_{t-1}, \tag{27}$$

$$P_t = B_0 + B_1 \hat{X}_t + B_2 I_{t-1} + B_3 Q_{t-1}, \tag{28}$$

where the constants A_i and B_i ($i = 0,...,3$) are non-linear functions of the parameters of the demand curve, the cost function and of the probability distribution of demand. Given Q_t, I_t is determined by identity (23). In this framework price and output decisions are recursive in the sense that each decision is one in a sequence of decisions and it is conditional on available information and on Q_{t-1} and I_{t-1}.

Hay's model of output and price determination is a further modification of an application of quadratic costs and linear constraints framework made by Childs (1967) whose model we shall consider first. He develops a framework within which the relations between production, orders and inventories can be explained. The decision-maker is assumed to take the product price as given and behaves so as to minimize the expected present value of costs associated with inventory, order and production. The cost of deviation of the actual level of unfilled orders from the optimal level is approximated by a quadratic function of the form

$$c_1(U_t - U_t^*)^2 = c_1(U_t - c_{13} - c_{14}Q_t)^2. \tag{29}$$

Similarly, inventory costs are approximated by

$$c_2(I_t - I_t^*)^2 = c_2(I_t - c_{21} - c_{23}N_t)^2, \tag{30}$$

where the desired inventory I^* depends on new orders net of cancellations. (In an alternative model, I^* depends on sales.) Finally, the costs associated with production are both direct costs and smoothing costs, once again approximated by the function

$$c_{32}Q_t + c_3(Q_t - Q_{t-1})^2.$$

The cost parameters $c_1, c_2, c_3, c_{14}, c_{23}, c_{32}$ are all assumed positive. The formal problem is one of minimizing

$$C = \sum_{t=1}^{T} \lambda^{t-1} \{c_1(U_t - c_{13} - c_{14}Q_t)^2 + c_2(I_t - c_{21} - c_{23}N_t)^2 + c_{32}Q_t$$

$$+ c_3(Q_t - Q_{t-1})^2\},$$

subject to

$$N_t - D_t = U_t - U_{t-1} \qquad (t = 1, \ldots, T) \left.\right\}$$
$$Q_t - D_t = I_t - I_{t-1} \qquad (t = 1, \ldots, T). \left.\right\}$$

The full derivation of the linear decision rules for U_t and I_t is given in Childs (1969). They take the form

$$U_t = A_{10} + A_{11}Q_{t-1} + A_{12}(I_{t-1} - U_{t-1}) + \sum_{i=0}^{T} B_{1i}N_{t+i}, \tag{31}$$

$$I_t = A_{20} + A_{21}Q_{t-1} + A_{22}(I_{t-1} - U_{t-1}) + \sum_{i=0}^{T} B_{2i}N_{t+i}, \tag{32}$$

where the coefficients in both decision rules are functions of the cost parameters.

The alternative model due to Hay contains costs associated with backlogs, inventory, variations in production and price changes.

First, it is assumed that the desired inventory at the end of period t relates linearly to shipments in that period

$$I_t^* = c_{23} + c_{24}X_t, \tag{33}$$

and the costs associated with inventory are represented by

$$c_{21} + c_2(I_t - c_{23} - c_{24}X_t)^2.$$

Second, the desired level of backlogs is made a linear function of the level of production in t, Q_t,

$$U_t^* = c_{13} + c_{14}Q_t,$$

are given by the quadratic term

$$c_{11} + c_1(U_t - c_{13} - c_{14}Q_t)^2.$$

Third, costs of changing the level of production are expressed as

$$c_3(Q_t - Q_{t-1})^2,$$

which implies that a unit change in the level of production is equally costly in either direction, large changes being more costly than small ones. The cost of price changes is assumed to be

$$C_4[(P_t - V_t) - (P_{t-1} - V_{t-1})]^2,$$

where V_t denotes the direct unit costs of production, labour and materials cost and user cost of capital. This suggests that there is little or no cost to the form of price changes which result from cost changes. Note that in this formulation price increases and reductions are treated symmetrically. The rationale behind this specification is that, in the absence of general cost changes, output price tends to be sticky insofar as there is a cost attached to changes in the mark-up $(P_t - V_t)$. Further, in accordance with some versions of full-cost pricing, there is assumed to be no cost attached to a change in price due to changes in direct cost. Empirical evidence on pricing policies as reported, for example, by Silbertson (1970) suggests, however, that the relevant measure of direct costs may not be those of the firm in question, but rather those of another firm, such as the least efficient firm or that of the price-leader in that group.

Finally Hay introduces a linear stochastic demand curve of the form

$$N_t = X_t - bP_t, \tag{34}$$

where N_t denotes new orders in t, P_t the price and X_t is a random variable. Hay argues that the randomness results from existence of factors which the firm cannot control but he does not sufficiently clarify, in the specification (34), what is assumed about the reactions of other firms.

The problem can now be cast in a profit maximizing framework where the decision-maker chooses values of inventories, outputs and prices such that the present value of expected profits over T periods is maximized subject to the appropriate constraints. The problem falls in the class of problems which was described earlier. Application of the methods mentioned there yields the three decision rules which are of interest. In particular, the decision rule for production is of the form

$$Q_t = f(Q_{t-1}, P_{t-1}, I_{t-1}, U_{t-1}, X_t, X_{t+1}, \ldots, V_{t-1}, V_t, \ldots). \tag{35}$$

The use of decision rules raises a number of interesting questions which are not without econometric implications. The sensitivity of responses in variables to changes in cost parameters, fluctuations in demand (correctly or incorrectly anticipated) and variations in the lag structure are important. For a thorough discussion of these issues based on a set of simulation experiments, the reader is referred to Hay.

2.4 INVENTORIES IN MACROECONOMIC MODELS

The significance of inventories stems from their short-run variability. By sensitively responding to changes in the level of aggregate economic activity, inventory changes contribute in turn to these fluctuations to an extent and in a manner which is difficult to ignore. This point has been repeatedly stressed in the literature. Lundberg (1968), for instance, provides a table which displays the variability of the growth of various expenditure components of GNP for fourteen countries over a period of fifteen years. This shows the inventory-investment component of gross national products (GNP) to be their most volatile part. Consumption is the most stable component. Behaviour of inventories over the cycle (rather than a calendar period) established this volatility even more clearly.

When the aggregate changes are analysed to see what categories of inventories contribute most to this variability, manufacturing inventory investment usually plays the major role. This arises partly from the larger proportion of total stocks there and partly from the fact that these stocks are probably more sensitive to fluctuations in demand than those of wholesalers and manufacturers. The latter could be due, in part, to the time-consuming nature of manufacturing processes which necessitates carrying stocks of finished goods, work in process and raw materials. Provided there is any conformity in the timing of response of these categories of stocks to demand fluctuations, the consequence would be an amplification in inventory fluctuations of much greater proportions than those emanating from the distributive sector.

In the specific context of business cycles, the roles of inventories as seen by Mitchell, Hawtrey, Keynes and Hansen have been described by Abramovitz (1950) and will not be repeated here. Instead, the important characteristics of six other models will be used to illustrate some of the developments and frontiers of research in the last three decades.

Metzler (one)

In his 1941 paper, Metzler considers a sequence of accelerator–multiplier models and shows, within the framework of these models, how fluctuations in aggregate output could originate from the attempts by firms to maintain a stable relation between their inventories and output. His discrete formulation is highly aggregative. No distinction in drawn between producer and consumption goods or between inventories at different stages of fabrication. Decisions relate to single periods and are based on information relating to past periods or expectations about future periods. The analysis provides an insight into period-by-period behaviour of aggregate output. The salient features of his models are considered here and in the following two sections.

Let Y_t, H_t and $\bar{I}$ denote output, stocks and investment, the last of which is exogenously given. Assume a one-period lag in consumption expenditures,

$$C_t = \beta Y_{t-1}, \qquad 0 < \beta \leq 1. \tag{36}$$

Beginning from equilibrium, suppose there is a change in the level of income brought about by a change in the level of autonomous investment $\bar{I}$. Suppose that holders of stocks attempt to maintain a constant level of stocks. Let the change in income in period $(t - 1)$ be $(Y_{t-1} - Y_{t-2})$; then, the consequent change in consumption is $\beta(Y_{t-1} - Y_{t-2})$, which is also the extent to which the stocks would change if the inventory holders remain passive. If, on the contrary, they attempt to bring back their stocks to the desired constant level by producing for stocks, H, precisely the extra amount $\beta(Y_{t-1} - Y_{t-2})$ in period t, that is

$$H_t - H_{t-1} = \beta(Y_{t-1} - Y_{t-2}), \tag{37}$$

the same additional output will be generated in that period. Using the income identity

$$Y_t = C_t + (H_t - H_{t-1}) + \bar{I}, \tag{38}$$

we obtain

$$Y_t = \beta Y_{t-1} + \beta(Y_{t-1} - Y_{t-2}) + \bar{I},$$
$$Y_t = 2\beta Y_{t-1} - \beta Y_{t-2} + \bar{I}. \tag{39}$$

It is possible that, following a change in autonomous investment, Y may or may not converge to a new equilibrium value. Where the model is stable, the convergence to the new level may be oscillatory or monotonic. The stability condition in the present case is that the roots of $z^2 - 2\beta z + \beta = 0$ shall lie within the unit circle of the complex plane. (See Rowley (1973), Ch. 3.) β lying between 0 and unity guarantees that the process is stable though convergence is oscillatory. This result can be easily understood. First, remember that the autonomous increase in investment leads to an increase in income and consumption initially but a decrease in stocks. In the following period an increase in production for sale and for stocks stimulates consumption via the multiplier effect, thus reducing stocks still further. However, given β less than unity, the successive increments to consumption become smaller and smaller until consumption levels off. Inventories, however, adjust with a lag so they continue to increase after consumption and income level off. Eventually the level of stock exceeds the desired constant level. Production is then reduced to attain the lower level of stocks. But this attempt to liquidate excess stocks is self-defeating in view of the operation of the multiplier process. A reduction in output reduces income and consumption thus starting the whole process in reverse.

This model illustrates the 'pure inventory cycle'—so called because the fluctuations in aggregate income are generated entirely from the attempts to maintain stocks at a constant desired level.

Metzler (two)

To increase generality, suppose that the desired stock is proportional to the expected value of consumption, $\hat{C}_t$. Let

$$\hat{C}_t = C_{t-1} = \beta Y_{t-1} \tag{40}$$

and

$$H_t^d = \alpha \hat{C}_t = \alpha\beta Y_{t-1}, \tag{41}$$

where H_t^d is the stock desired at the end of period t. α is the accelerator co-efficient. If we continue to assume that the entire discrepancy between desired and actual stocks is removed in any one period, production for stocks in period t is $(\alpha\beta Y_{t-1} - H_{t-1})$. If no unintended accumulation or depletion of inventories took place in period $(t-1)$, then H_{t-1} is $\alpha\beta Y_{t-2}$. Unintended change in inventories in period $(t-1)$ is $\beta(Y_{t-1} - Y_{t-2})$. Thus

$$H_{t-1} = \alpha\beta Y_{t-2} - \beta(Y_{t-1} - Y_{t-2})$$

and

$$
\begin{aligned}
H_t &= H_{t-1} + \text{planned change} + \text{unplanned change} \\
&= H_{t-1} + \alpha\beta(Y_{t-1} - Y_{t-2}) + \beta(Y_{t-1} - Y_{t-2}) \\
&= [(1+\alpha)\beta]\, Y_{t-1}.
\end{aligned}
$$

Substituting from the above equation in (38) and noting that C_t is βY_{t-1}, we obtain:

$$Y_t = [(2+\alpha)\beta]Y_{t-1} - [(1+\alpha)\beta]Y_{t-2} + \bar{I}. \tag{42}$$

The stability condition for this second-order difference equation is that the roots of the characteristic equation $z^2 - (2+\alpha)\beta z + (1+\alpha)\beta = 0$ shall lie within the unit circle of the complex plane. Condition $0 < \beta < 1$ is no longer sufficient to ensure stability. If the acceleration coefficient α exceeds $(1/\beta - 1)$, then the model is unstable. Even if one confines oneself to stable models, it is clear that the larger the value of α, the longer will be the duration of the inventory cycle. This model explains the role of the acceleration coefficient in the determination of the nature and duration of the inventory cycles.

Metzler (three)

In both of the earlier models the assumptions made with respect to expectations-formation were extremely simple. Suppose now that expected consumption for period t is given by the following weighted average of consumption for the past two periods:

$$
\begin{aligned}
\hat{C}_t &= (1+\eta)C_{t-1} - \eta C_{t-2} \tag{43} \\
&= [(1+\eta)\beta]Y_{t-1} - (\eta\beta)Y_{t-2},
\end{aligned}
$$

whereas actual sales in period t are given by

$$C_t = \beta Y_{t-1}$$

and so the sales forecasting error is

$$\hat{C}_t - C_t = \eta\beta(Y_{t-1} - Y_{t-2}). \tag{44}$$

Metzler calls η the 'coefficient of expectations'. The total production for stocks in period t is the sum of production to replace unanticipated inventory losses and to bring output to a given proportion of difference between expected sales in period t and in period $t - 1$, that is,

$$\alpha(1 + \eta)\beta Y_{t-1} - (1 + 2\eta)\beta Y_{t-2} + \eta\beta Y_{t-3}.$$

Unanticipated inventory losses are given by (44). The aggregate income is then given by

$$Y_t = \beta Y_{t-1} + [(1 + \eta)\beta]Y_{t-1} - \eta\beta Y_{t-2}$$
$$+ [(1 + \eta)\beta Y_{t-1} - (1 + 2\eta)\beta Y_{t-2} + \eta\beta Y_{t-3}] + \bar{I},$$
$$Y_t = [(1 + \eta)(1 + \alpha) + 1]\beta Y_{t-1} - [(1 + 2\eta)(1 + \alpha)\beta]Y_{t-2}$$
$$+ [(1 + \alpha)\eta\beta]Y_{t-3} + \bar{I}, \tag{45}$$

which is a third-order difference equation. The condition for stability of this equation is that the roots of the characteristic equation $z^3 - [(1 + \eta)(1 + \alpha) + 1]\beta z^2 + [(1 + 2\eta)(1 + \alpha)\beta]z - (1 + \alpha)\eta\beta = 0$ are within the unit circle on the complex plane. That is, using the Schur–Cohn criterion (see, for example, Rowley (1973, pp. 75–76))

$$[(1 + \alpha)\eta\beta]^2 > 1,$$
$$\{[(1 + \alpha)\eta\beta]^2 - 1\}^2 > \beta^2[3 + 2\alpha + 4\eta + 4\alpha\eta]^2$$

and

$$\beta^2[2(1 + \eta + \alpha\eta) + \alpha]^2 > [1 + \beta(1 + 2\eta)(1 + \alpha)]^2.$$

These conditions do not lend themselves to an easy interpretation in the present context, but they place severe restrictions on the relative magnitudes of α, β and η. If, for instance, expectations are formed by a straightforward extrapolation of the change in sales in the previous period so that η is unity, then a necessary condition for stability is for β to exceed $1/(1 + \alpha)$. If expectations are static in the sense that $\hat{C} = C_{t-1}$, so η is zero, then a necessary condition for stability is that β be less than $1/(3 + 2\alpha)$.

Metzler, unlike earlier trade-cycle theorists, regarded the economy as basically stable but with a structure such that increases in demand automatically set up oscillations around the new equilibrium value. His models generate a number of problems for empirical investigation. The maintained hypothesis that the change in production in any period is sufficient to eliminate the discrepancy between desired and actual inventories has raised questions about its empirical validity and related implications. Some studies have also concentrated on the nature of businessmen's expectations and the importance of extrapolative and regressive elements in them, on the existence of a stable relationship between stocks and expected sales, on the determinants of change of inventories in the short run, and on the question of whether historical evidence regarding short-term economic fluctuations is consistent with either the pure or modified inventory cycle hypothesis.

Bergstrom

Bergstrom (1966), modifies those assumptions of Metzler's models whereby investment was taken as exogenously given and consumption was assumed to depend upon output with a lag. His models are constructed in a continuous form and are for the most part linear in variables.

Consider first an aggregate model which consists of a consumption function, an investment function, a supply function, an inventory adjustment function and the national income identity.

Consumption is assumed to depend on income at all previous points of time with greater weight being attached to income in the nearer past. This is equivalent to having consumption determined by expected future income and the expectations are determined by historical levels of income. Let

$$\frac{dC}{dt} + \alpha C = \alpha(1 - s)Y + \alpha A, \quad 0 < s < 1$$

or, in operator notation,

$$(D + \alpha)C = \alpha(1 - s)Y + \alpha A. \tag{46}$$

α is the speed of response parameter and s is the saving propensity, C is aggregate real consumption expenditure and Y is aggregate real income.

The investment equation is a simple accelerator form,

$$DK = \gamma(vY - K), \quad Y, v, > 0. \tag{47}$$

v is the optimum capital-output ratio. The desired level of stock is assumed to vary linearly with total final expenditure $(C + DK)$,

$$S^* = \beta(C + DK) + K, \quad \beta, K, > 0. \tag{48}$$

The rate of change of output is given by the supply equation which is

$$DY = \lambda(C + DK - Y) + \mu(S^* - S), \tag{49}$$

where λ and μ are positive, $(S^* - S)$ measures the discrepancy between the desired and actual stocks and $(C + DK - Y)$ measures the excess of sales over output. The rate of change of output is positive when the desired stocks exceed actual stocks or when actual output is below the sales. The larger the value of coefficient μ the greater the speed at which output increases to remove the gap $(S^* - S)$.

Finally, the continuous income identity

$$Y = C + DK + DS \tag{50}$$

closes the model.

By substitution, we can reduce the system to one of three behavioural equations plus an identity. Note from (50) that in equilibrium C is equal to Y, and, from (46) and (48), that the equilibrium value of S, say S^e, is $(\beta A)/s + k$.

Let

$$\sum_{i=0}^{n} a_i z^{n-i} = 0$$

be the characteristic equation for the system with positive a_0. Applying the Routh–Hurwitz conditions (Baumol (1970, p. 303)), the necessary and sufficient conditions for stability are $a_1 > 0, a_4 > 0, (a_1 a_2 - a_3) > 0$ and $a_1 a_2 a_3 - a_3^2 - a_1^2 a_4 > 0$, where

$$a_1 = -[-\alpha - \gamma + \mu\beta\gamma v - \lambda(1 - \gamma v)],$$

$$a_2 = \alpha\gamma + \gamma\lambda + \alpha s\lambda - \alpha\gamma\lambda v + \mu(1 - \alpha\beta - \gamma v + \alpha s\beta - \alpha\beta\gamma v),$$

$$a_3 = \alpha\gamma\lambda s + \mu(\gamma + \alpha s - \alpha\gamma\beta - \alpha\gamma v + \alpha\gamma\beta s),$$

$$a_4 = \mu\alpha\gamma s.$$

(A derivation of these equations is provided in Chapter Three.) Observe that negative a_1 violates a stability condition, and this will occur if $(\alpha + \gamma + \lambda)$ is less than $(\gamma\lambda v + \mu\beta\gamma v)$ which inequality will be satisfied if μ is 'sufficiently large'. Thus a high rate of change of production for removing the discrepancy between S^* and S could cause instability. Ranges of values for coefficients μ and/or β can be constructed such that for given values of the remaining coefficients the behaviour of the system is damped and oscillatory.

Like Metzler's models, this model emphasizes the role which inventories could play in short-term fluctuations and focuses attention on parameters whose sizes determine dynamic behaviour of an economy.

Lovell

Lovell (1962) extends Metzler's analysis in two important directions. First, he considers the implications for stability of a multitude of firms simultaneously attempting to adjust their inventories to a level which is determined by expectations about the future. Second, he relaxes the assumption of full adjustment to the desired level within each time period and studies the consequences of letting firms adjust partially to their desired level of stocks. In his model the main reason for holding inventories is the buffer-stock motive. Prices are assumed to be rigid and constraints on capacity ineffective. This discrete model is restricted to stocks of final goods.

Let $I(t)$ denote the level of inventories and let superscripts p, a, d distinguish planned, actual and desired inventories respectively. Desired inventories at the end of time period t, i_t^d, are assumed to be a stable linear function of expected sales, $\hat{x}_t$,

$$i_t^d = \gamma + \beta\hat{x}_t. \tag{51}$$

The planned change in inventories is proportional to the discrepancy between i_t^d and i_{t-1}^a, thus

$$i_t^p - i_{t-1}^a = \delta(i_t^d - i_{t-1}^a), \qquad 0 < \delta \leq 1. \tag{52}$$

But by the identity between production in period t, q_t, sales, x_t and change in inventories we have

$$i_t^p - i_{t-1}^a = q_t - \hat{x}_t. \tag{53}$$

The stock level at the end of period t is the sum of the planned level and the error in forecasting sales,

$$i_t^a = i_t^p + (\hat{x}_t - x_t)$$
$$= \gamma\delta + (1 + \beta\delta)\hat{x}_t - x_t + (1 - \delta)i_t^a. \tag{54}$$

Substituting for $(i_t^p - i_{t-1}^a)$ and $(i_{t-1}^a - i_{t-2}^a)$ in (53), we obtain

$$q_i = (1 + \beta\delta)\hat{x}_t - (1 + \beta\delta)\hat{x}_{t-1} + (1 - \delta)q_{t-1} + \delta x_{t-1}. \tag{55}$$

If it is further assumed that $\hat{x}_t$ is x_{t-1}, $\hat{x}_{t-1}$ is x_{t-2}, and so on, this reduces to

$$q_t = (1 + \beta\delta + \delta)x_{t-1} - (1 + \beta\delta)x_{t-2} + (1 - \delta)q_{t-1}. \tag{56}$$

Next suppose that (56) describes the production behaviour of a typical industry and that the coefficients β and δ for all firms in a given industry are assumed to be the same. (This is Lovell's weak uniformity assumption.) Let $q_{it}^{(j)}$ and $x_{it}^{(j)}$ stand for production and sales of the ith firm in the jth industry $\{i = 1,...,n, j = 1,...,N\}$; then the output of the jth industry is

$$\sum_{i=1}^{n} q_{it}^{(j)},$$

as given by

$$\sum_{i=1}^{n} q_{it}^{(j)} = (1 + \beta^{(j)}\delta^{(j)} + \delta^{(j)})\sum_{i=1}^{n} x_{i,t-1}^{(j)}$$

$$+ (1 + \beta^{(j)}\delta^{(j)})\sum_{i=1}^{n} x_{i,t-2}^{(j)} + (1 - \delta^{(j)})\sum_{i=1}^{n} q_{i,t-1}^{(j)}. \tag{57}$$

Next define the following column vectors and matrices:

$$\mathbf{Q}_t = [\Sigma q_{it}^{(1)},...,\Sigma q_{it}^{(N)}], \mathbf{X}_t = [\Sigma x_{it}^{(1)},...,\Sigma x_{it}^{(N)}],$$

$$\mathbf{B} = \mathrm{diag}[\beta^{(j)}], \mathbf{D} = \mathrm{diag}[\delta^{(i)}], \mathbf{I} = \mathrm{diag}[1],$$

where $i = 1,...,$ $,j = 1,...,N$ and $\mathbf{I}$ is of order N. The diagonal $\mathbf{B}$ and $\mathbf{D}$ will be referred to, respectively, as matrices of marginal inventory sales coefficients and adjustment coefficients. In this notation output equations for all N industries may be written in the form

$$\mathbf{Q}_t = (\mathbf{I} + \mathbf{BD} + \mathbf{D})\mathbf{X}_{t-1} + (\mathbf{I} + \mathbf{BD})\mathbf{X}_{t-2} + (\mathbf{I} - \mathbf{D})\mathbf{Q}_{t-1} \tag{58}$$

or, under the assumption that $\hat{x}_t$ is x_t, $\hat{x}_{t-1}$ is x_{t-1}, and so on, by

$$\mathbf{Q}_t = (\mathbf{I} + \mathbf{BD})\mathbf{X}_t + (\mathbf{D} - \mathbf{I} - \mathbf{BD})\mathbf{X}_{t-1} + (\mathbf{I} - \mathbf{D})\mathbf{Q}_{t-1}. \tag{59}$$

To reduce these equations even further, Lovell introduces a system of equations linking the sales of each sector to the level of production in all other sectors.

Assuming technical conditions governing production are the same for all firms in a given sector, and that there are no stocks of intermediate goods, the purchases of goods for production purposes can be obtained by multiplying $\mathbf{Q}$, the vector of outputs, by $\mathbf{A} = (a_{ij})$, the matrix of input–output coefficients. (a_{ij} is the amount of jth good required to produce one unit of ith good, $a_{ij} \geq 0$.) Assuming also that there is a one-period delay in converting inputs to outputs, the sales-for-production component of total sales in period t is given by the product of $\mathbf{A}$ and $\mathbf{Q}_{t+1}$. Let $\mathbf{F}_t$ be the column vector whose ith element represents the quantity of final output of industry i demanded for purposes other than production. Then, we have, in matrix notation

$$\mathbf{X}_t = \mathbf{A}\mathbf{Q}_{t+1} + \mathbf{F}_t,$$

which when substituted in (58) yields

$$\mathbf{Q}_t = [\mathbf{I} - (\mathbf{I} + \mathbf{BD} + \mathbf{D})\mathbf{A}]^{-1}\{[\mathbf{I} - \mathbf{D} - (\mathbf{I} + \mathbf{BD})\mathbf{A}]\mathbf{Q}_{t-1}$$
$$+ (\mathbf{I} + \mathbf{BD} + \mathbf{D})\mathbf{F}_{t-1} - (\mathbf{I} + \mathbf{BD})\mathbf{F}_{t-2}\}, \tag{60}$$

which is a system of linear non-homogeneous difference equations explaining current levels of output in terms of past levels of output and past levels of final demand. This system of equations is a useful tool for studying the implications of alternative forecasting assumptions and/or alternative adjustment patterns for the dynamic stability of the economy. Lovell makes the assumption that the matrix $\mathbf{A}$ satisfies the Simon–Hawkins conditions before considering the question of dynamic stability; that is, the maximal characteristic root of $\mathbf{A}$ is within the unit circle on the complex plane.

Consider the case where $\hat{X}_t$ is X_{t-1} (naive expectations), $\mathbf{D}$ is $\mathbf{I}$ (full adjustment within the period) and $\mathbf{B} \geq 0$ (marginal desired inventory coefficient nonnegative). For stability, we require that the maximal characteristic root of A be less than $[3 + 2 \min (\beta^{(i)})]^{-1}$. Whether or not such a restriction is likely to be satisfied seems mainly an empirical matter. In another case where $\hat{X}_t$ is X_{t-1}, but adjustment partial, it can be shown that, under the assumption of strong uniformity, $(\beta\mathbf{I} = \mathbf{B}, \delta\mathbf{I} = \mathbf{D})$, 'the lower the marginal desired inventory coefficient, other things being equal, the larger the dominant root of $\mathbf{A}$ that is compatible with stability; the slower the speed of adjustment, provided it remains positive, the more likely the economy is to be stable', (see Lovell (1962, p. 288)). In a third case where perfect forecasts ($\hat{X}_t = X_t$) and full adjustment ($\mathbf{D} = \mathbf{I}$) are assumed, the model is found to be unstable if $\beta \geq 0$. Thus the conclusion of the foregoing analysis is that stability and time path of the economy depend upon the rate of adjustment and sales-forecast errors. This model does not allow for the existence of inventories of inputs, but Foster (1963) has put forward a model incorporating raw material inventories. He adopts a multisector framework and examines the effect of alternative forecasting assumptions for the stability of the economy, the main conclusion being that stability is sensitive to the forecasting assumptions employed.

A number of difficulties arise when the econometrician attempts to assess empirically the role of inventories in determining the stability of the economy, using as a basis a model such as that of Bergstrom or Lovell. One of these is the assumption of price rigidity, another is the lack of recognition of bottlenecks in supply, and these jointly preclude any adjustment on the part of the firm which takes form of longer order books or delivery lags or rationing arrangements. It is also realistic to allow for the possibility of interaction between between price changes and revision of inventory objectives. Finally, when unfilled orders and delivery lags are introduced, it is not clear that the positive feedback from higher output will take place as in Metzler's model, or if the accelerator-multiplier phenomenon will still operate as here. It is clear that the empirical investigator interested in the role of inventories in the short-run dynamics of the economy must follow a different approach from those outlined above.

Pearce

Pearce (1970a, b) provided an explicit statement of the manner in which inventories, especially the unplanned element, influence manufacturers' supply decisions, prices and exports and imports. His representation of these forces in a dynamic model of the United Kingdom is intended to serve as a basis for a large economy-wide econometric model. Here we shall be concerned with that part which relates stock-holding behaviour to other parts of the model. Some idea of the working of the whole system may be obtained by studying the flow chart given in Pearce (1970a). He has emphasized however that 'the system was constructed in the first instance partly on the basis of received economic theory with no regard whatever to the availability of adequate data'.

Using Pearce's notation the consumer demand functions are written in the form

$$X^c = X^c(q_i, Y), \tag{61}$$

where q_i is the set of all market prices, Y is aggregate expenditures, and the superscript c stands for consumers. The supply functions of the model are of the form

$$S^h = S^h(\Pi, \Sigma^u)$$

$$S_t^h = \alpha_2 \Pi + \alpha_2 \Sigma^u + S_{t-1}^h, \tag{62}$$

where Π represents 'excess profits', Σ stock changes, S^h the actual production of a particular industry in a particular time period, and the superscript u represents unplanned changes. Π and Σ^u are meant to be regarded as 'out of equilibrium' variables so that, in equilibrium, their values will be zero. Thus the suppliers produce the same quantity in successive periods unless both Π and/or Σ^u are different from zero. The higher the 'excess profit' the larger the supply, and conversely for unplanned stocks.

Total home demand, D^h, is defined as the sum of consumer demand, demand for capital items, demand for the commodity for intermediate use and demand by government agencies. Any particular component of the sum may, of course, be zero for a given commodity.

The identity:

$$x = S^h - D^h - \Sigma \tag{63}$$

yields either imports (if x is negative) or exports (if positive) as the difference between home supply and home sales plus inventory investment. In equilibrium, inventory investment will be zero and home supply would exactly match home sales and exports (or imports). Thus, in this model, given the above identity, a separate explanation for exports or imports is not called for. Given these relations which fix home supply and home demand, imports and exports simply appear as a by-product. This approach, which regards exports and imports as residuals, may be contrasted with one in which an explicit export or import demand function is specified and estimated using as explanatory variables relative prices and home demand. There is no demand function for imports, rather imports are 'a reflection of the activity of other elements in the system'. A more standard approach to the problem is based on the assumption that there exists a relationship between exports on one hand and terms of trade and home demand on the other. But the relationship between x, S^h, D^h and Σ given above is an identity and not a behavioural or casual relation. Pearce explains, 'There are in fact no parameters specifying the nature of the dependence to find. All response rates are just unity. Given S^h, D^h and Σ finding x is a matter of addition and subtraction.'

It may be expected that Pearce's approach to specification of import/export equation would aim at explaining a different type of phenomenon, for example, when importers may find it desirable to run down their stocks temporarily rather than buy abroad or when exporters find themselves holding stocks at a time when foreign demand is met out of foreign stocks. To this end, let the amount available for export be denoted by $S^h - (D^h + \Sigma^p)$ where Σ^p denotes planned inventory change. A parallel definition of the excess demand in the rest of the world (the superscript w denotes rest of the world) is $S^w - (D + \Sigma^p)^w$. Profitability of exporting is dependent on the difference between the foreign price net of transport cost and duty and the domestic price, being greater when the difference is greater. Thus exports depend upon home excess supply, foreign excess demand and the appropriate price ratio denoted by Ω. If Ω is greater than unity, exporting is profitable. As explained earlier, the relation

$$x = x[(S^h - D^h - \Sigma^p), \quad (S^w - (D + \Sigma^p)^w), \Omega] \tag{64}$$

also serves to explain imports. For instance, if home demand and productive capacity utilization are high, any further increase in demand is met by a higher level of imports. If imports are not forthcoming, then home stocks of the commodity would decline and the (assumed) pricing behaviour is such that domestic prices of that commodity will rise making it more profitable for the rest of the world to export it.

The equations determining prices are based on considerations akin to those considered in the 'target rate of return' pricing models. However, when actual stocks are in excess of planned stocks, this tends to dampen any potential price increases; conversely, if they are below the planned level the price change will be positive. Thus the price changes depend not only on profitability, changes in input prices and changes in taxes but also upon the level of stocks.

To empirically implement this model it is necessary to partition observed stock into the two unobservables—planned component, Σ^p, and the unplanned component, Σ^u. Difficult conceptual problems arise in taking account of expectations, price speculation and so on which are likely to affect planned stock-holding. The author's tentative solution is to set up as best as one can an equation which explains the way planned stock-holding—or the systematic component of stocks—is determined. So the level of stocks predicted by the equation would be identified as the planned stock and the residual, $(\Sigma - \Sigma^p)$, as the unplanned stock. One possibility is to treat regression residuals from the inventory equation as proxy for the unobserved category of unplanned stocks. This is clearly unsatisfactory since so much depends on the accuracy with which we can specify the determination of planned stocks. This in turn raises the difficult question of what exactly one might include in that category.

Conclusion

The business cycle theorists, such as Hawtrey and Mitchell, differed from Metzler in looking upon contractions and expansions as feeding upon themselves and incapable of being terminated except when constrained by forces which did not come into play at a late stage of each phase. Metzler was the first to satisfactorily explain the length and duration of inventory cycles. However, theoretical models do neglect many factors, such as unfilled orders, price adjustment, production to order, differences in behaviour of inventories at different stages of fabrication, the complexity of expectations formation, which are important in practice. The task of examining, econometrically, the importance of each of these factors is relatively easy within a single equation framework. It is, however, much less simple to determine exactly where this would leave the inventory cycle theory. It is an interesting question whether inventory cycles would still be realized. A closer look at this latter question is contained in the last chapter of this book. The more immediate questions of econometric specification and measurement of individual relationships are considered in intervening chapters.

CHAPTER 3

The Structure of Temporal Response

The temporal responses of investment in both inventories and real fixed capital assets to changes in their determining variables have been fruitful areas of econometric research. Some illustrations of current practice are given in the the six sections below. The first of these sections provides an introduction to the basic concepts and terminology associated with distributed-lag responses in both continuous and discrete forms. The second section gives a brief survey of the techniques that have been advocated for the estimation of responses, although restricted both to discrete forms (because of the nature of economic data) and to stationary ones. The latter restriction is then relaxed in the third section and variable responses are considered although not much progress has been made in this particular context. This is, perhaps, due to the attraction of the operational methods used with stationary responses but not easily extended to variable ones.

Clearly, if lags are not supply-determined, it is difficult to believe that patterns of temporal response will not vary between changes in different determining variables. This creates interpretative problems for models built by the two-stage procedure described in Chapter One, whereby lagged responses (or adjustment mechanisms) are superimposed upon expressions for desired capital stocks. A dispute concerning these problems is cited in the fourth section below. It is followed by a discussion of the stability of distributed-lag processes (not to be confused with the stationarity of weights in these responses) in both single-equation and multi-equation frameworks in the fifth section. Such stability is important for economic interpretations and, also, for the properties of particular estimation techniques.

Although we consider here many aspects of the potential complications that may arise with distributed-lag responses, we cannot adequately deal with all of them. One significant omission concerns errors of measurement in determining variables. Some insight into the effects of these errors in this particular

76

context may be derived from Grether and Maddala (1973) who suggest that, in the case of discrete models with no lags or finite lags, such measurement errors may lead to the spurious appearance of long adjustment lags even in large samples. Of course, with continuous models and discrete representations, some errors of measurement are inevitable. The final section below considers some aspects of this problematical area but its emphasis is on approximation rather than estimation.

3.1 DISTRIBUTED LAGS: BASIC CONCEPTS AND TERMINOLOGY

The literature on distributed lags and their applicability as characterizations for investment processes is particularly extensive. Surveys of interest here have been provided by Dhrymes (1971), Griliches (1967), Nerlove (1967, 1972), Rowley (1973, Ch. 3), Wallis (1969) and others. These authors emphasize the restricted specifications of temporal responses that can be appropriately represented by a sequence of weights for discrete and equi-spaced intervals. Within this class, several distinct approaches may be distinguished. A number of these will be mentioned below but first it is convenient to introduce some of the terms in common use. Since these are not necessarily restricted to investment, we use the notation y_t and x_t for arbitrary dependent and determining variables. There is no loss of generality in assuming a single determining variable.

The dependent variable responds with a discrete distributed lag to changes in the determining variable if

$$y_t = \sum_{j=0}^{\infty} \alpha_j x_{t-j}, \tag{1}$$

where the sequence $\{\alpha_j\}$ is a collection of fixed parameters. This sequence is often called the 'filter' or 'time-form' of the response and its individual members are 'reaction coefficients'. If the symbol B is used to represent both the lag operator and an arbitrary complex variable, the 'transfer function' of the response is the polynomial $\alpha(B)$, where

$$\alpha(B) \equiv \alpha_0 + \alpha_1 B + \alpha_2 B^2 + \ldots + \alpha_n B^n + \ldots, \tag{2}$$

so that y_t is $\alpha(B)x_t$. Equation (1) indicates that the observation for the dependent variable is the convolution of the filter and the sequence of current and past values for the determining variable. This specification is the basis for the very successful use of generating functions, such as $\alpha(B)$, since the convolution of sequences in the time domain is associated with the much simpler operation of multiplication of generating functions, or transforms, in the transform domain. This association has already been used in Sections 1.2 and 1.3 although it was not made explicit there. Its value should be apparent from the further manipulations of generating functions which are presented below.

The first reaction coefficient α_0 can be interpreted as an 'impact' multiplier for the temporal response. Thus, if a unit change occurs in the determining variable in any period, it leads to an immediate change of magnitude α_0 in the dependent variable. In the absence of further changes in the determining variable, later changes in the dependent variable will be α_1, α_2 and so on as successive periods elapse. Truncated sums of these coefficients represent the 'adjustment path' of the dependent variable to the initial unit change and the total or 'comparative-static' multiplier is the infinite sum $\alpha(1)$ if this exists. Members of the sequence which form the adjustment path are 'interim multipliers'. Let these be denoted by $\{(1 - \delta_s)$ for $s = 0, 1, 2, ...\}$. Then, for any non-negative integer s,

$$\delta_s \equiv 1 - \sum_{j=0}^{s} \alpha_j \tag{3}$$

and

$$\delta_{s+1} = \delta_s - \alpha_{s+1}. \tag{4}$$

Thus

$$\left(\sum_{s=0}^{\infty} \delta_{s+1} B^{s+1} \right) = B \left(\sum_{s=0}^{\infty} \delta_s B^s \right) - \left(\sum_{s=0}^{\infty} \alpha_{s+1} B^{s+1} \right)$$

and

$$[\delta(B) - \delta_0] = B\delta(B) - [\alpha(B) - \alpha_0] \tag{5}$$

if

$$\delta(B) \equiv \sum_{s=0}^{\infty} \delta_s B^s. \tag{6}$$

Rearranging the terms of (5) and recalling the equality of δ_0 and $(1 - \alpha_0)$, we obtain

$$(1 - B)\delta(B) = 1 - \alpha(B). \tag{7}$$

In the particular illustration where net investment $(I - R)_t$ responds to the changes in desired capital stock K_t^* with the transfer function $a(B)$,

$$(I - R)_t = a(B)(1 - B)K_t^*$$
$$= \alpha(B)K_t^*, \qquad \text{where } \alpha(B) \equiv a(B)(1 - B),$$
$$= \left(\sum_{i=0}^{\tau} \alpha_i K_{t-i}^* \right) + \left(\sum_{i=\tau+1}^{\infty} \alpha_i K_{t-i}^* \right).$$

Jorgenson and Stephenson (1967b) point out that, if a unit change in K^* occurred τ periods ago and the new level has persisted since,

$$(I - R)_t = \left(\sum_{i=0}^{\tau} \alpha_i \right) K_{t-\tau}^* + \sum_{i=\tau+1}^{\infty} \alpha_i K_{t-i}^*,$$

so

$$\frac{\partial (I - R)_t}{\partial K^*_{t-\tau}} = \left(\sum_{i=0}^{\tau} \alpha_i \right) = 1 - \delta_{\tau}.$$

These interim multipliers can be calculated using (7) if $\{\alpha_j\}$ are known or if appropriate estimates are available.

Suppose, in addition to (1), the sequence of reaction coefficients is non-negative and has a finite sum. Then, apart from a scale factor b, these coefficient weights correspond to the probability distribution of a non-negative, integer-valued, random variable. We may therefore write

$$\alpha(B) = b \sum_{j=0}^{\infty} w_j B^j$$

$$= bW(B), \text{ say,}$$

where $\{w_j\}$ are non-negative and sum to unity if b is $\alpha(1)$. It can readily be shown that the mean lag of response in this situation is the derivative of $W(B)$ with respect to B as evaluated for a unit value of B. Further, this is equal to $\delta(1)$, where $\delta(B)$ is redefined in terms of $\{w_j\}$ rather than $\{\alpha_j\}$.

Similar terms have been introduced for stable continuous patterns of temporal response. The differential operator D, representing differentiation with respect to time, fulfills an analogous role to that of the lag operator used for discrete patterns of response. For example, in Goodwin's presentation of the flexible accelerator in continuous form,

$$\dot{K} \equiv DK = \alpha(K^* - K), \tag{8}$$

where K is actual capital stock and K^* is its desired or target level. If K^* is assumed to be proportional to real output X, we might write

$$(D + \alpha)K = \alpha K^* = \alpha bX$$

and

$$K = b \frac{\alpha}{D + \alpha} X. \tag{9}$$

This specification is a 'simple exponential lag' since, if X is a constant, the solution of (9) is

$$K = (K_0 - bX)\exp(-\alpha t) + bX, \tag{10}$$

where K_0 represents the level of capital stock when t is zero. Clearly this specification may be extended to more complicated transfer functions. One obvious form is

$$K = b \left[\frac{\alpha m}{D + \alpha m} \right]^m X. \tag{11}$$

The references cited in Section 3.6 provide further specifications. In addition, Allen (1966, 1967) provides excellent surveys both of appropriate operational methods and of some continuous economic models.

In empirical work, it is always necessary to restrict the possible forms of transfer functions. Some of the forms which have been adopted are distinguished in the next section. Others are described in the surveys cited above. One particular choice, associated with reaction coefficients which decline as a geometric progression, has been especially popular in studies of investment. It can be derived from two distinct *ad hoc* models identified by the names 'adaptive expectations' and 'partial adjustment'. The former is defined by the two equations

$$y_t = bx_t^*$$ (12)

and

$$x_t^* - x_{t-1}^* = \gamma(x_t - x_{t-1}^*),$$ (13)

where x_t^* represents the expected value of the determining variable. Equation (13) is a generating process for expectations. The second approach is defined by

$$y_t^{**} = bx_t$$ (14)

and

$$y_t - y_{t-1} = \gamma(y_t^{**} - y_{t-1}),$$ (15)

where y_t^{**} is a target or 'equilibrium' level. The transfer function of response between y_t and x_t is $\gamma b / [1 - (1 - \gamma)B]$ in both cases so that reaction coefficients are $\{\gamma\beta(1 - \gamma)^j$ for $j = 0, 1, ...\}$.

In Section 1.3, we described the literature stemming from the seminal paper of Eisner and Strotz (1963). This attempted to clarify the constraints that must be placed upon decision-makers in an optimization framework in order to obtain the partial-adjustment form. Bases for the alternative adaptive-expectations form were established from the viewpoint of optimal forecasts. Muth (1960) initiated this development by pointing out that for a particular type of stochastic process, the simple adaptive-expectations specification is the conditional expectation of all future values of the determining variable x_t. This point was later clarified and extended by Nerlove and Wage (1964), Couts, Grether and Nerlove (1966) and Nerlove (1967). One important pitfall that is often forgotten in deriving transfer functions from models with optimal forecasting criteria has been stated by Sims (1971b) in a commentary upon such models. He pointed out that in these models 'there is never a difference between the time interval at which economic agents observe a series and the time interval at which the econometrician can observe it. But more often than not it is reasonable to assume that buyers and sellers observe the variables affecting their behavior at time intervals much finer than those separating published data.'

A further difficulty arises from aggregation if individuals' forecasting schemes are not identical. Thus, following Bierwag and Grove (1966), we can distinguish between individual responses and the aggregate one that is typically observed. Let y_{jt} and x_{jt} represent the variables pertaining to the jth individual. Further, let there be n individuals and let aggregative weights for all variables be $\{m_j\}$. Suppose the transfer function for the jth individual is $\gamma_j b/[1 - (1 - \gamma_j)B]$. Then,

$$\sum_{j=1}^{n} m_j y_{jt} = \sum_{j=1}^{n} m_j \frac{\gamma_j b}{1 - (1 - \gamma_j)B} x_{jt}. \tag{16}$$

The aggregate dependent variable $\Sigma m_j y_{jt}$ no longer has a simple transfer function to represent its temporal response to changes in the aggregative determining variable $\Sigma m_j x_{jt}$ unless γ_j is the same for all individuals. Even if x_{jt} is the same for these individuals, the transfer function will be a rational function of two polynomials in the lag operator.

In Section 1.1, rational transfer functions were introduced in the context of Jorgenson's neoclassical model. These are a simple generalization of the 'Koyck' form discussed in the last few paragraphs. Their principal advantage stems from the representation of temporal response in terms of a few 'intrinsic' parameters. Estimation is usually based upon separated forms for specifications. For example, the separated form for both the adaptive-expectations and partial-adjustment approaches is

$$y_t = (1 - \gamma)y_{t-1} + \gamma b x_t \tag{17}$$

and a derived estimate may be obtained for b by dividing an estimate for the regression coefficient of x_t by $\hat{\gamma}$, where this latter estimate is derived from the estimated regression coefficient of y_{t-1}. Some problems with the distributional characteristics of such derived estimates are assessed by Lianos and Rausser (1972).

Once estimates of intrinsic parameters have been calculated, they may be used to produce estimates of the filter. Unfortunately, the latter depend some-what critically both upon the techniques used to calculate initial estimates of regression coefficients and, also, upon the economic theory which is the basis for desired, equilibrium, expected or target levels. To illustrate the second factor, Griliches and Wallace (1965) used the same transfer function with two similar but non-identical theoretical bases. They found that despite their general similarity, these equations indicate very different distributed lag functions. More recently, Eisner and Nadiri (1968) re-assessed Jorgenson's results by making adjustments based upon logarithms of variables instead of his simple form. There is little to choose between these specifications on an *a priori* basis but the estimated mean lags of Eisner and Nadiri were much shorter. This seven-months difference would be critical if such rival estimates were used as the bases for governmental policy-making.

Finally, Muth (1961) also developed a more general theory for the generation of expectations. These 'rational' expectations were conditional forecasts based upon all observations both for the variable being forecast and other relevant variables. The decision-maker is assumed to have exact knowledge of the generating process for these variables. In this more general framework, the weights for a forecast need not necessarily sum to unity. Much depends on the historical patterns experienced by the determining variable and we may distinguish both 'regressive' and 'extrapolative' elements in the formation of expectations. See, for example, Modigliani and Bossons as cited in Chapter One and, also, Helliwell and Glorieux (1970).

3.2 PARTICULAR TECHNIQUES OF ESTIMATION

When Koyck (1954) introduced the simple transfer function cited above, he recognized both its convenience and the inconsistency of least-squares estimates of its separated form except in one very restricted case. Consider the specification

$$y_t = b \sum_{j=0}^{\infty} \gamma(1-\gamma)^j x_t + \varepsilon_t, \qquad 0 < 1 - \gamma < 1, \tag{18}$$

where ε_t is a random error with zero mean, constant variance and is non-autocorrelated. The sequence $\{\varepsilon_t\}$ is then called 'white noise'. The transfer function of dependence in (18) is $b\gamma/[1 - (1-\gamma)B]$. If both sides of the equation are multiplied by the denominator of this transfer function, its 'separated form' is obtained as

$$y_t = (1-\gamma)y_{t-1} + b\gamma x_t + \varepsilon_t - (1-\gamma)\varepsilon_{t-1}. \tag{19}$$

Least-squares estimates of regression coefficients for this form are affected both by the presence of y_{t-1} among its regressors and by the autocorrelation of the new error term $[\varepsilon_t - (1-\gamma)\varepsilon_{t-1}]$. Since y_{t-1} is contemporaneously correlated with this error, these estimates are both inconsistent and asymptotically biased. Koyck suggested an adjustment to the normal equations of the least-squares method which yields consistent estimates. An alternative procedure might be based on the use of x_{t-1} as an instrumental variable instead of y_{t-1}. Notice that, if ε_t is such that the sequence $\{\varepsilon_t - (1-\gamma)\varepsilon_{t-1}\}$ is non-autocorrelated instead of the untransformed error, this problem will not arise. This situation is compatible with the partial adjustment model.

Consider the more general specification provided by (1) and (2) if ε_t is added to the former. Jorgenson (1966) has suggested that $\alpha(B)$ can be represented by a rational function of two polynomials

$$\alpha(B) = \frac{m_0 + m_1 B + \ldots + m_p B^p}{1 - n_0 B - n_1 B^2 - n_{q-1} B^q} \tag{20}$$

$$= \frac{m(B)}{1 - Bn(B)}, \text{ say.}$$

Here $\{m_i\}$ and $\{n_s\}$ are 'intrinsic parameters', p and q are non-negative integers. The separated form for this transfer function is

$$y_t = n(B)y_{t-1} + m(B)x_t + \varepsilon_t - n(B)\varepsilon_{t-1}. \tag{21}$$

Clearly, if the initial error ε_t is non-autocorrelated, then the error for this form is autocorrelated. Further it is contemporaneously correlated with the regressors $y_{t-1}, y_{t-1}, \ldots, y_{t-p}$ and least-squares estimates do not satisfy properties that many econometricians consider desirable. These properties of consistency and asymptotic unbiasedness are not the only criteria than might be considered. Much depends upon the purpose for which the estimates are calculated. In any case, a recent emphasis in theoretical econometric literature has been the 'small sample' properties of estimators. Existing samples of data are usually small or affected by potential structural changes so that justifications of particular estimation methods in terms of 'asymptotic' properties may be questionable. Some interesting comments upon small-sample properties of estimates for the Koyck specification are provided by Morrison (1970). These estimates include those based on the separated form and others based upon truncations of the initial specification. We should also note the results of Merriwether (1973) which suggest that 'the errors resulting from lag structure misspecification are far greater than those resulting from the use of an estimator with the correct lag specification but without allowances for the unusual error term structure, such as an ordinary least squares estimation of the Koyck model'.

The induced autocorrelation of transformed errors and the introduction of lagged dependent variables do not arise if the denominator in (20) can be suppressed and $\alpha(B)$ is a polynomial of finite length. Then

$$y_t = \sum_{j=0}^{p} m_j x_{t-j} + \varepsilon_t. \tag{22}$$

Unfortunately, if p is large, estimates of $\{m_j\}$ may not be determined with an adequate degree of precision. After stochastic assumptions are introduced for the errors, it is often found that these individual coefficients are not significantly different from zero at conventional levels for inferential tests of significance. Let the vector y represent the T observations for the dependent variable, the matrix X represent the observations for $x_t, x_{t-1}, \ldots, x_{t-p}$, and ε represent the vector of errors. X has order T by $(p+1)$. Then, if m is the vector of reaction coefficients, (22) may be written in matrix notation,

$$y = Xm + \varepsilon, \tag{23}$$

where m has $(p+1)$ elements. Almon (1965) suggested that, when p is large, it may be appropriate to reparameterize the model by imposing linear restrictions of the form

$$m = A\delta, \tag{24}$$

where A is a known matrix with more rows than columns and δ is a vector of (new) unknown parameters. Technically, the constraint puts m in the 'range space' of A. δ may be estimated by the least-squares technique after we substitute $A\delta$ for m in (23). Then a derived estimate of m is

$$\hat{m} = A[(XA)'(XA)]^{-1}(XA)'y \tag{25}$$

and familiar statistical procedures may be followed using this. These procedures are, of course, dependent upon the constraint (24) being satisfied by the initial vector of reaction coefficients m.

In her initial formulation, Almon used interpolation polynomial formulae to generate her choice for A but a simpler and equivalent choice is given by

$$m_j = \sum_{i=0}^{s} \delta_{i+1} j^i \qquad \text{for } j = 1, 2, \ldots, (p+1) \tag{26}$$

$$= [1, j, j^2, \ldots, j^s] \delta$$

where there are $(s+1)$ elements in δ and s is less than p. This popular choice is frequently supplemented by 'endpoint restrictions' such as

$$m_{-1} = 0 = \sum_{i=0}^{s} \delta_{i+1}(-1)^i \tag{27a}$$

and

$$m_{p+1} = 0 = \sum_{i=0}^{s} \delta_{i+1}(p+1)^i; \tag{27b}$$

that is,

$$\begin{bmatrix} 0 \\ 0 \end{bmatrix} = \begin{bmatrix} 1 & -1 & \ldots & (-1)^s \\ 1 & (p+1) & \ldots & (p+1)^s \end{bmatrix} \delta$$

or

$$0 = C\delta, \tag{28}$$

with an obvious change in notation. If can be shown that (24) and (28) imply

$$m = A[I - C'(CC')^{-1}C]\mu = A_*\mu, \text{ say}, \tag{29}$$

for arbitrary μ. Thus endpoint restrictions simply modify the initial choice of A so as to represent the distributed-lag model (23) as a singular linear model

$$y = XA_*\mu + \varepsilon \tag{30}$$

for which an infinite number of least-squares estimates $\hat{\mu}$ can be calculated. Fortunately $XA_*\hat{\mu}$ is independent of the choice of $\hat{\mu}$ from amongst these estimates.

Three distinct streams of criticisms for this approach can be distinguished. First, the choices for both A and endpoint restrictions in many investment studies have been treated as if they were obviously acceptable and rarely justified. However evidence presented by Trivedi (1970b) and others suggests that the imposition of endpoint restrictions causes substantial biases in estimation. The same conclusion might be made about choices for A. Second, the Almon polynomial approximation leads to elements in XA that are substantially different in magnitude. Cohen et al. (1973) suggest that $(XA)'XA$ may therefore be difficult to invert accurately so that rounding errors may obscure estimates. Finally, certain plausible patterns of reaction coefficients do not lie on any polynomial of degree s, as postulated in (26). Modigliani and Shiller (1973) provide an illustrative criticism in this context. In their own work, they use an alternative bayesian approach, developed by Shiller, that imposes the condition of 'smoothness' on the transfer function for dependence. This condition assigns low probabilities to some of the derivatives of the transfer function when they are evaluated at all values for B.

These criticisms of the Almon procedure, although becoming more widely known, have not reduced the incidence of its use because none of the existing alternative procedures are fault-free. Jorgenson and Stephenson (1967a) described the essence of our current states of knowledge and practice. 'The choice of an appropriate specification for a distributed lag function....is a multiple decision problem of great complexity. No formal statistical procedure is available for such problems, so that the choice must be made on some basis other than the testing of a statistical hypothesis.' With their work using the class of rational or 'General Pascal' specifications (20) and (21), these two researchers illustrate the arbitrariness adopted by researchers in choosing particular transfer functions. For example, after some preliminary explorations but without any firm theoretical bases, they set q equal to two, p equal to at most seven and required the lag polynomial of the numerator to have at most four non-zero intrinsic parameters, all corresponding to successive powers. Within the restricted class of reduced forms (21) fulfilling these constraints, they chose the specification for which the least-squares fit minimized the standard error of regression and the leading non-zero coefficient in $m(B)$ is positive. An alternative bayesian illustration has been provided by Chetty (1971) for a class of transfer functions introduced by Solow (1960), where

$$y_t = b\frac{(1-\lambda)^r}{(1-\lambda B)^r}x_t + \varepsilon_t. \tag{31}$$

In Solow's initial discussion, b, λ and the positive integer r are population parameters to be estimated. By contrast Chetty suggests the use of either beta or uniform distributions for λ and r. For example, suppose gross investment expenditures I_t are related to appropriations A_t, as provided by the National Industrial Conference Board's survey, by

$$I_t = \frac{(1-\lambda)^r}{(1-\lambda B)^r}(b_0 + b_1 A_t) + \varepsilon_t. \tag{32}$$

Chetty demonstrates the estimation of this relationship where ε_t is generated by a first-order autoregressive process, b_1 and λ are distributed uniformly in the range $(0,1)$ and r ranges from 1 to 5 with equiprobable integral values. These choices would, of course, be modified if more prior information were available.

This arbitrariness is not restricted to econometric research. It also occurs under the heading 'the identification problem' in the modelling of many physical processes. Suitable surveys of the non-econometric literature have been provided by Astrom and Eykhoff (1971) and Mayne (1971). For appropriate econometric references in this context, Aigner (1971) and Pierce (1972) are worth consulting. (See Chapter Six for a brief discussion of diagnostic checks of distributed lag models.) We return to the question of choices between specifications in Chapter Four.

3.3 VARIABLE LAGS

The widespread acceptance and use of simple transfer functions to represent stable distributed-lag responses should not lead us to forget earlier discussions presented in Sections 1.3 and 1.5. One major conclusion of the former concerned the very restrictive nature of the assumptions that permit a stable Koyck transfer function to be derived from particular neoclassical optimization models. Recall also the important work of Treadway (1970) which demonstrates that dynamic 'target' ('equilibrium' or 'derived') variables are not necessarily consistent with the outcomes of static optimization models. Unfortunately, these outcomes have been linked with more complex transfer functions, for example those associated with Almon (1965), Jorgenson (1966), Solow (1960) and Tsurumi (1971), without appropriate qualifications to the two-stage procedure. Meyer and Glauber (1964) are excellent representatives of eclectic approaches as described in Section 1.5. They suggest that rates of adjustment by investment to its determining variables will usually depend upon a host of factors including competitive, financial and institutional constraints. Thus, for example, a decision-maker faced with a more competitive market may react quicker. He could seek the goodwill of his customers by making less use of order backlogs as a substitute for the expansion of productive capacity.

Before considering a few illustrative studies that have attempted to use variable patterns of response, it is convenient to cite three sources of variability. First, we should recall Sims' distinction between the time interval at which economic agents observe a series and the time interval at which the econometrician can observe it. The appropriateness of fixed sampling intervals had earlier been questioned by Fisher (1962) who also distinguished threshold effects for the stability of responses. Variability may thus stem from either an inappropriate approximation of individual response intervals by the researcher of from the intrusion of other factors than simply the length of a time interval. Second, seasonal variability may confound fixed response patterns. Third, decisions are critically affected by the lengths of forward horizons for decision-makers. In Muth's framework for rational expectations, it can be established that weights in fixed distributed-lag responses depend upon the prediction period for expectations.

Suppose a determining variable x_t has a time-path that can be represented by an autoregressive process of order $(p + 1)$ so

$$x_{t+1} = \sum_{i=0}^{p} m_i x_{t-i} + \eta_{t+1} = m(B)x_t + \eta_{t+1}, \tag{33}$$

where $\{\eta_t\}$ is a white-noise sequence and $\{m_i\}$ are parameters. Then, if $x_{t+1,1}^*$ is $E(x_{t+1}/x_t, x_{t-1} \ldots x_{t-p})$, one-period expectations formed via

$$x_{t+1,1}^* = m(B)x_t$$

will have minimum mean-squared errors. Further, the two-period expectations are given by

$$x^*_{t+2,2} = m_0 x^*_{t+1,1} + \sum_{i=0}^{p-1} m_{i+1} x_{t-i}$$

and

$$x^*_{t+2,2} = \sum_{i=0}^{p-1} (m_0 m_i + m_{i+1}) x_{t-i} + m_0 m_p x_{t-p}. \tag{34}$$

Notice the weights for (34) are markedly different from those of (33) so that a shift from one-period to two-period expectations changes the transfer fuction from $bm(B)$ to $b\{m_0 m(B) + [m(B) - m_0]/B\}$ if (12) is the basic relationship. Clearly variable patterns of response will occur either if an individual decision-maker adjusts his planning horizon within a sample period or if the relative contributions of distinct decision-makers with different fixed horizons vary over time.

Many separate approaches to the introduction of variability in distributed-lag responses may be discerned in econometric literature. Three of the simplest and more popular ones are presented here. It should be recalled from Section 1.3 that, in Chenery's formulation of the flexible accelerator model, investment is proportional to the difference between desired capital stock and actual capital stock, suitably scaled to reflect excess capacity made desirable by economies of scale and perhaps lagged:

$$(I - R)_t = b(K_t^* - \lambda K_{t-1}).$$

Greenberg (1964) modified this in a number of ways to obtain a variable-reaction, non-linear model. His basic model uses gross investment as its dependent variable. Both K^* and K are defined in terms of the ratio of sales (S) to capacity utilization (C) using the McGraw-Hill surveys of expected and actual series. Finally, the variability in response is introduced by making the natural logarithm of b equal to a linear combination of profit variables (lagged one and two periods) and Moody's indexes for common stock prices and for the average price of new money capital. Thus, after a logarithmic transformation, his model is

$$\log I_t = \beta_0 + \sum_{j=1}^{g} b_j(B) z_{jt} + \beta_{g+1} \log \left[\frac{S^*}{C^*} - \lambda \frac{S}{C} \right], \tag{35}$$

where $\{b_j(B)\}$ are lag polynomials, $\{z_{jt}\}$ represent the collection of financial variables, and the asterisks denote expected values as recorded in the surveys.

Another illustration of simple modifications to the flexible accelerator is provided by Grossman (1973). He introduces variability asymmetrically by making the changes in the manufacturing industries' inventory proportional to the difference between the product of a cyclically variable factor with the desired level of inventory (assumed to be proportional to anticipated sales) and actual inventory. Thus variability is associated only with the desired level and not with its actual level. The cyclically variable factor depends linearly upon a lagged value of the ratio of unfilled orders to sales.

A second approach to the introduction of variability has often been combined with the Almon restrictions but is not necessarily associated with it. Essentially this approach extends that illustrated above beyond the framework of the flexible accelerator and to more variable parameters. If the specifications by Tinsley (1967) and Trivedi (1970a) are combined, they yield a model of the general form

$$y_t = \sum_{j=0}^{p} m_{j,t} x_{t-j} + \varepsilon_t, \tag{36}$$

where

$$m_{j,t} = m_j + \bar{m}_j z_{t-j} \qquad \text{for all } j, t. \tag{37}$$

$\{m_j\}$ and $\{\bar{m}_j\}$ are two collections of $(p+1)$ parameters and z_t is a supplemental variable. Substitution yields

$$y_t = \sum_{j=0}^{p} m_j x_{t-j} + \sum_{j=0}^{p} \bar{m}_j x_{t-j} z_{t-j} + \varepsilon_t \tag{38}$$

or

$$y = Xm + (X^*Z)m + \varepsilon \tag{39}$$

in matrix form. m and $\bar{m}$ are parametric vectors of length $(p+1)$, X and ε are defined as for (23), Z is the matrix with typical row $(z_t, z_{t-1}, \ldots, z_{t-p})$ and (X^*Z) is the Schur Product of X and Z. This product is formed by multiplying each element in X by the element in the same row and column in Z. (See Rowley (1973), Ch. 7.) The final equation is in a convenient form for estimation of m and $\bar{m}$ Sometimes the researcher may wish to further constrain these parameters. For example, Tinsley suggests unit and zero values for the sums of $\{\bar{m}_j\}$ and $\{\bar{m}_j\}$ respectively. Clearly the model might also be reparametrized in the fashion of Almon. Thus, if A and $\bar{A}$ are known matrices of appropriate sizes, we might restrict m and $\bar{m}$ to lie within their respective range spaces. (39) would then become

$$y = XA\mu + (X^*Z)\bar{A}\bar{\mu} + \varepsilon, \tag{40}$$

where the Almon restrictions are

$$m = A\mu \qquad \text{and} \qquad \bar{m} = \bar{A}\bar{\mu}$$

for arbitrary (new) parametric vectors μ and $\bar{\mu}$. In this case, Tinsley's restrictions suggest unit and zero values for the sums of the elements in $A\mu$ and $\bar{A}\bar{\mu}$ respectively.

The choice of the supplemental variable (or, in an easy extension, supplemental variables) depends upon the contect. Trivedi suggested a cyclical variable similar to that described for Grossman's paper. Tinsley used both this variable and another representing capital utilization. Earlier, Popkin (1966) had used this framework to link investment expenditures and appropriations, with backlogs providing the variability component. Later, Pesando used seasonal dummy variables here. A further illustration is provided by Ellison and Stafford (1973).

The final approach to variability in our short list can be represented by Jack (1966). This involves threshold variables making gross investment depend upon a distributed lag of the differences between sales and the maximum level of sales in the previous four periods if this difference is non-negative, and zero otherwise. Similarly, the influence of liquidity upon investment expenditures is represented by a simple dummy variable. This has a unit value only if the earnings/dividends ratio of the firm being observed exceeds 1·5, the average ratio of the sample less its standard deviation.

3.4 DIFFERENTIAL RESPONSES

In the first section of this chapter, the discussion was restricted to a specification with only a single determining variable. No loss of generality was involved there since the primary purpose of this discussion was to introduce terminology in common use. However, in the absence of very strong assumptions with little empirical validity, it is clear that investment in either fixed real capital assets or inventory may be associated with markedly different patterns of response to changes in distinct determining factors. Thus, for example, if rational polynomials in the lag operator $\{m_i(B)/n(B)\}$ are appropriate transfer functions, we might specify

$$n(B)y_t = \sum_{i=1}^{h} m_i(B)x_{it} + \varepsilon_t, \qquad (41)$$

where $\{x_{it}\}$ are a collection of additive determining variables and $n(B)$ is a composite polynomial formed from the denominators of transfer functions for these variables. An illustration of this specification is provided by Hickman (1965), who used a neoclassical model similar to that of Jorgenson as represented by equation (11) of Section 1.1. Clearly, from this equation and in the notation defined there but using a logarithmic transformation, we obtain

$$\log K_{jt}^* = \sigma \log \left(\frac{p}{c_j}\right)_t + \sigma(\gamma - 1)\log Q_t.$$

Hickman added a time trend to represent neutral technical progress and interpreted the determining variables as expectational ones. If this interpretation is acknowledged by the notational device of an asterisk, his specification is

$$\log K_{jt}^* = \sigma \log \left(\frac{p}{c_j}\right)_t^* + \sigma(\gamma - 1)\log Q_t^* + \alpha t + \varepsilon_t, \qquad (42)$$

where a Koyck transfer function associates $\log K_j^*$ and $\log K_j$. In addition,

$$\log \left(\frac{p}{c}\right)_t^* = m_1(B)\log \left(\frac{p}{c}\right)_t \qquad (43a)$$

and

$$\log Q_t^* = m_2(B)\log Q_t. \qquad (43b)$$

When choosing 'best fits' to annual post-war data for 19 industrial sectors in the United States, Hickman decided that $m_1(B)$ should be zero for 12 sectors. A similar result was obtained by Schramm (1972) for parts of the French economy after adjustments for the possible non-exogeneity of output Q and market imperfections in the product market. The first adjustment may be based upon equations (9) and (10) of Chapter One after the choice of a suitable production function and elimination of output. Schramm concluded that his empirical results 'raise serious questions about the adequacy of these investment models in explaining actual French investment behaviour' principally because of the inadequate performance of neoclassical price variables in contrast to output.

In all of the investment studies by Jorgenson and his associates, a single determining variable was used but this was a composite formed from the product of real output with the ratio of output price to the user-cost of investment goods. Thus, in effect, they were suggesting that the temporal responses of investment to separate changes in output or relative prices are similar apart from scale factors. The results of Hickman and Schramm may indicate that the role of relative prices is exaggerated by Jorgenson's restrictive assumptions. His single (composite) determining variable would, if this criticism were correct, be subject to errors of measurement which would affect the validity of his estimates of temporal responses. Some further questioning of these estimates has been presented in this context by Eisner and Nadiri (1968, 1970), Bischoff (1969, 1971b), and Flemming and Feldstein (1971). Bischoff introduced a putty–clay hypothesis according to which relative prices, including tax credits, interest rates and depreciation rules appear to affect equipment spending with a much longer lag than do changes in output. Further, for expenditures on equipment in the United States, Bischoff's empirical results suggest 'the short-run elasticity of equipment demand with respect to output substantially exceeds the long-run elasticity' which is in marked contrast both with his estimates for price influences and with other researchers' estimates. In particular, these estimates should be contrasted with alternative results offered by Jorgenson and Stephenson (1969), and Eisner and Nadiri. The outcome of this dispute is unclear but our personal assessment is that the existence of differential responses seems relatively well-established, although the empirical relevance of the putty–clay hypothesis (with its comparative constraints upon responses to changes in relative prices and output) remain questionable.

Some of the results of Eisner and Nadiri are cited in Chapter Four, were model choices are discussed. These should also be read in the original source if only to established the persistence of very large areas of disagreement amongst prominent researchers in this area. Similarly, the work by Flemming and Feldstein contains relevant material for areas of research besides that of immediate concern here. In particular, it provides a rare application of the Pascal transfer function, which we identified with Chetty's illustration in Section 3.2, and also it attempts to introduce more realistic aspects of corporate finance than usually are found in most empirical models of either fixed capital or inventory formation.

Clearly it is unfair to single out the work of Jorgenson and his associates as a possible framework for the introduction of differential responses. Other researchers have often adopted such responses, frequently using linear models with separate Almon-type transfer functions for different determining variables. However, it is important to stress the difficulties of reconciling theoretical models, which give inadequate attention to dynamic patterns of adjustment, with empirical evidence. These difficulties have been raised at a number of points in the preceding pages and will dominate applied econometric work in the future. Jorgenson's initial work and its successors give immense attention to fiscal detail but wholly fail to capture dynamic constraints except as appendages for empirical work. The elegance of its theoretical model of net-worth optimization, which permits analytic results to be derived, may have discouraged developments in alternative frameworks. Any assessment of the combination of elegance with more realistic restrictions, as perhaps represented in current investigations of the role of adjustment costs in the determination of investment, is premature. If optimization-models really are to be of value, they should be able to utilize feedback from empirical fits. Thus, we must seek to develop models that are capable of generating both variable lags and differential responses.

3.5 STABILITY

Separated forms were introduced in a number of earlier sections without their essential characteristics being made explicit. Similarly, in Section 2.4 where several macroeconomic models involving inventories were described, stability conditions were introduced without a clear statement that they must be based upon separated forms. Appropriate definitions of both separated and resolved or final forms are given in Rowley (1973, pp. 102–107). For our purposes, it is sufficient to assume that the distinction between endogenous and exogenous variables in linear interdependent systems is widely-known. An equation in a given system is then said to be in separated form if it associates a single endogenous variable with only its own lagged values, exogenous variables and errors. When the lagged values are eliminated by repeated substitution, a resolved form is obtained. The collections of coefficients in this form are the filters of the temporal responses of the endogenous variable to changes in the exogenous variables.

The three deterministic Metzler models of Section 2.4 can be manipulated to yield second or third-order difference equations in aggregate income Y_t; namely, equations (39), (42) and (45). Consider the last of these

$$Y_t = [(1+\eta)(1+\alpha)+1]bY_{t-1} - [(1+2\eta)(1+\alpha)b]Y_{t-2} + [(1+\alpha)\eta b]Y_{t-3} + I,$$

where $\bar{I}$ is exogenously given investment and other symbols represent structural parameters of Metzler's third model. With an obvious change in notation, this may be written as

$$Y_t + a_1 Y_{t-1} + a_2 Y_{t-2} + a_3 Y_{t-3} = \bar{I}, \tag{44}$$

or

$$(1 + a_1B + a_2B^2 + a_3B^3)Y_t \equiv a(B)Y_t = \bar{I}.$$

Notice that this is in a separated form even though it contains no error term. Its characteristic equation is defined by

$$z^3 + a_1z^2 + a_2z + a_3 = z^3a\left(\frac{1}{z}\right) = 0. \tag{45}$$

The dynamic behaviour of Y_t is wholly determined by the three parameters (a_1, a_2, a_3) and the dynamic behaviour of investment. Stability is usually discussed in terms of the former or, alternatively, in terms of the three alternative complex parameters which are roots of (45). Let these roots be denoted α_1, α_2 and α_3 so that

$$z^3a\left(\frac{1}{z}\right) = (z - \alpha_1)(z - \alpha_2)(z - \alpha_3) = 0 \tag{46}$$

and

$$a(B) \equiv \prod_{j=1}^{3}(1 - \alpha_jB)Y_t = \bar{I}. \tag{47}$$

Notice that $(1 - \alpha_jB)\alpha_j^t$ is zero for all j. Thus premultiplication by $a(B)$ annihilates any linear combination of α_1^t, α_2^t and α_3^t. If these roots are both distinct and real, the general solution of (44) is the sum of an arbitrary linear combination of $\{\alpha_j^t\}$ and a particular solution of (44). Clearly, if any of the roots $\{\alpha_j\}$ exceeds unity in absolute size, the associated component in the general solution will increase without bound over time. More generally, for repeated and complex roots, stability of the solution depends upon all of these roots falling within the unit circle of the complex plane. This condition for stability is inconvenient when the characteristic polynomial is of high order. An alternative condition, the Schur–Cohn criterion, is defined in terms of the parameters $(a_1, a_2, a_3,...)$ and may be more useful when only qualitative information about their values is available. This is illustrated in Section 2.4. With numerical estimates of the parameters, this criterion is often less useful than that given above. (See Rowley (1973, Ch. 3) for description of the Schur–Cohn criterion.)

For linear differential equations with constant coefficients, similar sets of stability conditions can be derived. Consider Bergstrom's model which was introduced in Section 2.4. This deterministic model was a complete collection of five differential equations, (46)–(50) inclusive in that section, associating consumption C, income Y, the stock of fixed capital assets K, the stock of inventory S and the desired stock of inventory S^*. If a superscript e is used to represent 'equilibrium' values, defined by equating actual to desired stock of inventory and by setting all derivatives equal to zero, these equations indicate that

$$C^e = Y^e = \frac{A}{s},$$

$$K^e = \frac{vA}{s}$$

and

$$S^e = \frac{bA}{s} + k.$$

These equilibrium values are introduced so that the system can be expressed in a homogeneous form. After elimination of S^* by substitution, this form is given by

$$(D + \alpha)(C - C^e) = \alpha(1 - s)(Y - Y^e) \tag{48a}$$

from (2.46),

$$D(K - K^e) = \gamma v(Y - Y^e) - \gamma(K - K^e) \tag{48b}$$

from (2.47),

$$(D + \lambda)(Y - Y^e) = (\lambda + \mu b)[(C - C^e) + D(K - K^e)] - \mu(S - S^e)$$

from (2.48) and (2.49), and

$$(Y - Y^e) = (C - C^e) + D(K - K^e) + D(S - S^e)$$

from (2.50). That is, with rearrangement and elimination of $D(K - K^e)$ from the right-hand side of these equations, (48a), (48b),

$$[D + \lambda - (\lambda + \mu b)\gamma v](Y - Y^e) = (\lambda + \mu b)(C - C^e) - \mu(S - S^e)$$
$$- (\lambda + \mu b)\gamma(K - K^e) \tag{48c}$$

and

$$D(S - S^e) = (1 - \gamma v)(Y - Y^e) - (C - C^e) + \gamma(K - K^e). \tag{48d}$$

Suppose $\mathbf{y}$ is used to represent the column vector with four elements $(C - C^e)$, $(K - K^e)$, $(Y - Y^e)$, $(S - S^e)$. Then the system (48a–d) can be written in the form

$$\mathbf{Dy} = \mathbf{Fy} \tag{49}$$

where

$$\mathbf{F} \equiv \begin{bmatrix} -\alpha & 0 & \alpha(1 - s) & 0 \\ 0 & -\gamma & -\gamma v & 0 \\ (\lambda + \mu b) & -(\lambda + \mu b)\gamma & -\lambda + (\lambda + \mu b)\gamma v & -\mu \\ -1 & \gamma & 1 - \gamma v & 0 \end{bmatrix} \tag{50}$$

The stability of this model depends upon the elements of $\mathbf{F}$. In particular, it is stable if and only if the characteristic roots of $\mathbf{F}$ have negative real parts. These roots are the solution of the determinantal equation $|\mathbf{F} - z\mathbf{I}| = 0$. Clearly the determinant is a fourth-order polynomial in z,

$$\sum_{i=0}^{4} a_i z^{4-i}$$

say. It may be confirmed that the coefficients $\{a_i\}$ are given by the expressions presented in Section 2.4. Both Baumol and Rowley give alternative sets of stability conditions and indicate the simple relationship between these conditions for difference and differential systems.

Why bother with stability? There are two bases for such concern. First, the stochastic properties of estimators may be affected by instability. (See, for example, Rao (1961).) Second, any change in a determining variable could eventually lead to an infinite change in the dependent variable. No finite comparative-static multiplier exists and conventional static theory cannot prove useful for model specification. Notice also that the stability criteria cited above are dependent upon the parameters from all equations of an interdependent set, whether of difference or differential types. Despite this dependence, dynamic multipliers have frequently been derived from single equations even where these could possibly involve a non-resolved form.

3.6 CONTINUOUS MODELS AND DISCRETE APPROXIMATIONS*

Theoretical models of economic behaviour are often framed in continuous rather than discrete time. The advantages of doing so have been stressed by Koopmans (1950). Econometric models on the other hand continue to be predominantly discrete largely because the data available to the econometrician refer to discrete intervals. Now it may very well be the case that, in many situations, the choice of a discrete rather than continuous model can be justified as a natural choice insofar as economic decisions may genuinely be discrete in character. On the other hand, when one is dealing with an aggregate whose components take as their decision period some discrete time interval which itself may be different for different units, it is appropriate to consider the aggregate as varying continuously.

Consider the relationship between production, Q, and final sales, X, when sales vary continuously. If it is assumed that producers react to a single change in X at a point in time $t = 0$ by changing Q at different points in time in the interval $t = 0$ and $t = p$, the value of Q at t can be written in the form of an integral equation

$$Q(t) = \int_{\tau=0}^{p} w(\tau)X(t-\tau).d\tau + \varepsilon(t), \tag{51}$$

where $w(\tau)$ denotes the dependence of Q at time t on X at time $(t-\tau)$ and $\varepsilon(t)$. This specification assumes linearity; the constant term is omitted for convenience. Beginning with equilibrium values (Q^*, X^*), the time-form of response of Q to a unit change in X is given by $w(t)$ since

$$\frac{dQ}{dt} = w(t), \qquad 0 \le t \le p. \tag{52}$$

What determines the goodness of a discrete approximation to the true time form of response? Are any inferences drawn regarding that time form on the basis of a discrete model likely to be seriously misleading? Phillips (1956) has considered this problem in the following way.

Suppose that Q and X are flows per discrete unit of time and discrete periods of length Δt are indexed sequentially from 0, 1, 2 and so on. Thus the period between $t = 0$ and $t = \Delta t$ is numbered period 0, that between $t = \Delta t$ and $t = 2\Delta t$ is numbered period 1, and so on. Then,

$$Q_j = \int_{t=j\Delta t}^{(j+1)\Delta t} Q(t)dt \tag{53}$$

and

$$X_j = \int_{t=j\Delta t}^{(j+1)\Delta t} X(t)dt. \tag{54}$$

Phillips argued that if Q_t and X_t are found to be contemporaneously related in empirical work, this in itself does not provide sufficient grounds for inferring

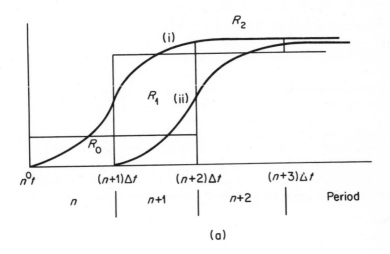

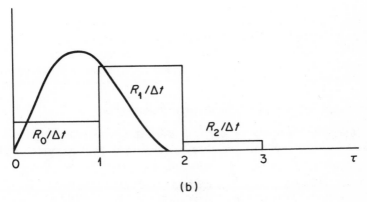

Figure 2.

the existence of a similar relationship in the continuous process. No unique relation between the observed Q and X will prevail because the observed values of Q in a period j depend not only on the observed values of X_j, X_{j-1} and earlier values, but also on the values taken by X within the period. If and only if X has a definite intra-period time form, the same for all periods, will there be a determinate relation between Q_t and X_t. As an illustration suppose that $X(t)$ changes only at the very end of each period so that $X(t)$ is $X_j/\Delta t$ for the range $j\Delta t \le t \le (j + 1)\Delta t$. Given that the basic model is linear, the value of X_j can be thought of as being a sum of step functions, a step from 0 to $X_j/\Delta t$ at time $j\Delta t$ and a step from $X_{j+1}/\Delta t$ at time $(j + 1)\Delta t$. The two curves (i) and (ii) in Figure 2(a) represent, respectively, the direct response of Q to a unit step in X at time $j\Delta t$ and the response to a unit change in X at $(j + 1)\Delta t$. The latter curve is, of course, merely the former one shifted a period along the time axis. The rectangles R_0, R_1 and R_2 represent, respectively, the resultant production in periods j, $(j + 1)$ and $(j + 2)$. Production of period j resulting from demand in period $(j - 1)$ is $(X_{j-1}/R_1\Delta t)$ and production in period $(j - 2)$ is $(X_{j-2}/R_2\Delta t)$. The discrete relationship between Q and X is then

$$Q_j = \frac{R_0}{\Delta t}X_j + \frac{R_1}{\Delta t}X_{j-1} + \frac{R_2}{\Delta t}X_{j-2} + \varepsilon'\Delta t. \tag{55}$$

Comparison between $w(\tau)$ and the histogram (see Figure 2(b)) representing the coefficients of the discrete relationship shows that the latter is indeed a poor approximation to the former. The figure also illustrates that the relationship in discrete time is over at least two periods except when the reaction in the continuous model is instantaneous. Thus the approximation procedure itself induces a moving average form in the X variable. If the observation period is small, then the discrete formulation is one in which Q_j is related to, say, r values of X through the equation

$$Q_j = \alpha_0 X_j + \alpha_1 X_{j-1} + \ldots + \alpha_r X_{j-r} + \varepsilon'\Delta t, \tag{56}$$

where $p/\Delta t \le r \le (p/\Delta t + 1)$. From Figure 2, it is clear that with a reduction in the length of the period, the sequence $\{\alpha_j\}$ provides a much better approximation to the time-shape $w(\tau)$.

In practice the intra-period time-form of X will not be definite. Phillips remarks that for this reason the $\{\alpha_j\}$ on the discrete relationship will not be strictly determinate. This can be regarded as a consequence of time aggregation.

Derivation of discrete models from continuous models

Consider the problem of deriving difference equations from differential equations. In econometrics, we always deal with stochastic models so let both the differential and difference equations be stochastic. As illustrations, we shall only consider the special cases of first- and second-order differential equations since these demonstrate the essential nature of the problem involved here. Any reader who is interested in pursuing these in greater generality and rigour should refer to Bartlett (1946), Phillips (1956, 1959), Durbin (1961), Bergstrom (1966), Sargan (1974), Wymer (1972), Phillips (1972) and Yaglom (1962).

Case A: Pure first-order stochastic differential equation

Consider the equation

$$\dot{y}(t) + \alpha_1 y(t) = \varepsilon(t) \tag{57}$$

or

$$Dy(t) + \alpha_1 y(t) = \varepsilon(t), \tag{58}$$

where D is the differential operator and α_1 is a constant, $\varepsilon(t)$ is a random impulse function which changes $y(t)$ discontinuously. $Dy(t)$ may be regarded as formally defined by the (58) in terms of $\varepsilon(t)$ which is an improper function possessing a proper integral

$$\int^t \varepsilon(v)dv = u(t).$$

$u(t)$ is a homogeneous random process such that

$$E[u(t)] = 0 \qquad \text{for all } t$$

and

$$E[\{u(t_1) - u(t_2)\}\{u(t_3) - u(t_4)\}'] = 0 \qquad \text{for } t_1 > t_2 \geq t_3 > t_4.$$

Since

$$\lim_{h \to 0} E\left\{ \left| \frac{u(t+h) - u(t)}{h} - Du(t) \right|^2 \right\}$$

does not exist, $u(t)$ is non-differentiable and so the process $\varepsilon(t)$ cannot be rigorously defined.

The solution of the differential equation is

$$y(t) = \int_{u=-\infty}^{t} e^{-\alpha(t-u)}.\varepsilon(u).du, \tag{59}$$

whence it follows that, at time $(t + h)$,

$$y(t+h) = \int_{-\infty}^{t+h} e^{-\alpha_1(t+h-u)}.\varepsilon(u).du$$

$$= e^{-\alpha_1 h} \int_{-\infty}^{t+h} e^{-\alpha_1(t-u)}.\varepsilon(u).du$$

$$= e^{-\alpha_1 h} \left[\int_{-\infty}^{t} e^{-\alpha_1(t-u)}.\varepsilon(u).du + \int_{t}^{t+h} e^{-\alpha_1(t-u)}\varepsilon(u)du \right].$$

$$y(t+h) = e^{-\alpha_1 h}y(t) + z(t+h), \tag{60}$$

where

$$z(t + h) = \int_t^{t+h} e^{-\alpha_1 (t-u)} . \varepsilon(u) . du. \tag{61}$$

If observations are collected for y at equispaced intervals of length h, then in view of (60), they will satisfy a difference equation of the form

$$y_{t+h} - a_1 y_t = z_{t+h}, \tag{62}$$

where $a_1 = e^{-\alpha_1 h}$, with an obvious change in notation. Thus, if we are mainly interested in observations spaced at intervals of length h, then (62) is exactly equivalent to the stochastic differential equation (58).

To relate differential and difference equations it is useful to use the formula of Lagrange

$$B^h = e^{-hD}$$

associating the lag and differential operators. (See Brown (1965, p. 157).)

Case B: Pure second-order stochastic differential equation

Consider the equation

$$D^2 y(t) + \alpha_1 D y(t) + \alpha_2 y(t) = \varepsilon(t) \tag{63}$$

or

$$y(t) = [D^2 + \alpha_1 D + \alpha_2]^{-1} \varepsilon(t). \tag{64}$$

Assuming that the polynomial in D has two distinct real roots μ_1 and μ_2, we can factorize it into $(D - \mu_1)(D - \mu_2)$.

The solution of the differential equation is

$$y(t) = \int_{-\infty}^t C_1 e^{\mu_1 (t-u)} . \varepsilon(u) . du + \int_{-\infty}^t C_2 e^{\mu_2 (t-u)} . \varepsilon(u) . du, \tag{64}$$

where $C_1 = (\mu_2 - \mu_1)^{-1} = -C_2$.

Using (64) it can be shown that

$$y(t + 2h) = (e^{\mu_1 h} + e^{\mu_2 h}) y(t + h) + (e^{(\mu_1 + \mu_2)h}) y(t) + z(t + 2h), \tag{65}$$

where

$$z(t + 2h) = \int_{t+h}^{t+2h} \varepsilon(u) \left[\frac{e^{-\mu_1 (t+2h-u)} - e^{-\mu_2 (t+2h-u)}}{\mu_2 - \mu_1} \right] . du \\ + e^{-(\mu_1 + \mu_2)h} \int_t^{t+h} \varepsilon(u) \left[\frac{e^{-\mu_1 (t-u)} - e^{-\mu_2 (t-u)}}{\mu_2 - \mu_1} \right] . du. \tag{66}$$

Given (65), observations at equi-spaced intervals of length h will satisfy the second-order difference equation

$$y_{t+2h} + a_1 y_{t+h} + a_2 y_t = z_{t+2h} - a_2 z_{t+h}, \tag{67}$$

where

$$a_1 = -(e^{\mu_1 h} + e^{\mu_2 h}), a_2 = -e^{(\mu_1 + \mu_2)h}, \tag{68}$$

$$z_{t+2h} = \int_{t+h}^{t+2h} \varepsilon(u)\left[\frac{e^{-\mu_1(t+2h-u)} - e^{-\mu_2(t+2h-u)}}{\mu_2 - \mu_1}\right]du \tag{69}$$

and

$$z_{t+h} = \int_{t}^{t+h} \varepsilon(u)\left[\frac{e^{-\mu_1(t-u)} - e^{-\mu_2(t-u)}}{\mu_2 - \mu_1}\right]du. \tag{70}$$

The main difference from case A is that the exact difference-equation equivalent of the equation (63) involves a stochastic term which is generated by a first-order moving-average process. Even if the $\{z_t\}$ process is serially uncorrelated, moving-average terms of the type $(z_{t+2h} + a_1 z_{t+h})$ are correlated. In conclusion, therefore, the second-order stochastic differential equation behaves like a second-order difference equation with a first-order moving average error; the parameters of the difference equation are non-linear functions of the parameters in the differential equation. Using similar methods it can be shown that the continuous linear rth-order process behaves like a discrete linear rth-order process with a stochastic term which is generated by a moving-average process of order $(r-1)$.

Case C: Continuous time distributed lag model and its discrete representation

Consider the continuous time model

$$Dy(t) = Ay(t) + Cx(t) + \varepsilon(t), \tag{71}$$

where $y(t)$ is a vector of length n and $x(t)$ is a vector of k exogenous variables, independent of the disturbance vector $\varepsilon(t)$ which is assumed to be a Gaussian white noise process so that $E[\varepsilon(t)]$ is O and $E[\varepsilon(t), \varepsilon'(\tau)]$ is $\Omega\delta(t - \tau)$. Here $\delta(t - \tau)$ is the Dirac delta function. A and C are matrices of unknown parameters.
    The choice of a first-order system involves no loss of generality since higher-order systems can be reduced to the first-order case. Restrictions may be introduced on the matrix A such that (71) defines a recursive model. [See Bergstrom (1966).] The solution of the above differential equation takes the form

$$y(t) = \Phi(t,t_0)y(t_0) + \int_{t_0}^{t} \Phi(t,\tau)[Cx(\tau) + \varepsilon(\tau)]d\tau, \tag{72}$$

where $D\Phi(t,\tau) = A\Phi(t,\tau) = Ae^{A(t-\tau)}$ and $\Phi(t,\tau)$ is a matrix of order n by n.
    Assume, somewhat restrictively, that the stimulus variable $x(t)$ is held fixed at a given level in the interval $[t_0,t] = [t_i,t_{i+1}]$. Then

$$y(t_{i+1}) = \Phi(t_{i+1},t_i)y(t_i) + \left[\int_{t_i}^{t_{i+1}} \Phi(t_{i+1},\tau)Cd\tau\right]x(t_i)$$

$$+ \int_{t_i}^{t_{i+1}} \Phi(t_{i+1},\tau)\varepsilon(\tau)d\tau \tag{73}$$

which may be written in the form

$$y(i + 1) = \Phi(i + 1, i)y(i) + \theta(i + 1, i)x(i) + \varepsilon^*(i), \tag{74}$$

where

$$\Phi(i + 1, i) = \Phi(t_{i+1}, t_i),$$

$$\theta(i + 1, i) = \int_{t_i}^{t_{i+1}} \Phi(t_{i+1}, \tau)C d\tau,$$

$$\varepsilon^*(i) = \int_{t_i}^{t_{i+1}} \Phi(t_{i+1}, \tau)\varepsilon(\tau).d\tau.$$

ε^* is a Gaussian white noise sequence defined in discrete time.

To rewrite the above equations in a more convenient form we define $h = t_{i+1} - t_i$ and $\Phi(t, \tau) = e^{A(t-\tau)\tau}$, $\Phi(i + 1, i) = e^{Ah}$. The matrix term e^{Ah} may be expanded as an infinite series thus:

$$e^{Ah} = I + Ah + A^2\frac{h^2}{2!} + A^3\frac{h^3}{3!} + \dots \tag{75}$$

which may be approximated by the first two terms (say) if h is sufficiently small, that is

$$e^Ah = I + Ah + O(h^2) \simeq I + Ah. \tag{76}$$

Here $O(h^2)$ denotes terms at most of order h^2. The symbol O denotes stochastic order of magnitude. A term $f(h)$ is said to be of $O(h^k)$ if

$$\lim_{h \to 0}(h^{-k}|f(h)|)$$

is finite. Now

$$\theta(i + 1, i) = \int_{t_i}^{t_{i+1}} \Phi(t_{i+1}, \tau)C d\tau$$

$$= \int_{t_i}^{t_{i+1}} [I + A(t_{i+1} - \tau)]C d\tau$$

$$\simeq Ch + ACt_{i+1}h - AC\int_{t_i}^{t_{i+1}} \tau.d\tau$$

$$\simeq Ch + AC\frac{h^2}{2!} = Ch + O(h^2). \tag{77}$$

Substituting for θ in (74) we obtain

$$y(i + 1) = e^{Ah}y(i) + [Ch + O(h^2)]x(i) + \varepsilon^*(i). \tag{78}$$

(78) is a discrete-time approximation to $O(h^2)$ to the original continuous model. It illustrates the point that the nature of the relationship between the two sets of parameters is complex, but the problem of estimating the continuous

time model is essentially a computational one. Furthermore, the size of the coefficients depends upon the interval between observations.

Approximation problems

If the variable x is of the instantaneous type, then an approximation to x_τ in the interval $t - 1 < \tau < t$ is given by

$$x_{t-1+} \simeq \frac{x_t + x_{t-1}}{2}.$$

Such an approximation is used by Houthakker and Taylor (1966). This process of averaging can be thought of as a process of centering the observation in period t. If the variable y is also of an instantaneous type then its value at time τ in the same interval can be similarly approximated. An approximation to the rate of change of variable in a single time period is then simply the first difference. In making such as approximation we introduce into our model arbitrary errors of approximation which might be assumed random. Such errors will be added to errors on equations leading to a new compound disturbance. (We ignore this complication below by suppressing the error term.)

Thus we set

$$\int_{t-h}^{t} Dy(s)ds \simeq \frac{1}{h}[y_t - y_{t-1}] = \frac{1}{h}(1 - B)y_t \tag{79}$$

and

$$\int_{t-h}^{t} y(s)ds \simeq \frac{1}{2h}[y_t + y_{t-1}] = \frac{1}{2h}(1 + B)y_t. \tag{80}$$

Using these approximations, we obtain a discrete approximation to the continuous model

$$(D + \alpha)y(t) = \beta x(t). \tag{81}$$

This approximation is

$$\left(1 + \frac{\alpha h}{2}\right)y_t = \left(1 - \frac{\alpha h}{2}\right)y_{t-1} + \frac{\beta h}{2}(x_t + x_{t-1}), \tag{82}$$

which may be compared with the exact discrete equivalent (62) after scaling the latter by a factor $(1 + \alpha h/2)$. This operation yields

$$\left(1 + \frac{\alpha h}{2}\right)y_t = \left[\left(1 + \frac{\alpha h}{2}\right)e^{-\alpha h}\right]y_{t-1} + \left[\left(1 + \frac{\alpha h}{2}\right)\beta(1 - e^{\alpha h})\right]x_{t-1+}.$$

Expanding $e^{-\alpha h}$ as a power series, we see that

$$e^{-\alpha h}\left(1 + \frac{\alpha h}{2}\right) = 1 - \left(\alpha h - \frac{\alpha h}{2}\right) + \left(\frac{\alpha^2 h^2}{2} - \frac{\alpha^2 h^2}{2}\right)$$
$$- \left(\frac{\alpha^3 h^3}{6} - \frac{\alpha^3 h^3}{4}\right) + \left(\frac{\alpha^4 h^4}{24} - \frac{\alpha^4 h^4}{12}\right) - \cdots$$

$$= \left(1 - \frac{\alpha h}{2}\right) - \left(\frac{\alpha^3 h^3}{12}\right) + O(h^4),$$

where $O(h^4)$ denotes terms at most of order h^4. The symbol O denotes stochastic order of magnitude. Comparing the result with (82), it is clear that the difference in the coefficient of the lagged dependent variable in the approximate and the exact versions is

$$\frac{(1 - \alpha h/2) - e^{-\alpha h}(1 + \alpha h/2)}{h} = \frac{1}{12}\alpha^3 h^2 + O(h^3), \tag{83}$$

which will be small if h is small. Thus the approximation suggested above while being computationally easier will yield good approximations to the exact equivalent. A similar expression can also be derived for the approximation error in the coefficients of x_t. Reflection on this point will indicate, however, that the error of approximation will depend on actual values of x. The smaller the length of h, the closer would the approximation $1/2 (x_t + x_{t-1})$ be to x_{t-1+}.

What is the gain through using data at, say, interval h rather than $2h$? For the approximate model the coefficient of the lagged dependent variable will have an error (neglecting $O(h^3)$) of the order $1/12\alpha^3 h^2$ compared with $(1/12\alpha^3)(4h^4)$ whence we see that the error is proportional to the square of the length of the sampling interval.

This discussion suggests only the nature of a possible approach to the problem. It should be noted that the problem is rather complex especially if we entertain the possibility that $x(t)$ is a stochastic but integrable variable. (See Astrom (1970) for an introduction to the concept of stochastic integration.) In that case there are at least two questions which we have to face. First, does the nature of the stochastic process generating the $x(t)$ make any difference to the goodness of an approximation of the type discussed above? Second, what is the difference in the misspecification bias arising from application of alternative estimators if several are available? We shall not go into the matter here. The interested reader will find an extensive treatment in Sargan (1974).

CHAPTER 4

Problems of Specification: Some Basic Choices

All areas of applied econometrics provide illustrations of tentative rules for action that have been adopted despite their questionable bases. Faced with persistent demands for criteria to govern the optimal conduct of research, econometricians have usually responded with behavioural rules that appear to be reasonable (at least to their proponents) in the context of our present state of knowledge. The following sections describe certain of these rules and illustrate some particular choices in studies of investment. Thus, they reflect operational patterns of conduct rather than either economic or statistical theories even though many rules are partially rationalized in theoretical terms.

4.1 EXPLANATORY VARIABLES IN 'INCOMPLETELY-SPECIFIED' MODELS

Many terms have been introduced to denote classifications of variables included in statistical fits. Although this multiplicity can be confusing, it serves as a useful reminder that there exist many distinct motives for computing such fits. Models have been developed for the control of particular variables of interest (dependent or endogenous variables), the prediction of their levels in changed circumstances, and the explanation of past levels in specific historical periods. Clearly the optimal choice of variables in any research circumstance will not necessarily be independent of the purpose for which they are being considered. Lindley (1968) illustrates this simple proposition in a bayesian framework for the twofold alternatives of control and prediction.

Often we know even less about economic structures than assumed by Lindley in the illustration cited above. Bancroft (1944) introduced the apt description of 'incompletely specified' for the models that typically occur in practical situations. He initiated an important stream of analyses, which explored some popular operational rules for choice of explanatory (determining, exogenous or predictor) variables. We consider some aspects of this stream in the next chapter. Notice the classical linear model and its multi-equation extensions, which dominate theoretical discussions in econometrics, presume a knowledge of the variables to be included in their specifications. In fact, the econometricians' concept of identification, which logically precedes estimation in systems of equations, depends critically upon such knowledge. (See Rowley (1973, Ch..4).)

The focus of this section is on practical matters. First, some references are provided for efficient computational procedures for the estimation of specifications with different collections of explanatory variables. Second, some popular rules for selection of explanatory variables in single-equation cases are cited.

For many years, calculations were severely restricted by inadequacies in computational facilities. Now, although developments in the past two decades have substantially reduced computational burdens, there remains a constant need for the efficient use of existing facilities to reduce computational costs and possible numerical inaccuracies. Garside (1971) describes some of the more important considerations that should be noted in this context. Earlier papers by Garside (1965) and Schatzoff, Tsao and Fienberg (1968) indicate relatively efficient approaches to the enumeration problem for least-squares estimates associated with alternative specifications. These approaches are based on the principle of the 'Hamiltonian Walk' as it applies to the calculation of least-squares estimates for the parameters of all possible subsets of explanatory variables from a given collection of candidates. If there are k possible explanatory variables, the alternative choices for subsets of these variables may be represented by the vertices of a k-dimensional hypercube with sides of unit lengths. Clearly the coordinates of any vertex are either unity or zero and signify the inclusion or exclusion of particular variables in any specification. As Garside suggests, a Hamilton Walk provides a systematic method of examining all vertices without repetition so that the regression submodels at two successive steps differ by the inclusion, or exclusion, of just one variable . Garside's second paper deviates from the Walk principle but provides an alternative and relatively efficient algorithm for full enumeration of all specifications.

Often these algorithms calculate alternatives that would be immediately discarded. To eliminate these unnecessary calculations, several tree-searching approaches have been suggested. These involve the partial enumeration of specifications with screening of potential branches (disjoint classes of vertices in the illustrative framework given above) by comparative statistics and arbitrary cut-off rules. All of these procedures are based on comparisons of residual sums of squares, coefficients of multiple determination or similar indicators. See, for example, the three rules proposed by Beale, Kendall and Mann (1967) and the use of Mallow's c statistic as described by Daniel and Wood (1971, Ch. 6). Notice that sometimes the problem of choice has been expressed as one of 'optimal regression' whereby the researcher seeks to choose a fixed number of non-zero parametric estimates from a larger class of potential candidates. Beale (1970) illustrates this approach and extends it to include non-negativity constraints on some parameters.

Clearly enumeration of alternative specifications will provide a background for choice and some indication of the sensitivity associated with particular choices but the researcher usually needs to adopt one specification in preference to all others. Thus enumeration must be combined with a criterion function for this final choice. Typically, this is based upon arbitrary statistical criteria after pre-screening of alternatives that obviously conflict with prior notions. (An example of such prescreening is provided by the omission of any specification for an investment equation which leads to a negative estimate for the accelerator coefficient.) Amongst the statistical criteria most frequently cited for final choice may be found the stepwise use of Student's t statistics, maximization of coefficients of multiple determination (in both adjusted and unadjusted forms), minimization of standard errors of regression, and minimization of mean squared forecast errors based on truncated samples.

Stepwise use of Student's statistics ('stepwise regression') appears to have been first systematized by Efroymson (1960) although the exclusion and inclusion of explanatory variables on this basis has a long history. Valid criticisms of this criterion, which were begun as early as 1944 by Bancroft, will be described in the next section in the context of some specific estimators. In stepwise regression, three critical values for indicators are used. Two of these establish the 'statistical significance' of particular conditional parameters and the other signals the end of the search for the optimal specification. Thus significant variables (according to the first critical value) are singly introduced into the estimated equation. Other variables are omitted as they become insignificant (according to the second critical value) until an 'equilibrium' point is reached. Arrival at this point is indicated by the favourable comparison of the change in a simple measure (such as R^2 or the sum of squared residuals) with the third critical value. Unfortunately the equilibrium point for this 'forward-selection' (or 'step-up') procedure often differs from the alternative 'backward-selection' (or 'step-down') procedure in which insignificant variables are singly omitted and we have no basis for choosing between them. Further the equilibrium points may be markedly affected by extensions to data. An excellent survey of these procedures and their uses is provided by Draper and Smith (1966, Ch. 6).

The coefficient of multiple determination, R^2, has been used as a crude indicator of the proportion of sample variation in a dependent variable explained by an estimated linear combination of explanatory variables. The 'adjusted' form $\bar{R}^2$ was introduced because increases in the number of explanatory variables will usually increase R^2 and will never decrease it in least-squares fits. (See Rowley (1973, Ch. 1).) The approach to choice of specification based on the maximization of $\bar{R}^2$ is not entirely independent of the stepwise procedures cited above. In particular, if a unit level is set for the first critical value, formal linkages can be established between the alternative approaches. These are clarified by Dhrymes (1970), Bacon (1972) and Valentine (1972). However, the value of establishing such linkages appears small given the fragile theoretical bases for both approaches. In addition, as indicated by Koerts and Abrahamse (1970) the distribution of R^2 sensitively depends upon the observations for explanatory variables in particular samples as well as upon the unknown parametric vector and common variance of the errors in the classical linear model. Some Monte-Carlo evidence on the deficiencies of these criteria in distributed-lag models has been presented by Cohen *et al.* (1973). This pessimistic evidence appears to be typical of published investigations.

Minimization of the estimated standard errors of regressions for alternative specifications has been illustrated by Jorgenson and Stephenson (1967a). Some possible power calculations for this third approach are provided by Schmidt (1973) for the situation where lagged dependent variables are absent. Clearly it suffers from similar shortcomings to those indicated for the other criteria cited above. Ignorance and incomplete specification may preclude development of simple statistical indicators for general use in discrimination between different specifications. It may be that only sequential modelling, with careful experimentation between any two stages and the deliberate introduction of perturbations, can offer much chance of successful choices between alternative collections of explanatory variables. Unfortunately, econometricians seldom enjoy the control opportunities of system engineers who face similar problems and who have begun to develop sequential procedures of this type.

4.2   ESTIMATORS

The choice between different estimators, even for a given specification of explanatory variables, is as difficult a problem as that indicated above for the choice of explanatory variables. Our elementary textbooks usually define certain properties of estimators and indicate the relationships between mean squared errors, variances, biases and efficiencies but, in practical situations, these descriptions are often inadequate bases for choice. Our principal deficiencies may stem from an inflexible theoretical preoccupation with mean values instead of other measures of location or centrality and with normally distributed errors. As Anscombe (1967) suggested, 'The disposition of present-day statistical theorists to suppose that all 'error' distributions are exactly normal can be ascribed to their ontological perception that normality is too good not to be true.' Fortunately more exploratory research has begun into a number of areas that formerly lay outside the mainstream of activity. Since some of these areas are of relevance for the choice between estimators, they are described below.

The assumption of normally distributed errors for investment equations is especially significant in the choice of estimators. Its adoption frequently leads the researcher directly towards the least-squares estimates. Yet there is ample evidence to suggest that the assumption may be unwarranted for some economic phenomena. Thus, for example, it has been suggested that, in models with the ratio of investment to capital stock as their dependent variable, alternative distributions may be more appropriate. This point is simply clarified by Smith (1973). When other distributions are considered, many of our standard indicators lose their relevance and the choice of estimation techniques can range over a much longer list of alternatives. Some of these alternative techniques are briefly cited below.

In the classical linear model with identically and independently distributed errors, least-squares estimators are optimal in the restricted sense that they have minimum variances amongst the class of estimators that are linear functions of the observations for the dependent variable. They are also maximum-likelihood estimators and normally distributed if, in addition, the errors are normally distributed. These properties and computational simplicity are the principal justifications for the use of least-squares estimators. Two qualifications are necessary. First, definitions of the classical model frequently understate the importance of assuming finite variances for errors. Often errors are described as the representations of a large number of omitted variables, with small individual significance, and the assumptions of normality and finite variances for the errors are justified in terms of the central limit theorem. However the appropriateness of this theorem depends critically upon the existence of finite variances for the componental variables forming the errors. Second, ease of computation is no longer as critical a factor as it was when calculations were only made with hand-operated machines. This development has considerably increased the number of feasible estimators. For example, least-lines (or MAD) estimators, which minimize the sum of absolute residuals and which had been explored as early as 1818 by Laplace, were often dismissed as impracticable until the criterion was reformulated as a simple problem in linear programming and the simplex algorithm became familiar to researchers.

The normal distribution is one particular member of the class of 'stable' distributions which are reproduced by weighted addition. (See Feller (1971, ch. 6).) Thus, if the errors of any model are independent drawings from a given stable distribution, then any linear combination of the errors will have the same distribution apart from location and scale parameters. The central limit theorem indicates that the normal distribution is the only stable distribution with finite variances. For other stable distributions, which cannot be rejected *a priori*, this justification excludes finite variances and the Gauss–Markov theorem, which clarifies the optimality of least-squares estimators, does not apply. This has influenced other researchers to consider alternative approaches to estimation.

Blattberg and Sargent (1971) considered the properties of both least-squares and least-line estimators in the situation where errors follow a distribution with fatter extreme tails than the normal distribution. Since less weight is attached to extreme observations by a least-lines estimate, they suggested that it seems a natural estimator to apply in cases where extreme observations occur more frequently than where the disturbances are normally distributed. Indeed the evidence from their Monto–Carlo study confirms a marked superiority for the least-lines estimator. It is, also, known that this estimator is a maximum-likelihood estimator if the errors are drawn from a double exponential distribution; Smith and Hall (1972) provide additional evidence for this situation. However, earlier work by Ashar and Wallace (1963) suggests a substantial loss of efficiency if least-lines estimators are used instead of least-squares estimators when the errors really are normally distributed. With respect to bias, some relevant results are cited by Kiountouzis (1973). Least-lines estimators are not linear functions of the observations for the dependent variable and their statistical properties are difficult to establish, but it is known that, in the classical linear model with symmetrically distributed errors, there exist least-line estimators which are symmetrically distributed about the parametric vector. Thus, for example, if the Cauchy distribution is appropriate for the errors, there exists a least-lines estimator which is symmetric about its median even though its moments will not exist. Kiountouzis' investigation indicates some small deviations from the sample median even with symmetric error distributions and large samples. This apparent contradiction is resolved by the potential non-uniqueness of the least-lines estimators. Multiple solutions occur if least-lines fits do not pass through a number of observational points equal to the number of unknown parameters for explanatory variables.

These results indicate that choice between least-lines and least-squares estimators critically depends upon the unknown distribution of the errors. Clearly, the popular framework provided by the representation of mean squared biases is irrelevant here. The trade-offs between efficiency (as reflected in variances) and biases do not exist if errors have a stable but non-normal distribution.

A final piece of evidence concerning least-lines estimators is given by Meyer and Glauber (1964). They used various methods to calculate estimates for a model of investment expenditures and made post-sample predictions with these. In checks of prediction errors, the least-lines estimates were judged to be superior to others including least-squares estimates. The linear-programming representation for the least-lines criterion is described by Fisher (1961).

The least-lines estimators are not the only ones that can be based upon mathematical-programming techniques. Meyer and Glauber also illustrate the use of quadratic programming where least-squares estimators are to be constrained by parametric inequalities, based on either *a priori* or extraneous information. Another alternative is provided by the Chebyshev criterion whereby estimates are chosen to minimize the largest absolute residual. Algorithms for this approach are indicated by Duris and Sreedharan (1968) and Wagner (1959) but it is seldom used perhaps because of the difficulties experienced in attempts to establish distributional characteristics for the Chebyshev estimators.

When errors are normally distributed and variances exist (as we shall assume throughout the remainder of this section), we might use relative efficiency in the mean-squared-errors (MSE) sense as an indicator of optimality for estimators. For example, if least-squares estimators are unbiased and have large variances, it may be both possible and preferable to use alternative estimators that are biased but have variances which are sufficiently small that their mean squared errors are smaller than those of least-squares estimators. If $\mathbf{y}$ and $\mathbf{X}$ represent observations for the dependent and explanatory variables, respectively, least-squares estimators of the parametric vector β are solutions of the normal equations

$$\mathbf{X'X}\hat{\beta} = \mathbf{X'y}. \tag{1}$$

Such solutions always exist but often the diagonal elements of the inverse for $\mathbf{X'X}$ (when it exists) are large. Then the variances and mean squared errors of $\hat{\beta}$ are also large. Suppose, instead, the normal equations are amended by supplementing the principal diagonal of $\mathbf{X'X}$ with positive entries. This yields

$$(\mathbf{X'X} + \Lambda)\hat{\beta} = \mathbf{X'y}, \tag{2}$$

where Λ is a diagonal matrix formed from the additional entries. The introduction of this 'ridge' will make the estimators biased but it may also reduce the mean squared errors. Suppose the data have been previously scaled so that the principal diagonal of $\mathbf{X}\,\mathbf{X}$ has unit elements. Then the choice of the scalar matrix $k\mathbf{I}$ (with arbitrary constant k fixed in advance of estimation) for Λ yields a specification that has been called 'ridge regression'. Marquardt (1970) provides a survey of the properties of this class of estimators while Lindley and Smith (1972) illustrate a possible basis for them from a bayesian framework. It can be shown that a ridge estimator of this class is MSE-efficient relative to the least-squares alternative for some choices of k. Unfortunately, these choices depend on the values of β and $\mathbf{X}$. No rule has been established for ensuring that an appropriate choice for k will be made in practical situations and some Monto–Carlo evidence is available that shows marked inefficiency with particular choices.

The obvious arbitrariness which is involved in the use of ridge regression has restricted its adoption in applied econometrics but it has been widely used in other areas such as chemical engineering. Econometricians have turned instead to other approaches which also involve bias. Thus, for example, they may cite MSE-efficiency as a justification for imposing exact restrictions which are only approximately valid (or even patently false) or for adopting the range-space requirement associated with the Almon technique. The researcher hopes that, in such cases, decreases in variances more than compensate for increases in squared biases but, as with ridge regressions, no practical rules guarantee reasonable chances of success here.

Several other biased but relatively MSE-efficient estimators have been sought with a variety of two-stage procedures. These stem in part from the seminal criticism by Bancroft (1944), cited above, of the use of preliminary tests of significance in the choice of variables. For many years, it has been a common practice amongst econometricians to calculate two (or more) statistical fits where variables are omitted from the final specification on the bases of their coefficients' lack of statistical significance or inappropriate signs in an earlier fit. The resulting 'conditional omitted variable' (or COV) estimators are biased and conventional computational programmes will fail to take account of the consequences of the two-stage procedure in calculating their estimated standard-errors and Student's statistics associated with simple zero hypotheses.

With respect to the first-stage use of t statistics, Bancroft (1972) has provided both a brief survey of commentaries in this area and a simple statement of the attendant inferential difficulties. 'In using inference procedures incorporating preliminary test(s) of significance the experimenter behaves as if the null hypothesis of the preliminary test is true if it is not rejected. This is contrary to the inference philosophy advocated in many texts in applied statistics to the effect that failure to reject a null hypothesis does not imply that it is true. Such texts imply that failure to reject the null hypothesis can be attributed to a small sample size and/or lack of power.' Some statistical properties of these COV estimators are described by Bock, Judge and Yancey (1973a, b; 1974). With respect to the first-stage use of post-fit inequality constraints (for example, where variables are later omitted when their estimated coefficients in the first stage have the 'wrong' sign), Lovell and Prescott (1970) illustrate that 'this procedure causes bias and can lead to inefficient parameter estimates' and, also, that 'grossly exaggerated statements concerning significance levels are likely to be made when other regression coefficients in the model are tested with the final regression obtained after deleting variables with incorrect sign'.

Several conclusions with respect to the choice of estimators might be drawn from the preceding account. First, the distribution of the errors is a critical factor in this choice. The Gauss–Markov theorem for the optimality of least-squares estimators is distribution-free but its relevance depends upon the existence of finite variances for error terms. Thus the theorem is irrelevant for some distributions that have been considered by economists. Second, there exist a large number of alternative estimators and there is no obvious need for the researcher to consider only one particular approach. Finally, if multi-stage procedures are followed, there is a danger that inappropriate formulae will be used. The distribution of an estimator derived sequentially will depend upon decision rules applied at earlier stages in its derivation.

4.3   MODELS AND MULTIPLE COMPARISONS

Frequently many economic models appear compatible with the same body of statistical data. Unfortunately, as might be expected from the earlier sections of this chapter, there exist no sound bases to indicate how a choice should be made between these alternative models in such circumstances. Instead a conventional collection of indicators is usually calculated and assessments are made within this somewhat fragile framework of indicators. The following account cites many of these indicators. It should be supplemented with some of the many comparative studies which are available for models of investment expenditures. In view of the emphases on neoclassical, accelerator and eclectic models in Chapter One, appropriate comparisons are provided by Bischoff

(1971b), Gould and Waud (1973), Jorgenson, Hunter and Nadiri (1970a, b), Jorgenson and Siebert (1968b), Kuh (1963, Ch. 8) and Meyer and Glauber (1964, Ch. 9).

Although statistical indexes are often the primary basis for choice, there are some critical questions that must also be considered. First, why were alternative models built? As suggested earlier for the choice between different collections of explanatory variables, there is a critical difference between the motives of control, explanation and prediction. Box–Jenkins and purely autoregressive models, which embody no economic mechanisms, might be appropriate choices if only simple predictions are sought. However, some form of economic structure seems to be needed for adequate use in control or explanations. Here prior notions concerning desirable qualitative features must be satisfied. For example, when the role of fiscal factors in the determination of investment is of concern, a reasonable requirement for model is that the influence of changes in capital allowances on investment should depend upon the level of corporate tax rates.

Second, are the alternative models different in any important way given the use to be made of the final choice? If they are similar in this context, a lack of sensitivity might suggest that any of the models is sufficient and choice is trivial. Third, are data measured in a manner consistent with structural components of the economic model? Jorgenson (1971) illustrates this problem using the proportionality hypothesis for replacement which implies the use of a net stock concept. He indicates several studies which are inconsistent in the sense that this hypothesis and gross stocks are jointly used.

Once estimates of coefficients have been calculated, graphical displays can have a useful role in both discriminating between models and choosing between them. For example, plots of sample residuals which have been ordered according to the movements of other factors can indicate deficiencies of particular models and potential hazards for particular techniques of estimation, which are adversely affected by the presence of outliers in data. In addition, if enough additional observations become available after estimates have been calculated, predicted values from the fitted models can be compared with actual values. A four-quadrant diagram has proved very popular in this context. Its axes record predicted and actual values on the same scale. Ideally the points for post-sample predictions should be tightly clustered around the positive 45-degree line for this diagram. If points are also identified according to additional criteria, their patterns may suggest enlargements of models or their rejection if erratic patterns dominate the tightness of clustering.

One problem with graphical displays in their use of all points as if they were equally important. A familiar argument in macroeconomics is that it is especially important to be able to predict 'turning points' in the paths of dependent variables. Thus, it is argued, such points should be given extra weight in assessing models. In an extreme scheme, turning points could be given unit weights while other points are given zero weights and ignored. This is the background for one statistical index for comparing models. Counts of successful predictions of turning points form simple indices and have been widely used, often severely adjusted for 'false' predictions where turning points are identified but directional predictions are incorrect.

Statistical indexes based on sample evidence include coefficients of multiple determination, standard errors of regressions, Durbin–Watson statistics, estimated autoregressive parameters, partial correlation coefficients and other indicators cited above for the choice of variables. These goodness-of-fit statistics are usually combined with post-sample evidence such as sums of squared (or absolute) prediction errors, correlation coefficients between predicted and actual values of investment, and other measures of tracking ability. The two studies by Jorgenson, Hunter and Nadiri provide convenient illustrations of these two sources of choice criteria. In addition to the indexes cited above (which are widely known), they use Scheffé's S-method of multiple comparison. An appropriate description of this method and its modification is provided by Scheffé (1970), while a survey of 'the present state of multiple comparison methods' and an extensive bibliography are given by O'Neill and Wetherill (1971). Finally, the integration of the choice criteria cited here and in earlier sections of the chapter for both single-equation and multi-equation models is attempted by Dhrymes *et al.* (1972).

There is however a sense in which the model selection problem has a well defined structure, and this occurs when the alternative or competing models are 'nested' within some maintained model form. In such cases the classical Neyman–Pearson hypothesis testing procedures are appropriate, though rarely have they been vigorously applied in econometric studies. Excellent discussions of the principles involved can be found in Seber (1966) and Silvey (1970).

Competing hypotheses which are ordered, for example hypotheses concerning the order of a polynomial regression or the maximum lag in a finite distributed-lag model, are important special cases of general nested hypotheses since it is usually only in such cases that the classical theory of hypothesis testing can be applied without complications. In the absence of an ordering of the competing hypotheses, although they may all be nested within the maintained hypothesis, it is possible that the general model selection problem of having to discriminate between competing and yet non-nested hypotheses may be encountered, and the statistical theory in this area is not well developed. An important area in which choices between non-nested hypotheses have to be made is that of the choice of functional forms, which is a very common problem in all areas of applied econometrics including studies of investment behaviour.

4.4 FUNCTIONAL FORMS

Two important aspects of the choice of functional forms have been especially prominent in recent studies of investment. First, there is the question of specifying the final form for use in empirical fits as illustrated below by the choices between ratio and simple linear forms and between different adjustment mechanisms. Second, there is the problematical choice of componental forms for economic models which may be based upon both prior notions and extraneous empirical evidence. One illustration of such choices is provided by the topic of the production function.

Ratio models have often been identified with the problem of heteroscedastic errors. Consider the linear model

$$y_t = \beta_0 + \beta_1 x_{1t} + \beta_2 x_{2t} + \varepsilon_t, \tag{3}$$

where x_{1t} and x_{2t} are explanatory variables, y_t is the dependent variable, ε_t is a random error and the other symbols represent unknown parameters. Suppose this model satisfies all classical conditions except the requirement that the errors be homoscedastic. Instead suppose $E(\varepsilon_t \varepsilon_s)$ is $\sigma^2 z_t^2$, for some non-stochastic variable z_t, if t and s are equal, and zero otherwise. In particular cross-sectional studies of gross expenditures, the levels of capital stock of firms have been identified with $\{z_t\}$. Since the errors in (3) are heteroscedastic, least-squares estimators based on this linear specification may be relatively inefficient. Consider the alternative ratio models with 'deflated' variables.

$$\frac{y_t}{z_t} = \beta_0 \frac{1}{z_t} + \beta_1 \frac{x_{1t}}{z_t} + \beta_2 \frac{x_{2t}}{z_t} + \frac{\varepsilon_t}{z_t} \tag{4}$$

and

$$\frac{y_t}{z_t} = \gamma_0 + \beta_1 \frac{x_{1t}}{z_t} + \beta_2 \frac{x_{2t}}{z_t} + \varepsilon_t^*, \tag{5}$$

where $\{\varepsilon_t^*\}$ is implicitly defined by comparison of (3) and (5). Equation (4) satisfies all classical properties and least-squares estimators based on it will be identical with the efficient Aitken estimators based on (3). Notice that the ratio model has the same deflator in the denominators of all its explanatory variables. This contrasts with the augmented accelerator model of Eisner, which was cited in Section 1.3, where capital stock data were used to deflate some explanatory variables and the dependent variable, gross investment, but reference sales were used to deflate the acceleration terms. In addition, Eisner uses a constant term which is absent in (4), unless z_t is either x_{1t} or x_{2t}, but present in (5). This term accounted for twenty percent of investment in his study. However, as Belsley (1972) points out, least-squares estimates based on (5) when (3) is correct will be both biased and inconsistent. Hence the interpretation of a fitted constant term is unclear. Deflation by a measure of capital stock is also problematical in another respect. Since such measures are generally based upon past values for the dependent variable, it is difficult to treat them as non-stochastic. Deflation by a non-stochastic factor will change the distributional properties of the error terms. In particular, it can eliminate normality, zero means and independence of the errors.

When these statistical complications are ignored (as usually occurs), researchers use indicators of the types cited in earlier sections. Unfortunately, we have no sound basis for comparing coefficients of multiple determination for either different dependent variables or different collections of explanatory variables (see Pesaran (1974). Goodness-of-fit becomes then a very subjective means of assessment. In addition, suppression of a constant term may make R^2s have a non-unit upper bound. Clearly transformations of models should be explicitly taken into account if more rigorous bases for choices are to be found. Some further aspects of this problem of comparison are provided by Teekens and Koerts (1972), who consider the specific effect of logarithmic transformations of multiplicative models on errors' properties. Their work is also of direct significance for assessing the worth of extraneous empirical information in the choice of componental forms for economic models.

A second illustration of choice for the specification of final forms for empirical fits is provided by the use of adjustment mechanisms. In Chapter One, Jorgenson's neoclassical model was represented as a two-stage procedure, which first expresses desired capital in terms of a collection of variables and then introduces an adjustment mechanism to associate desired and actual magnitudes. It will be recalled that, for a Cobb–Douglas production function, the first stage of this procedure yields

$$K_j^* = \frac{p}{c_j} Q \tag{6}$$

as an expression for the desired level of the stock for the jth capital asset, where p, c_j and Q are the price of output, the user-cost of the jth asset and real output, respectively. A logarithmic transformation yields a linear relationship between the logarithms of these variables. This form is especially convenient for estimation if a simple adjustment mechanism is associated with it instead of with the initial multiplicative specification. In addition, the logarithmic form can be used to investigate the appropriateness of the Cobb–Douglas assumption. Consider equation (11) of Chapter One. This represents desired capital stocks for the alternative Constant-Elasticity-of-Substitution characterization of production. A logarithmic transformation yields a linear relationship with estimable parameters which may be identified with specifications for the returns-to-scale in production and the elasticity of substitution. As indicated in Chapters One and Three, markedly different estimates of behaviour were obtained for these two alternative choices and for the further adjustment approach used by Thurow.

Another problem should also be raised here. Jorgenson used only a subset of the external conditions to obtain his optimality rule which was the basis for his particular definitions of desired stocks. These conditions also include the production function so output may not be an exogenous variable. When the adjustment mechanism is associated with the logarithmic transformation, after elimination of output using the production function, actual capital stocks are determined only by price-ratios. In this form, Jorgenson's model has always fitted badly. An alternative approach to the exogeneity of output is provided by Sims (1972) who uses spectral techniques to assess behaviour in U.S. manufacturing industries. He confirms the insignificance of price-effects and his results for output suggest that this variable may, in fact, have an exogenous role in investment equations.

Turning specifically to the problem of choice of production functions, we should notice the British evidence offered by Rowley (1970, 1972b), who investigated this choice without using the logarithmic transformation. Suppose $\{x_s\}$ are a collection of n arbitrary explanatory variables. Then, we can approximate the product

$$\prod_{s=1}^{n} x_s^{\alpha} \simeq 1 + \sum_{s=1}^{n} \alpha_s \log_e x_s, \tag{7}$$

so that

$$\prod_{s=1}^{n} x_s^{1+\alpha} \simeq \prod_{s=1}^{n} x_s + \sum_{s=1}^{n} \alpha_s \left(\prod_{i=1}^{n} x_j\right) \log_e x_s, \tag{8}$$

where the $\{\alpha_s\}$ are parameters. If these variables are identical with (p/c_j) and Q, we obtain

$$\left(\frac{p}{c_j}\right)^{1+\alpha_1} Q^{1+\alpha_2} \simeq \frac{1}{\alpha} K_j^* + \alpha_1 K_j^* \log_e \frac{p}{c_j} + \alpha_2 K_j^* \log_e Q. \tag{9}$$

Thus the multiplicative form for desired capital stocks is represented as the sum of the expression for desired stocks in the Cobb–Douglas case and additional factors. If the adjustment mechanism is associated with this approximation, the parameters α_1 and α_2 can be subjected to significance tests relative to the zero values identified with the Cobb–Douglas specification. In particular, α_1 will not be zero for the CES characterization and α_2 will be zero with constant returns to scale. The evidence of Rowley and of Eisner and Nadiri (1970) who used the logarithmic transformation indicate some doubts about the use of the Cobb–Douglas specification in this context.

As a partial response to such evidence, Jorgenson (1972) surveyed the empirical literature on production functions with the purpose 'to select an appropriate description of technology on the basis of empirical evidence for United States manufacturing industries'. He concluded that the evidence 'is consistent with a production function characterized by elasticity of substitution equal to unity and constant returns to scale'. However the evidence may not be as clear-cut as he suggests. The reader should make his own assessment. One additional point should be made. It is not clear that the point-input–point-output production function is a good characterization of the productive process. For some purposes, it may be a useful artefact but it is not obvious, even then, that appropriateness in one area is sufficient for global appropriateness. Ideally all economic theories should perhaps be consistent with one overall framework. Unfortunately, the nature of this framework is extremely uncertain and the relationships between its parts are, consequently, very tentatively expressed by current economic literature.

Finally, it is important to note that there have been attempts to provide a statistical framework for discriminating between alternative models or functional forms when the implied hypotheses are non-nested. The seminal work in this area is that of Cox (1961, 1962), who attempted to develop systematic procedures for testing 'separate families of hypotheses' as represented by alternative choices for functional forms and collections of parameters, but the problem has received attention from others more recently. In particular, the papers by Atkinson (1970), Quandt (1974) and Pesaran (1974) illustrate new approaches to the problems of discrimination.

4.5 DATA

The problems of measurement cannot be separated either from economic theory or from estimation and statistical inference. As indicated in our Introduction, most researchers are persistently confronted by these problems even though they often appear to receive inadequate attention in published reports. A number of simple procedures associated with data collection and manipulation are described here. They represent a small but illustrative sample of approaches which have been adopted in particular studies of investment. Clearly our brief account should be supplemented by direct contact with the references cited both here and in the Introduction. We only consider five topics.

First, the eclectic studies of Meyer and Kuh (1957, Ch. 3), Kuh (1963, pp. 60–62, 91–96) and Meyer and Glauber (1964, Ch. 3) provide excellent illustrations of various attempts to obtain sample homogeneity before the calculation of estimators. Consider, for example, their approaches to the problems raised by mergers when economic theories of investment are associated with the behaviour of either a single decision-maker or firm. Meyer and Kuh omitted observations for any firms involved in mergers during the years in which the mergers took place whereas Meyer and Glauber omitted observations on these firms completely. Kuh imposed the rule that firms 'could not be parties to mergers destructive of their identity' although 'firms that bought out or merged others into themselves were left in the sample'. Investment in the assets of other firms is an alternative to investment in fixed real assets or inventory. Omission of particular observations may therefore appear a reasonable procedure if the theories being considered do not allow for this additional dimension of entrepreneurial choice.

Both Meyer and Kuh and Meyer and Glauber also modified traditional industrial product groupings in their searches for homogeneity in particular parts of their samples. Although they used different numbers of groups in the two studies, the same criterion was used in this context. Thus 'definitions of industry groups were altered so as to achieve a reduction in the within-group variance of the capital to output ratio' on the basis that this ratio is 'known to have a particularly important or sensitive influence in the behavioural relationship under study'. In another respect, the pre-screening of the two studies differed. Rapidly growing firms, whose investments for any given year exceeded more than a half of their existing gross fixed assets at the beginning of the year, were omitted from the sample of the earlier study but included in the latter one (only after a detailed investigation of simple correlations and partial regression estimates).

These restrictions to data inclusion are especially severe. For example, Kuh used only a final sample of sixty firms out of an initial collection of several hundred. Heterogeneity due to inappropriate 'pooling' of observations will lead to relatively inefficient estimators if errors are heterogeneous and to substantial biases if different parametric structures are appropriate for different parts of the pooled sample. Omission of data will eliminate these statistical difficulties but restricts the applicability of the fitted relation also. As Kuh suggests for his sample, they are 'all capital goods producers, are small and middle sized, two-thirds having 1955 gross fixed assets worth less than \$30 million, measured in 1953 prices. ... They are likely to be more stable firms and because big mergers are excluded, the least dynamic.'

A second important aspect of data selection is very closely related to that of homogeneity but it is convenient to discuss this separately by reference to time-series data and a simple procedure for discarding data. This procedure requires that we do not use any observations for periods associated with substantial changes in variables which are relevant for the determination of investment but excluded from specifications being considered by the researcher. In practice, this principle usually involves the truncation of samples rather than the assembly of a collection of disjointed ones. Consider, for example, the illustration provided by Rowley (1972a) from postwar British investment data. He ignored observations for the period before the third quarter of 1957 on the basis that his model was derived from a theory of demand for investment goods whereas this early period was characterized by severe restrictions on the supply of these goods. In addition, since the model involved many features of British corporate tax practices, he terminated the sample when these practices were substantially changed by the introduction of a new Corporation Tax and the expansion of regional selectivity in the system of Investment Grants. Similar truncations were made in a different U.S. context by Modigliani and Shiller (1973), who argued that the Korean boom and the price controls of 1971 would both markedly affect the structure of price expectations.

The advantages of this discarding procedure are similar to those indicated for the homogeneity checks described above since they reduce the possibility of biases in estimates. However, as Fisher (1962) clearly indicates, selectivity in using data means that 'we shall not be able to give an unambiguous interpretation to the probability statements'. Clearly this is a contentious area since we usually associate additional data with further 'information' and truncation, therefore, with a loss of information. A possible resolution of this contention might be based upon the argument that truncation is only a provisional approach to be adopted until our economic models are enlarged to explicitly include all significant factors.

A less familiar problem in the choice of data concerns the timing of changes in corporate tax rates and capital allowances. This did not arise until Jorgenson made popular more complex specifications for the roles of fiscal factors in the determination of investment. An illustration of a typical choice-situation is provided by Bischoff (1971b, p. 33), who sought to take account of the removal of the U.S. Tax Credit in 1969. 'Although the administration's intention to seek permanent repeal of the tax credit was announced April 21, 1969, and the repeal was eventually made retroactive for all equipment ordered after April 18, it was not passed until December 1969. There was a large bulge in orders in the months between announcement and passage, which affected expenditures into 1970. ... By only gradually reducing the credit parameter to zero, ... I have taken account of business skepticism about the passage and effective date of the repeal.' Clearly there is wide scope for such manipulations of data which again are associated with developments not directly considered in the prior specification of models.

Two other aspects of data choice will concern us in the remainder of this section; namely, the post-fit elimination of 'outliers' or eccentric points and the problematical general area of measurement of the prices for investment goods (and, hence, also of capital stocks). An outlier is a point of observation which appears to be substantially apart from other observations in a given sample. Sometimes such points can be anticipated before estimates for regression coefficients are calculated. For example, Eisner (1962) omitted firms from his sample who were associated with very small values of some of his explanatory variables. However recognition of an outlier is usually based upon inspection of regression residuals. The absolute size of particular residuals or their size relative to others are common reference points. Sometimes the presence of large residuals indicates computational blunders in the arithmetical reduction of original data or the impact of omitted but identifiable factors. But, as Kruskal (1960) pointed out, sometimes an 'apparently wide (or otherwise anomalous) observation is a signal that says: "Here is something from which we may learn a lesson, perhaps of a kind not anticipated beforehand, and perhaps more important than the main object of the study". Examples of such serendipity have been frequently discussed—one of the most popular is Fleming's recognition of the virtue of penicillium.'

In practice, researchers have been rather pessimistic about outliers especially since their presence in a sample markedly affect the values of least-squares estimators. Often the corresponding observations are omitted either by reference to *ad hoc* inspection of residuals or by the use of rejection rules. (See, for examples of the latter, the account by Anscombe (1960).) An alternative approach might involve the subjective weighting of observations as to their reliability and the use of weighted least-squares estimators. However there is much to be said for following Kruskal's practical suggestion. 'My own practice in this sort of situation is to carry out an analysis both with and without the suspect observations. If the broad conclusions of the two analyses are quite different, I should view any conclusions from the experiment with very great caution.'

Difficulties in establishing theoretical bases for measurement are immense and will not be discussed here. Instead we briefly focus attention on the problems of collecting appropriate data where specific theoretical bases are accepted. These problems are currently being discussed due particularly to the release of the Searle Report in the United States and the recent higher rates of inflationary changes in prices, which have varied substantially between different types of assets. A comprehensive account of these problems (and perhaps the best starting point for the detailed investigation of this area) is contained in the earlier report of the Price Statistics Review Committee (1961). However, with our severely restricted aims, it is convenient to simply cite some of the results of Gordon (1971, 1973), which suggest that transaction prices of capital goods in the United States exhibit procyclical fluctuations relative to list prices. 'Machinery prices appear to have been considerably more flexible downward during the periods of weak investment demand between 1957 and 1963 than indicated by the Wholesale Price Index, and more flexible upward during the subsequent expansions during 1963–69.' If the assertion of additional flexibility is correct, the official deflators for producers' durable equipment are biased. This has two important consequences for the earlier period of slump. The supply of investment goods did not fall by as much as official indexes indicate and the ratio of producers to consumers good prices varied more than shown in these indexes. Clearly these consequences affect our interpretation of empirical results based on the unadjusted official indexes. In particular, they could explain the generally insignificant estimates for separate price effects on investment. The principal results to emerge from the recent and earlier debates are the confirmation of our uncertainties as to how to collect data and the cyclical sensitivity of our conventional investment series to particular choices.

4.6 STRUCTURAL CHANGES AND SEASONALITY

A 'structural change' is usually said to have occurred if the set of parameters characterizing a particular model in one part of a given sample of data is not identical with the set of parameters characterizing the same model in a second part of the sample. Clearly, although we have not explicitly used this term in earlier sections of this chapter, structural changes are an important aspect of our discussion in many instances as, for example, in the search for homogeneous data and the truncation of data. Although eclectic models for investment in fixed real capital, which are described in Section 1.5, are the most obvious illustrations of models which use structural changes as an intrinsic part of their theoretical frameworks, the initial emphasis in the account provided below primarily concerns inventory. This selection attempts to avoid repetition. However, one example drawn from the eclectic models might suffice as an indication of their significance in this respect.

Meyer and Glauber (1964, pp. 159–160) outline upturn and downturn models since 'under the accelerator-residual funds theory the expectation would be that a capacity utilization variable would dominate the upswings while the residual funds variable would provide the best explanation of investment in the downswing.' Accordingly, 'the sample, of course, must be bifurcated into its component upswing and downswing periods before the models themselves can be fitted.' The principal difficulty in practice is to decide switching points between their two models. They used a critical level for the McGraw-Hill index of capacity-utilization as the basis for partitioning their sample but this choice is not necessarily ideal. Here there are always several views as to the timing of historical switch-points.

For both inventories and their determinants, structural instabilities can be associated with very marked seasonal patterns of behaviour. In anticipation of heavy demand at Christmas retailers increase their stocks of goods in the preceding months. Similarly the incidence of other public holidays in particular months leads to marked seasonality in both sales and inventories of retailers. Moriguchi (1967) illustrated such seasonal shifts in U.S. manufacturing industries also. In the cement industry, demand shows both a sharp seasonal peak coincident with the peak in construction activity and a substantial decline in winter months. Manufacturers, however, do not directly vary their production with these fluctuations. Rather they attempt to smooth production in face of this fluctuating demand. Inventories accumulate in the slack season for demand and they are reduced in peak seasons. Thus inventories absorb many of the effects of seasonal fluctuations as well as those of unforeseen changes in sales. In the U.S. timber industry, production is additionally conditioned by the less-predictable climatic considerations and demand is thus met out of either stocks or imports.

These and other similar considerations raise important issues for the researcher as to how he should allow for seasonality in his use of the regression framework. Nerlove (1964) has emphasized that seasonality only corresponds to approximate and not exact periodicity. Thus even the same calendar months in two different years are not strictly comparable due to possible differences in the number of working days, end-of-month weekdays and other factors. Nevertheless a mechanistic 'seasonal adjustment' is frequently made to suppress complications arising from seasonal variabilities. Clearly one might ask how an appropriate adjustment should be carried out and, also, whether it introduces any problems for either statistical inference or economic interpretation. Some relationships between the optimality of particular types of seasonal adjustment and techniques of estimation for use with adjusted data are described by Rowley (1973, Ch. 7).

A view which is sometimes put forward in this context is that data ought not to be seasonally adjusted prior to their use in estimation. First, the adjustment procedure may eliminate from them more than the seasonal component, thereby altering the observed relationship between several series. Second, it is argued that seasonality in the dependent variable ought to be explained by seasonality in the explanatory variables. Thus insofar as seasonality in inventory investment is caused by seasonality in sales it should be so explained. In this vein, Wallis (1966) observed that 'the comparative amplitudes of seasonal fluctuations in the various series then constitute useful information about the economic processes of which our model is a representation, and the use of seasonally adjusted data amounts to throwing away this information'.

Once structural instability (whether seasonal, cyclical or from some other source) is acknowledged, there remains the problem of modelling its role. Two simple procedures have enjoyed widespread popularity. Both can be identified with enlargements of the number of explanatory variables by the introduction of supplemental dummy variables. These additional variables are based upon a rule whereby unit values are recorded during a particular season (a state of cyclical activity) and zero otherwise. The simplest procedure modifies the parameter of the constant term. Let 'seasons' be used as a generic term for groups of observations indicated by structural instability. Consider the simple relationship (4) introduced in the fourth section above,

$$y_t = \beta_0 + \beta_1 x_{1t} + \beta_2 x_{2t} + \varepsilon_t.$$

With this specification β_0 depends upon the value of t for the framework of this first procedure. It can assume any one of four distinct values depending upon the seasons during which the observations are collected. This instability can be represented by the enlargement

$$y_t = \left(\sum_{j=1}^{4} \beta_{0j} \delta_{jt} \right) + \beta_1 x_{1t} + \beta_2 x_{2t} + \varepsilon_t, \tag{10}$$

where, for any given observation, one and only one of the 'new' variables $\{\delta_{jt}\}$ has a unit value and the remainder have zero values. The parameters $\{\beta_{0j}\}$ are generally different. If the tth observation falls in the ith season, δ_{it} has a unit value and

$$y_t = \beta_{0i} + \beta_1 x_{1t} + \beta_2 x_{2t} + \varepsilon_t.$$

The sample can be partitioned into four groups which may be characterized by the four sets of parameters generated by shifts between β_{01}, β_{02}, β_{03} and β_{04}.

A second procedure generalizes this approach to changes in other parameters, perhaps to all parameters. For notational simplicity, consider only changes in β_1. Then, using the notation introduced above,

$$y_t = \beta_0 + \left(\sum_{j=1}^{4} \beta_{1j} \delta_{jt} \right) x_{1t} + \beta_2 x_{2t} + \varepsilon_t \tag{11}$$

and, for the tth observation falling in the ith season, the specification of the model is

$$y_t = \beta_0 + \beta_{1i} x_{1t} + \beta_2 x_{2t} + \varepsilon_t.$$

One illustration of this second procedure is provided by Johnston (1961) who advanced an interesting argument, based upon production-smoothing considerations, to suggest that the desired inventory–sales ratio may vary seasonally. Empirical results of Lovell (1968) have also established seasonal variation in the parameters of inventory equations for departmental stores.

The researcher has several options in estimation when structural changes recognized. First, he may choose to fit separate equations for each season as, for example, was done by Johnston, and Modigliani and Sauerlander (1955). Second, provided the variances of errors in all parts of the sample are appropriately assumed equal, the distinct parts may be 'pooled' using dummy variables as indicated above. Estimation may then be based on this augmented specification. Finally, the technique of 'covariance transforms' might be used to transform the augmented specification into a simpler form associating seasonally adjusted data; this latter form may then be fitted. The transforms are obtained by taking the residuals from a collection of preliminary least-square fits of all variables as explained by only seasonal effects and other relatively minor factors. Here the residuals can be considered as seasonally adjusted variables. (See Rowley (1973, Ch. 7).)

Prior adjustment of data, as involved in this third approach to estimation, will affect assessments of goodness-of-fit as, for example, reflected by coefficients of multiple determination. In addition, when an analysis is based upon the use of seasonally adjusted data, then an appropriate adjustment to the computed standard errors (and other statistics based on them) must be made in order to indicate the loss of degrees of freedom due to the prior seasonal adjustment. This point is discussed by Lovell (1963). A survey of consequences for statistical inference is also provided by Thomas and Wallis (1971), who discuss further developments not cited here. Although our examples have been exclusively linked with time-series data, the problems of structural instability are just as important for cross-sectional data. Kuh (1963, Ch. 5) provides an excellent account of them in this context. His description also suggests how conventional tests of significance can be used to assess whether there are structural shifts between different industrial groups.

4.7 EXPECTATIONAL VARIABLES

The problem of relating the behaviour of economic units, both individually and collectively to their expectations about future developments is a central feature of many econometric studies. Examples can be found in models of inflation, the term structure of interest rates, consumption behaviour as well as in models of investment. This problem often necessitates the specification of functions to explain how expectations are generated. We outlined some aspects of this problem is Section 1.4, where the primary focus of attention was investment in fixed real assets. In this section, we supplement our earlier outline by considering the choice between alternative hypotheses and models of inventory investment to the extent that they concern the formation of anticipations, expectations and plans.

If relevant anticipatory data are available on the same basis as other data, they may be used directly in inventory equations. Unfortunately, data for anticipations are frequently subject to errors of measurement which, if substantial, can lead the researcher to a choice between the direct use of these data and the use of alternative procedures involving proxies.

The terms 'expectations' and 'anticipations' are used interchangeably below. They represent magnitudes of variables which are expected to prevail in future periods. In practice, expectations need not be precise. It is common to suppose that expectations are based on past experience and that they may contain 'extrapolative', 'regressive' and trend elements. The extrapolative element represents a tendency to expect recent changes to persist in future periods. In contrast, the regressive element represents a tendency to expect a reversal to levels considered to be 'normal' in some sense and, thus, associates less weight to recently observed changes as compared with normal values. The mixture of these three elements in the generation of expectations may actually vary over time, which would create further difficulties for econometric modelling.

Early and influential studies of anticipations data are those of Ferber (1953, 1960), who analysed Railroad Shippers' Forecasts and highlighted their regressive characteristic. He considered that, in analysing the firms' forecasts, it was appropriate to regard them as forecasting seasonally unadjusted sales; an allowance for seasonality being made by modifying the figure for the corresponding period in the previous year in light of a recently observed trend. Thus, for example, in explaining quarterly sales, X_t, he used a model of the form:

$$\hat{X}_t = b_0 + b_1 X_{t-4} + b_2 X_{t-4} \frac{X_{t-1} - X_{t-5}}{X_{t-5}} \tag{12}$$

or

$$\hat{X}_t = b_0 + b_2 X_{t-1} \frac{X_{t-4}}{X_{t-5}} - (b_1 - b_2)(X_{t-1} - X_{t-5}) \frac{X_{t-4}}{X_{t-5}} \tag{13}$$

where $(\hat{\;})$ denotes a forecast value. A similar model for monthly forecasts is obtained by replacing the subscripts $(t - 4)$ and $(t - 5)$ in (12) by $(t - 12)$ and $(t - 13)$ respectively. The second term on the right-hand side of (12) represents the purely seasonal element in the forecast whereas the third term applies a correction to X_{t-4} equal to the percentage change in the value for the previous quarter over the corresponding quarter in the previous year.

Most of Ferber's fits suggest that b_1 exceeds b_2. Thus, from (13), this implies that the recent trend, as expressed by the difference $(X_{t-1} - X_{t-5})$, is given a negative weight in the formation of expectations; that is, $\hat{X}_t$ regresses towards X_{t-4}. This result in the interpreted by Ferber as indicating the fundamentally regressive nature of expectations. It stimulated a number of subsequent researchers to further explore the data for alternative explanations. In particular, the appearance of regressivity might be due to inaccuracies in the data. On analysing the Railroad Shippers' Forecasts, Hart (1960) finds them to be so regressive that he is led to suggest they ought to be reconstituted before being used in econometric work. Lovell (1964) examines this suggestion for the specific case of the cement industry and concludes that the Railroad Shippers' data were not suitable for judging the accuracy of anticipations held by businessmen.

More recently, Hirsch and Lovell (1969) re-examine Ferber's 'law of expectations' using a new body of data provided by Manufacturers' Inventory and Sales Expectations Survey of the Office of Business Economics, U.S. Department of Commerce. Availability of this data enables the authors to examine both alternative hypotheses regarding formation and accuracy of expectations and their impact on inventory and production decisions at firm level and at aggregate level. Their detailed analysis reveals a number of characteristics which are at variance with those in Ferber's earlier work but, again, anticipations are found to be regressive. Combined with the finding that anticipations appreared to be accurate, the inevitable conclusion is that regressivity and accuracy are not mutually contradictory.

Proxy procedures for quantifying expectations

The purpose of this section is to survey and assess various proxy procedures which one has to consider when anticipatory data are not available. Some alternatives purport to explain or describe the process generating expectations and others which simply describe an *ex post* relationship between actual and anticipated sales regardless of the underlying mechanism generating expectations. The econometrician's choice is usually dictated by a combination of factors of statistical tractability, economic realism and optimality in a well-defined sense. Broadly speaking the dividing line appears to be between those who bypass the specification problems using a theoretical argument establishing the equivalence between observed and expected values and those who specify an extrapolative mechanism. Though it is not true that all expectations can be represented by lag distributions, the use of lags has been the most widely used method of quantifying expectations.

If the data used by the econometrician have trend and seasonal components, he may wish to specify a model which generates expectations including 'seasonal' or trend variations. If such components are removed or filtered out prior to econometric modelling than one might simply consider autoregressive models of differing degrees of complexity. However, there appear to be good reasons for wanting to specify models which generate, say, sales expectations including seasonal variations since it is quite realistic to imagine economic agents behaving in this manner. By the same reasoning if the nature of seasonality is varying, that too may be incorporated into the model; furthermore, if the stochastic disturbances or forecast errors tend to be autocorrelated, then it may be that these too are taken account of by the agent. If we confine ourselves to the case in which anticipations (or forecasts) are conditional simply on the past observed values of that variable, and/or past forecast errors, a class of models elaborated by Box and Jenkins (1970) suggests a large number of feasible alternatives. Indeed, we might interpret specifications adopted in much of the applied econometric work on inventories as simply special cases of the class of models described below.

Suppose y_t is the series to be forecast, ε_t is the stochastic term identically and independently distributed with zero mean and common variance σ^2, and B is the backward shift or lag operator. Then consider the model

$$(1 - B^s)^D (1 - B)^d (1 - \phi_1 B - \dots - \phi_p B^p)(1 - \Psi_1 B^s - \Psi_2 L^{2s} \dots - \Psi_P B^{Ps}) y_t$$
$$= (1 - \theta_1 B - \dots - \theta_q B^q)(1 - \xi_1 B^s - \dots - \xi_Q B^{Qs}) \varepsilon_t, \tag{14}$$

where the successive polynomials in the lag operator B may be called the non-stationary seasonal part, the regular non-stationary part, the seasonal autoregressive part, the regular moving-average part, and the seasonal moving-average part respectively. Each model belonging to this general class may be characterized by the seven parameters p, d, q, P, D, Q and s which denote the following: p is the number of regular autoregressive parameters $(\phi_1, \dots, \phi_p)$, d is the number of regular differences, q is the number of regular moving average parameters $(\theta_1, \theta_2, \dots, \theta_q)$, P is the number of seasonal autoregressive parameters $(\Psi_1, \Psi_2, \dots, \Psi_p)$, D is the number of seasonal differences, Q is the number of seasonal moving-average parameters and s the order of the seasonal. s equals four if we have quarterly observations, or twelve if they are monthly.

To obtain further insight into this specification consider the following special cases:

$$D = 0, \, d = 1, \, p = 0, \, P = 0, \, q = 0, \, Q = 0; \tag{15}$$

$$y_t - y_{t-1} = \varepsilon_t.$$

$$D = 0, \, d = 0, \, p = 1, \, P = 0, \, q = 0, \, Q = 0; \tag{16}$$

$$y_t - \phi_1 y_{t-1} = \varepsilon_t.$$

$$D = 0, \, d = 0, \, p = 1, \, P = 1, \, q = 0, \, Q = 0, \, s = 4; \tag{17}$$

$$y_t - \phi_1 y_{t-1} - \psi_1 y_{t-4} + \phi_1 \psi_1 y_{t-5} = \varepsilon_t.$$

$$D = 0, \, d = 1, \, p = 1, \, P = 1, \, q = 1, \, Q = 1, \, s = 4; \tag{18}$$

$$\Delta y_t - \phi_1 \Delta y_{t-1} - \psi_1 \Delta y_{t-4} + \phi_1 \psi_1 \Delta y_{t-5}$$
$$= \varepsilon_t - \theta_1 \varepsilon_{t-4} - \xi_1 \varepsilon_{t-4} - \theta_1 \xi_1 \varepsilon_{t-5}.$$

(15) corresponds to the assumption that forecast value differs from the previous observed value by the random disturbance ε_t (the so-called 'naive' forecast); (16) posits a first-order autoregressive model and assumes that forecasts are generated using one lagged value—a procedure that may provide a reasonable approximation if y exhibits neither seasonality nor trend-type behaviour. If seasonal variation is quite pronounced, and the (quarterly) series exhibits autoregressive behaviour then (17) may provide an economical representation of the generation process since it takes account of relationships between the same quarter in successive years and between successive quarters in the same year. (This idea was also stressed by Ferber in his 1953 and 1960 studies.) Thus the lag of four periods in (18) represents a seasonal autoregressive effect, the lag of one period represents the regular autoregressive effect and the five-

period lag the interaction between the two. If, in addition, the y_t series exhibits trend-type behaviour (or non-stationarity), and the trend is approximately linear, the same specification will still apply but the y_t series will need to be replaced by its first difference. A further elaboration of this specification is obtained by replacing the independent error term ε_t by a moving average scheme with the same lag structure as on the RHS of (17), see (18). In a forecasting context the stochastic part can be given an interpretation in terms of updating of forecasts, i.e. the forecasts generated by the autoregressive part are 'updated' by taking account of the forecast errors in $t-1$, $t-4$, $t-5$, the last two representing respectively, the error due to a changing seasonal pattern ($Q = 1$) and its interaction with the regular first-order moving average.

By a suitable choice of a $(p, d, q)(P, D, Q)^s$ model it would be possible to gene-rate many more autoregressive–moving-average models that could provide reasonable proxies for the unobservable expectations variable. The attractive-ness of the procedure lies in its simplicity, but unnecessary elaboration will lead to an overparametrized model. To use these proxies one may substitute a chosen scheme for $\hat{y}_t$ (the expectational variable), or use a two-stage procedure which consists of fitting a variety of autoregressive–moving-average models to y_t and generating a series of 'forecast' values which constitute a proxy for the unobservable anticipations. However, the statistical consequences of such a two-stage procedure have not been fully investigated. Direct substitution has the disadvantage that if there is, for example, a distributed lag response of (say) z_t to y_t, then the occurrence of the lagged y's in the equation explaining z_t may cause identification problems. Finally it may be observed that this approach may be validly criticized on the grounds that it uses too little infor-mation regarding the input into the expectations generation process.

Next we turn to the work of Muth (1962), Mills (1962) and Lovell (1962) who have all suggested proxy procedures which bypass the question of how anticipations are formulated. Nevertheless they suggest procedures which can be and have been used in empirical work on inventory behaviour. Muth shows that if disturbances are independently normally distributed, certainty equi-valents exist for variables to be predicted, and all the formulae (including the the expectations generating formula) in the model are linear, then the predictions of the firm, say $\hat{y}_t$, conditional on all available information is 'rational' and should be distributed about the actual value y_t as follows:

$$y_t = \hat{y}_t + \varepsilon_t, \qquad E(\varepsilon_t) = 0, \qquad E(\hat{y}_t \varepsilon_t) = 0. \qquad (19)$$

Rational expectations are expectations conditional on all information available on the variable of interest and on related equations and not only on past values of that variable. Assuming that expectations are rational in the sense of Muth amounts to assuming that the economic units forming expectations have knowledge of the relevant structural equations and use them. Nerlove (1967) has extended Muth's results to a wider class of stationary and non-stationary time series. However, it is still necessary to retain the assumption that economic units have knowledge of the relevant structure and react to conditional forecasts generated by that structure. An econometric implication of (19) is that in the absence of anticipatory data on, say y_{T+1}, we should substitute in the model the realized value of that variable. This procedure amounts to having an error in variable. This implication has been criticized by Carlson (1967) on the grounds that the argument about rational expectations is relevant only to simple microeconomic situations. He explicitly rejects the notion that feedback from aggregated individual decisions can be readily enough perceived by individual decision-makers for them to make appropriate adjustments in their forecasts. Pashigian (1965) and Hirsch and Lovell (1969) regard the rational expectations hypothesis as basically an empirical question to be answered by examining anticipatory data at aggregated and disaggregated levels to see if they display the characteristic of 'rationality'. Using OBE–SEC survey data on sales expectations at 2-digit industry level Pashigian found some empirical evidence in support of rational expectations hypothesis. Hirsch and Lovell (1969) have tested the hypothesis that in making forecasts, firms make full use of all information available to them. In analysing the short sales anticipations (quarterly) they fitted the equation

$$X_t = \beta_1 + \beta_2 \hat{X}_t + \beta_3 X_{t-1} + \beta_4 X_{t-4} + \varepsilon_t. \tag{20}$$

Under the rational expectations hypothesis, $\beta_2 = 1$ and $\beta_1 = \beta_3 = \beta_4 = 0$, and cov $(\hat{X}_t, \varepsilon_t) = 0$. The hypothesis was tested using data for seven 2-digit industries in the durables group and seven in the non-durables group. Although β_2 was frequently close to unity, β_3 and β_4 were often significantly different from zero thus casting doubt on the adequacy of the model (19). When anticipations relating to the 2-quarter horizon were analysed, the previous conclusion remained substantially unchanged. Mills (1962) has advocated what he calls the 'implicit expectations' approach which he contrasts with the 'explicit approach' that underlies any attempt at describing the formation of expectations. Any error in the specification of the expectations generating mechanism leads to an error in the estimate of $\hat{X}_t$. Further, finding the appropriate specification is not straightforward and a simple specification will not take account of all the factors which a decision-taker may take account of. Mills has argued that in presence of these difficulties one may approach the matter indirectly and assume that statistically expectations are stable in the sense that the mean and variance are stable through time. It would be appropriate then to make some assumption about the distribution of forecast errors. Mills, therefore, makes the same assumptions as Muth, see (19), and argues that the consequences of such an assumption being a bad approximation are not much different from those resulting from a misspecification of the structure generating anticipations. The main difference between Mills and Muth is that the latter assumes cov $(\hat{y}_t, \varepsilon_t) = 0$ while the former assumes cov $(y_t, \varepsilon_t) = 0$.

Lovell (1962) has suggested the use of the proxy formulation

$$\hat{X}_t = (1 - \rho)X_t + \rho X_{t-1}, \qquad 0 \le \rho \le 1, \tag{21}$$

which does not explain how expectations are formed. Rather it is based on a hypothesis that the forecast value $\hat{X}_t$ *turns out to be* a weighted average of the actual value in periods t and $t - 1$; $\rho = 0$ corresponds to 'perfect' forecasts whereas $\rho = 1$ corresponds to 'naive' forecasts. Lovell explained that this assumption was motivated by a remark attributable to Keynes that it is sensible for producers to base their expectations on the assumption that the most recently realized results will contrive except insofar as there are definite reasons for expecting a change. Note the absence of an error term in (21) which implies that it is not reducible to either Mills' or Muths' model. If the unknown parameter could be estimated it would provide an indication of the extent of 'regressiveness' of expectations. In Hirsch and Lovell (1969) it was found that expectations were sufficiently accurate for the anticipated change in sales to be closely approximated by the actual change. The authors have suggested that this result casts doubt on a fairly common assumption that expectations are formed by extrapolating from past data. Once this is accepted, use of a Lovell-type proxy procedure seems a superior alternative to use of autoregressive formulae, though it may introduce additional estimation problems. Nevertheless, it is possible that the proxy procedure is still an inferior procedure to using anticipated data directly.

Although we have discussed the problem of sales forecasting in terms of a one-period horizon it is not necessary to be so restrictive. If we admit the possibility that inventory changes in a single period may be determined by expectations relating to several future periods, it is a straightforward matter to generalize the proxy procedures outlined in the previous subsection.

In conclusion to this section it is especially worth noting that introduction of expectations in a model, and the possibility that expectations may be disappointed, is perhaps the most important method of introducing truly dynamic elements in a model. In econometric work it is necessary to go from the unobservables of theory to observable variables and the most common way of doing this appears to have been the replacement of the unobservable by its predictor — usually a linear predictor. Where the predictor used is a minimum mean-square-error predictor, it is equivalent to knowledge of the relevant structure. Use of predictors typically involves lagged values, but these lags are *conceptually distinct from lags of adjustment*. We have given a number of illustrations to show that it may be *empirically* difficult to separate the two sources of lags, but logically the two are distinct, see Nerlove (1972).

The treatment of expectations above suffers from one important limitation in that it deals with essentially short-term and relatively small changes rather than large, discontinuous changes such as outbreaks of wars, occurrence of natural disasters or calamities, technological breakthroughs or changes in government policies. When dealing with fixed investment, expectations of such events are of course of major importance, both in themselves and in the way they interact with reactions to changes in other determinants. For example, a firm's reaction to increases in investment incentives may depend upon how long the incentive schemes are expected to last as well as on future expected demand, the response to the same incentives being quite possibly different under two alternative sets of demand expectations. This illustrates that in econometric work expectations in a much broader sense are relevant; theoretical models which spell out implications of these observations are discussed by Sumner (1973), Nickell (1974a, 1974b), Ando *et. al.* (1974). Simple extrapolative schemes do not in general adequately represent the more indirect and subtle influences of expectations such as those elucidated in the above mentioned works.

CHAPTER 5

Aggregation

The term 'aggregation' has often been associated with the voluminous body of economic literature which attempts to assess the 'existence' of both neoclassical production functions and capital indexes to serve as arguments in these functions. Our earlier chapters provide many instances whereby algebraic symbols are used to represent such entities. In fact, most studies of real fixed capital formation assume that net investment is equivalent to the net change in some capital index, appropriately measurable. The existence of capital measures has almost always been investigated in the context of efficiency prices given by an assumption of competitive equilibria. However, as we saw in both Chapters One and Three, many empirical studies of fixed investment include distributed lags to represent disequilibria in capital-goods markets as well as other dynamic factors. The brief historical survey and new results of Gorman (1968) suggest that aggregation of capital goods into stock indexes is possible outside equilibrium only in rather special cases. Such incongruencies between theory and practice will not be discussed here. They raise important issues which are beyond the scope of this text. Of course, our neglect does not reduce the marked significance of these issues.

Two surveys of aggregation theory are provided by Ijiri (1971) and Theil (1962). Our account emphasizes only some statistical aspects of particular areas of this theory. Economic aspects are wholly ignored so that a specialist source such as Green (1964) should be consulted to overcome our omissions. Six sections are given below. The first of these deals with the properties of least-squares estimators after aggregation over either different or similar structures. This is followed by a discussion of partial aggregation, which is the name given to a situation familiar to most econometricians whereby data are adjusted (for example, by the central collecting agencies to preserve the confidentiality of their sources) before their use by researchers. Although aggregative weights may be known, the losses in dimension due to this form of prior adjustment are irreversible. The third section describes an approach, due to Zellner (1969), which uses so-called 'stochastic parameters' to avoid some of the problems raised in the first section but may introduce further complications.

Aggregation can lead to complications in specification as well as for estimation. Section Four illustrates the former by reference to a temporal problem whereby data are sampled at longer intervals than are indicated by structural models. This problem has important consequences both for the choice of explanatory variables and for the specification of an appropriate error-generating process at the level of available data. The fifth section deals with tests of the homogeneity of aggregated structures for different types of assets, industrial categories or regions. Finally, some consideration is given to autocorrelation and the combination of spatial data for which no natural ordering may exist.

5.1 SOME STATISTICAL CONSIDERATIONS

Consider the following statistical model of linear aggregation which is described by Theil (1954) and, in matrix form, by Kloek (1961). Assume that there exist p distinct 'micro-relations' which are derived from the predictions of economic theory for p economic agents, assets, industrial sectors or regions

$$\mathbf{y}_i = \mathbf{X}_i \beta_i + \mathbf{u}_i \qquad \text{for } i = 1, 2, \ldots, p, \tag{1}$$

where $\mathbf{y}_i$ and $\mathbf{u}_i$ are column vectors with T stochastic elements and $\mathbf{X}_i$ is a non-stochastic matrix of order T by K. Aggregate variables are calculated as linear combinations of $\mathbf{X}_i$ and $\mathbf{y}_i$ which have scalar non-stochastic weights $\{w_{1i}, w_{2i}\}$ for $i = 1, 2, \ldots, p$.

$$\mathbf{y} \equiv \sum_{i=1}^{p} w_{1i} \mathbf{y}_i, \quad \mathbf{X} \equiv \sum_{i=1}^{p} w_{2i} \mathbf{X}_i. \tag{2}$$

These aggregate variables are used to derive a single 'macro-relation', which is investigated by the econometrician as if it were a relation indicated by his theory. Let this be represented as

$$\mathbf{y} = \mathbf{X}\beta + \mathbf{v}, \tag{3}$$

where β is any column vector with K elements and $\mathbf{v}$ is defined implicitly for any given choice of β by the consistency of these three equations. Notice that we have only introduced one collection of weights $\{w_{2i}\}$ for aggregation of the explanatory variables. Our account could be extended (perhaps using the Schur product introduced in Chapter Three) to allow for K distinct sets of aggregative weights for these variables.

Define a least-squares estimator $\mathbf{b}$ for the macro-relation

$$\mathbf{b} = (\mathbf{X}'\mathbf{X})^{-1} \mathbf{X}'\mathbf{y}. \tag{4}$$

Theil sought the optimal choice of the 'macro-parameter' β where optimality is characterized by the condition that $\mathbf{b}$ is an unbiased estimator of this parameter. Clearly, by substitution, we obtain

$$\mathbf{b} = (\mathbf{X'X})^{-1}\mathbf{X'} \sum_{i=1}^{p} w_{1i}\mathbf{y}_i$$

$$= \sum_{i=1}^{p} [w_{1i}(\mathbf{X'X})^{-1}\mathbf{X'X}_i]\beta_i + \sum_{i=1}^{p} w_{1i}(\mathbf{X'X})^{-1}\mathbf{X'u}_i$$

or

$$\mathbf{b} = \sum_{i=1}^{p} \phi_i \mathbf{X}_i \beta_i + \sum_{i=1}^{p} \phi_i \mathbf{u}_i, \tag{5}$$

where

$$\phi_i \equiv w_{1i}(\mathbf{X'X})^{-1}\mathbf{X'}. \tag{6}$$

Thus $\mathbf{b}$ is an unbiased estimator of β only if this latter vector is defined as the following optimal choice

$$\beta \equiv \sum_{i=1}^{p} \phi_i \mathbf{X}_i \beta_i, \tag{7}$$

which is a linear combination of the 'micro-parameters' $\{\beta_i\}$. Notice that $\phi_i \mathbf{X}_i$ is w_{1i} if any $\mathbf{X}_i$ is equal to $\mathbf{X}$. In many investment studies using aggregate data but explicitly based on a theory of the 'firm', this condition is unlikely to be satisfied since the matrices $\{\mathbf{X}_i\}$ should contain observations specific to individual firms. Hence, even if the scalar weights $\{w_{1i}\}$ are fixed, the aggregative weights for the macro-parameters $\{\phi_i \mathbf{X}_i\}$ will usually vary between samples.

Suppose that the vectors of micro-parameters are equal, denoted as β_0, but the micro-observations $\mathbf{X}_i$ are not necessarily identical. Then,

$$\beta = \left(\sum_{i=1}^{p} \phi_i \mathbf{X}_i \right) \beta_0,$$

$$\sum_{i=1}^{p} \phi_i \mathbf{X}_i = \sum_{i=1}^{p} w_{1i}(\mathbf{X'X})^{-1}\mathbf{X'X}_i$$

$$= \mathbf{I} - \sum_{i=1}^{p} (w_{2i} - w_{1i})(\mathbf{X'X})^{-1}\mathbf{X'X}_i, \quad \text{Using (2),}$$

and

$$\beta = \beta_0 - \sum_{i=1}^{p} (w_{2i} - w_{1i})(\mathbf{X'X})^{-1}\mathbf{X'X}_i \beta_0. \tag{8}$$

Thus the least-squares estimator is not an unbiased estimator for the common value of micro-parametric vectors β_0 unless the same collection of scalar weights is used for all variables that are specific to the micro-units. Again this condition may not be satisfied in aggregative studies of investment.

The potential instability of the optimal macro-parameter also creates difficulties for the use of prior information from theoretical sources. Such information is applicable at the micro-level but is frequently used at the macro-level to constrain a parameter which may bear no stable relation to those parameters which are theoretically appropriate. Clearly this problem leaves uncertain the roles of tests of hypotheses and selective rules based on this type of information. The dispersion matrix $\mathscr{D}(\mathbf{b})$ of the least-squares estimator is given by

$$\mathscr{D}(\mathbf{b}) = E\left[\sum_{i=1}^{p} w_{1i}(\mathbf{X}'\mathbf{X})^{-1}\mathbf{X}'\mathbf{u}_i\right]\left[\sum_{j=1}^{p} w_{1j}(\mathbf{X}'\mathbf{X})^{-1}\mathbf{X}'\mathbf{u}_j\right]' \qquad (9)$$

$$= \sum_i \sum_j w_{1i}w_{1j}(\mathbf{X}'\mathbf{X})^{-1}\mathbf{X}'\boldsymbol{\Omega}_{ij}\mathbf{X}(\mathbf{X}'\mathbf{X})^{-1},$$

where $\boldsymbol{\Omega}_{ij}$ is $E(\mathbf{u}_i\mathbf{u}_j')$. The elements of $\mathscr{D}(\mathbf{b})$ may differ markedly from those that would be considered if the researcher ignored aggregation and erroneously assumed that the macro-error vector $\mathbf{v}$ satisfies classical conditions. Thus, quite apart from the difficulties of reconciling theoretical constraints with the macro-parameter, conventional test statistics associated with tests of these constraints cannot be calculated unless sufficient information is available with respect to the correlation of errors for different micro-equations. Further discussion of this latter difficulty is presented in the third section below.

Theil described the difference between the (least-squares-optimal) macro-parameter and the average of micro-parameters as 'aggregation bias'. In empirical studies for which micro-data are available, it is convenient to use this term for the difference between an aggregate estimator (based on data which have been aggregated before estimation) and the average of micro-estimators (based on separate samples of micro-data). If this difference is divided by the average of micro-estimators, we can refer to the resulting ratio as 'relative aggregation bias'. Kuh (1963) illustrates this concept in his comparison of several distinct specifications for the determinants of investment. His results suggest that such bias is severe for the particular fits that he considers. Another illustration is provided by Boot and de Wit (1960) using investment data and stock-market valuations for ten large U.S. companies. They also give a valuable clarification of the nature of the macro-errors' distribution.

In contrast to aggregation bias, Grunfeld and Griliches (1960) suggested that aggregation can be desirable since the constituent micro-equations should not be assumed to be perfectly specified. They claimed that aggregation of economic variables can, and in fact frequently does, reduce these specification errors and aggregation does not only produce an aggregation error, but may also produce an aggregation gain. This claim can also be extended to the situation where the measurement of macro-data is superior to that of micro-data. The possible occurrence of this situation is often surprising but arises when published micro-data do not reflect constituent building-blocks of the macro-data but rather are derived from the latter by arbitrary rules of assignment.

Other aspects of aggregation concern the relative efficiency and predictive success of different least-squares estimators when parameters for the micro-equations are identical. Grunfeld and Griliches used coefficients of multiple determination for sample periods to indicate the occurrence of aggregation gain. They compared the R^2 for a macro-equation with a composite given by the amount of sample variance in the aggregate dependent variable explained by the sum of the fitted micro-equations. Later studies shifted attention to other indicators such as the mean-squared-errors of post-sample forecasts and standard errors of parametric estimates in Monte-Carlo studies. See, for example, the contributions of Orcutt (1965, 1968) and Edwards and Orcutt (1969) for presentations of particular empirical results and discussions of related matters. The specific framework of identical micro-equations' parameters is also used in Sections 5.2, 5.4 and 5.5 below.

Throughout this discussion, we have considered only least-squares estimators. In fact, it should be recalled that Theil defined the optimal choice of a macro-parameter in terms of these estimators. This was a convenient starting point for investigations of aggregation problems. It was subsequently supplemented by Theil (1959) with a similar approach embodying a two-stage least-squares macro-estimator, and obviously further extensions are possible. However, this second step does not appear to have generated any widespread interest and it has not led to any significant applications of this theory at least in the general area of investment studies.

5.2 PARTIAL AGGREGATION

One important difficulty facing many researchers stems from the forms in which data are available. Both private and governmental data-collecting agencies frequently adjust their compilations to reduce manipulation costs, to preserve the confidentiality of their sources, and to eliminate seasonality and other secular instabilities. In addition, individual researchers may make further adjustments to annihilate the influences of 'secondary variables' (that is, variables that are relevant for particular studies but are not the primary concern of researchers). These adjustments may affect both the distributional properties of estimators and the interpretation of statistical tests of significance based on the adjusted or aggregated data. The term 'partial aggregation' has been introduced to describe situations in which prior adjustments do not wholly distort the results of conventional procedures. In this section, we illustrate the consequences of partial aggregation by considering the effects on data of pre-multiplication by a linear transformation. Questions of bias are eliminated by the use of the same non-stochastic transformation for all variables in the framework where the pre-adjusted data satisfy the conditions of the classical linear model.

Suppose, Y denotes a vector containing N_1 observations for the dependent variable in a particular study and let Z represent a matrix, of order N_1 by K and rank K, which contains observations for K explanatory variables. Both Y and Z are assumed to be either unavailable or unused by preference of the researcher. Instead these data have been subjected to a prior transformation with known elements. This transformation can be represented by a non-stochastic matrix **G**, say, which has order N by N_1 and rank N. Then the elements of **GY** and **GZ** represent the data in the form in which they are available for use. **GZ** is assumed to have rank K initially but this assumption will be amended later when we discuss one particular form of prior adjustment that has been in widespread use.

Again in contrast to earlier usage of our notation, a 'micro-equation' (10) and a 'macro-equation' (11) must be distinguished. The former is the specification which would be used if data were available in an appropriate form whereas the latter is the specification which is actually used:

$$\mathbf{Y} = \mathbf{Z}\beta + \mathbf{u}, \tag{10}$$

where β is a vector of K parameters and **u** is a vector of random errors, and

$$\mathbf{GY} = \mathbf{GZ}\beta + \mathbf{Gu}. \tag{11}$$

The model described in Section 5.1, when the micro-parameters of p individual micro-relations are equal, can be expressed for example in the framework provided by (10) and (11). Exact equivalence can be established by the choices of $[w_{11}\mathbf{I}; w_{12}\mathbf{I}; \dots; w_{1p}\mathbf{I}]$, $[\mathbf{y}'_1, \mathbf{y}'_2, \dots, \mathbf{y}'_p]$ and $[\mathbf{X}'_1, \mathbf{X}'_2, \dots, \mathbf{X}'_p]$ for **G**, **Y**′ and **Z**′, respectively. The identity matrix **I** here has order T by T. N is T and N_1 is Tp. Thus,

$$\mathbf{GY} = \sum_j w_{1j}\mathbf{y}_j = \mathbf{y}$$

and

$$\mathbf{GZ} = \sum_j w_{1j}\mathbf{X}_j = \mathbf{X}$$

with these specifications. Notice that the transformation **G** is irreversible and that, for this particular illustration, **GG**′ is a scalar matrix $(\Sigma_j w_{1j}^2)\mathbf{I}$. If the p collections of errors $\{\mathbf{u}_j\}$ are mutually uncorrelated and individually satisfy classical conditions with the same variance σ^2, then $E[(\mathbf{Gu})(\mathbf{Gu})']$ or $E(\mathbf{vv}')$, the dispersion matrix of the aggregate errors, is also a scalar matrix $\sigma^2(\Sigma_j w_{1j}^2)\mathbf{I}$. Thus both the micro-errors and the macro-errors will satisfy classical conditions in these very restrictive conditions. Least-squares estimators of β based upon the 'macro-equation' (11) will, in the terms of the Gauss–Markov theorem, be relatively efficient amongst the linear estimators of β where linearity is defined by reference to **GY**. (See Rowley (1973, Chs. 1 and 7).) Notice, however, the loss of efficiency of the estimators in comparison with least-squares estimators based upon the 'micro-equation' (10). Orcutt suggests that this loss may be substantial and that it often results in a restricted ability to discriminate between alternative hypotheses. In the specification being considered here (11), conventional tests of significance will also be applicable without modification if the errors are normally distributed.

In more general situations, the dispersion matrix of **Gu** will not be a scalar matrix and, since **G** is known, equation (11) will satisfy instead the conditions for Aitken's generalization of the classical linear model. Estimation and tests of significance should be based on the generalized least-squares estimator, $\hat{\beta}$ say, where

$$\hat{\beta} = [(\mathbf{GZ})'(\mathbf{GG}')^{-1}(\mathbf{GZ})]^{-1}(\mathbf{GZ})'(\mathbf{GG}')^{-1}\mathbf{GY} \tag{12}$$

or

$$\hat{\beta} = (\mathbf{Z}'\mathbf{G}'(\mathbf{GG}')^{-1}\mathbf{GZ}]^{-1}\mathbf{Z}'\mathbf{G}'(\mathbf{GG}')^{-1}\mathbf{GY}.$$

The product $\mathbf{G}'(\mathbf{GG}')^{-1}$ is the Moore–Penrose inverse of $\mathbf{G}$ and may be denoted by $\mathbf{G}^-$. That is, $\mathbf{G}^-$ is the unique matrix such that $\mathbf{GG}^-$ and $\mathbf{G}^-\mathbf{G}$ are both symmetric,

$$\mathbf{G}^-\mathbf{GG}^- = \mathbf{G}^-$$

and

$$\mathbf{GG}^-\mathbf{G} = \mathbf{G}.$$

It may be confirmed that the Aitken estimator is identical with the least-squares estimator based upon the equation that results when (11) is subjected to a further transformation; namely, pre-multiplication by $\mathbf{G}^-$.

$$\mathbf{G}^-\mathbf{GY} = \mathbf{G}^-\mathbf{GZ}\beta + \mathbf{G}^-\mathbf{Gu}. \tag{13}$$

This final specification indicates a general principle to be followed in cases of prior adjustment. $\mathbf{G}^-\mathbf{G}$ is symmetric and is unaltered if multiplied by itself (idempotent). These properties are sufficient for the relative optimality of least-squares estimators based upon (13). The simple procedure to be followed if the researcher is faced by a 'macro-equation' (11) requires calculation of the Moore–Penrose inverse $\mathbf{G}^-$, pre-multiplication of all data by it, and then use of a convenient least-squares computational package with (13) as if this final specification satisfies the classical linear model. It can readily be confirmed that $\mathscr{D}(\mathbf{G}^-\mathbf{Gu})$ is $\sigma^2\mathbf{G}^-\mathbf{G}$ but the potential autocorrelation and heteroscedasticity, somewhat surprisingly for those unused to this formulation, do not affect the validity of familiar test statistics. (A good account of the properties of $\mathbf{G}^-$ and other less-restrictive inverses is provided by Graybill (1969).) The effects of the initial aggregation often cannot be eliminated since $\mathbf{G}$ is not necessarily a square matrix and reversible. Instead an additional transformation is used to put the equation into a form that can be used without the deficiencies attributable to (11). Notice however that important modifications to this approach must be made if the micro-errors are either heteroscedastic or autocorrelated. Some discussions of related nature are given in Sections 5.4 and 5.5. Two important references worth consulting are Prais and Aitchison (1954) and Feige and Watts (1972).

So far we have ignored the annihilation of data in prior adjustment. This occurs if $\mathbf{GZ}$ has columns of zeros and is a very common feature in econometric studies. Suppose $\mathbf{Z}$ is partitioned into $[\mathbf{Z}_1 : \mathbf{Z}_2]$ where $\mathbf{Z}_1$ and $\mathbf{Z}_2$ have K_1 and

and K_2 columns respectively. Then if $\mathbf{G}$ is the square matrix $(\mathbf{I} - \mathbf{Z}_1(\mathbf{Z}_1'\mathbf{Z}_1)^{-1}\mathbf{Z}_1')$, $\mathbf{GZ}_1$ is a null matrix. If β is partitioned conformably,

$$\mathbf{GY} = \mathbf{GZ}_1\beta_1 + \mathbf{GZ}_2\beta_2 + \mathbf{Gu} = \mathbf{GZ}_2\beta_2 + \mathbf{Gu}. \tag{14}$$

The effects of the first K_1 variables appear to have been eliminated but, clearly, the effects have been spread throughout the data by use of the $\mathbf{G}$-transformation. The macro-data $\mathbf{GY}$ and $\mathbf{GZ}_2$ are described as 'covariance transforms' of $\mathbf{Y}$ and $\mathbf{Z}_2$ by reference to $\mathbf{Z}_1$. If $\mathbf{Z}_1$ is simply a vector of constants $\mathbf{1}$, $\mathbf{G}$ is $(\mathbf{I} - (1/T) \mathbf{11}')$ and the covariance transforms represent observations as deviations from sample means for variables. With dummy variables for 'firm effects', 'industry effects' or 'seasonal effects', the transforms are more complicated expressions involving various means. (See Kuh (1963).) However this type of adjustment is quite general and does not necessarily involve data composed solely of unit or zero elements.

Equation (14) is similar to (11) but has one important difference. $\mathbf{G}$ in (14) is already symmetric and idempotent so that no further transformation is necessary. $\mathbf{G}$ is also its own Moore–Penrose inverse and $\mathbf{G}^-\mathbf{G}$ is $\mathbf{G}$ with this choice for $\mathbf{G}$. Aitken estimators of β_2 and least-squares estimators based on (14) are the same, but the usual formula for the Aitken estimator has to be revised since $\mathbf{G}$ is singular. Although least-squares computational packages can be used in conjunction with (14), they must be adjusted to take account of the so-called 'loss of degrees of freedom' due to the prior adjustment. For example, suppose Z_1 contains observations for four seasonal dummy variables, each taking a unit value in a particular season and a zero one otherwise. Then, the residual sum of squares $\mathbf{S}$ for a least-squares fit given by

$$\mathbf{S} \equiv (\mathbf{GY} - \mathbf{GZ}_2\hat{\beta}_2)'(\mathbf{GY} - \mathbf{GZ}_2\hat{\beta}_2) \tag{15}$$

is proportional to a chi-square variable with $(T - K_1 - K_2)$ degrees of freedom if the original errors u are independently and identically distributed as normal variables. With our seasonal illustration K_1 is 4 and standard programmes will proceed as if the degrees of freedom were $(T - K_2)$, the difference between the number of observations and the number of explanatory variables explicitly included in (14).

In conclusion, aggregation of data can critically affect the validity of popular procedures. It may introduce autocorrelation and heteroscedasticity. Further, it may mislead the researcher into an inaccurate calculation of degrees of freedom for tests of significance. However, for prior adjustments of the type considered in this section, all inferential difficulties can be eliminated by clear statements of these adjustments and appropriate supplemental transformations in some cases. There will persist possibilities of substantial losses in efficiency for estimators based upon macro-data provided there are no specification errors. In many instances, this is unfortunate but cannot be avoided since micro-data are not available to the researcher.

5.3 STOCHASTIC PARAMETERS

In the first section of this chapter, we introduced Theil's approach to the interpretation of a macro-equation based on aggregate data when economic theory indicates p micro-equations of the form

$$\mathbf{y}_i = \mathbf{X}_i \beta_i + \mathbf{u}_i \qquad \text{for } i = 1, 2, \ldots, p. \tag{1}$$

Zellner (1969) indicated an alternative specification, using 'stochastic para-meters', which may resolve Theil's problem of aggregation bias. Within this alternative framework, Swamy (1971) provides an illustration of estimation for an aggregate investment function, with eleven constituent micro-equations representing the investment behaviour of large U.S. corporations. He suggests that, for his data, inferential tests suggest that we should not treat the coefficient vector of the investment vector as fixed and the same for all items. This vector exhibits substantial variations across firms. In our following account, we describe two simple models extending (1) in the spirit of Zellner's proposal.

Suppose we suppress the errors $\mathbf{u}_i$ in (1). This deletion will be of little consequence in view of other modifications to be introduced below, provided each $\mathbf{X}_i$ contains a vector of constants. In addition, we first suppose that the para-meters β_i are not fixed but instead are stochastic variables with the same mean vector, $\bar{\beta}$ say, so that

$$\beta_i = \bar{\beta} + \mathbf{e}_i \qquad \text{for } i = 1, 2, \ldots, p, \tag{16}$$

where $\{\mathbf{e}_i\}$ are p mutually independent collections of random errors with zero means and dispersion matrices $\mathscr{D}(\mathbf{e}_i)$ equal to $\alpha_i \mathbf{I}$. The p additional parameters $\{\alpha_i\}$ are unknown scalars. Substitution for β_i in (1) yields

$$\mathbf{y}_i = \mathbf{X}_i \bar{\beta} + \mathbf{X}_i \mathbf{e}_i, \tag{17}$$

so we may specify a (new) macro-equation

$$\mathbf{Y} = \mathbf{Z} \bar{\beta} + \mathbf{w}, \tag{18}$$

where $\mathbf{Y}$ and $\mathbf{Z}$ are as defined in the previous section. $\mathbf{w}'$ is a new vector of macro-errors, of length pT, as given by $[(\mathbf{X}_1 \mathbf{e}_1)', \ldots, (\mathbf{X}_p \mathbf{e}_p)']$. Clearly the mean value of this vector is zero and its dispersion matrix $\mathscr{D}(\mathbf{w})$ is a block-diagonal matrix. That is, apart from p blocks of elements clustered along its principal diagonal, its elements are zero. A typical block is given by $\alpha_i \mathbf{X}_i \mathbf{X}_i'$. In the simplest case where there exists only one observation on each micro-agent ($T = 1$), the matrix $\mathscr{D}(\mathbf{w})$ would be a diagonal matrix with elements $\alpha_1 \mathbf{X}_1 \mathbf{X}_1'$, $\alpha_2 \mathbf{X}_2 \mathbf{X}_2'$, ..., $\alpha_p \mathbf{X}_p \mathbf{X}_p'$ along its principal diagonal and all other elements would be zero. Then there would be little purpose in using any complicated method of esti-mation since the model may be characterized by $(K + p)$ parameters but the data contains only p observations. More generally, one would require T to be sufficiently large to eliminate this 'overfitting difficulty'. Notice, however, that it is unnecessary for there to exist the same number of observations for each micro-agent. We have retained this assumption solely to simplify notation.

This example of Zellner's specification eliminates aggregation bias but this improvement is made by introducing heteroscedasticity and autocorrelation (except in the extreme one-observation case cited above). The new model represented by (18) is similar to Aitken's generalization of the classical linear model except for the 'intrusion' of the unknown parameters $\{\alpha_i\}$. Least-squares estimators of $\bar{\beta}$ will be unbiased but their efficiency is uncertain without knowledge of these supplemental parameters. Several alternative estimators have been proposed for this situation. These are based on simple two-stage procedures. First, estimators for the supplemental parameters $\{\alpha_i\}$ are calculated using least-squares residuals. Then these are used instead of true values in the formula for Aitken's generalized least-squares estimator. The resulting 'feasible Aitken estimators' will, of course, only have asymptotically optimal properties. They will usually be consistent but biased.

A more general example of stochastic parameters may be obtained by introducing more random errors. Suppose, in the absence of u_i, a typical observation in (1) may be written in the form

$$y_{it} = \sum_{j=1}^{K} X_{ijt}\beta_{ijt} \qquad \text{for } t = 1, 2, ..., T, \tag{19}$$

where

$$\beta_{ijt} = \bar{\beta}_j + e_{ijt}. \tag{20}$$

Again $\bar{\beta}_j$ are assumed to be mean values and the errors $\{e_{ijt}\}$ are assumed to have zero means. Substitution yields

$$y_{it} = \sum_{j=1}^{K} X_{ijt}\bar{\beta}_j + \sum_{j=1}^{K} X_{ijt}e_{ijt} \qquad \text{for } t = 1, 2, ... T \tag{21}$$

or

$$\mathbf{y}_i = \mathbf{X}_i\bar{\beta} + \mathbf{w}_{0i}$$

where $\mathbf{w}_0$ is a more complicated expression than before. In terms of the Schur product, $\mathbf{w}_{0i}$ is $(\mathbf{X}_i * \mathbf{E}_i)$ where $\mathbf{E}_i$ is a matrix of errors; a typical jtth element of which is e_{ijt}. Stochastic assumptions must again be introduced if feasible Aitken estimators are to be obtained by the same procedural stages described above.

In recent years, a substantial number of papers discussing these estimators have been published. Suitable starting points for further reading are provided in the special issue on Time-Varying Parameters of the *Annals of Economic and Social Measurement* (October 1973). Some finite-sample properties are indicated by Froehlich (1973) and Maddala and Mount (1973). The latter conclude that in the absence of lagged dependent variables, which complication we have omitted in the account provided above, there is nothing much to choose among these estimators. Finally, we should add that these models may often be extended without difficulty, for example by making the $\bar{\beta}_j$ elements linear combinations of other known factors.

5.4   TEMPORAL AGGREGATION*

In Section 3.o, we described some of the problems that arise when discrete data and models are used to approximate the relationship indicated by continuous models. This is an extreme case of situations that frequently occur in research. Here data which are available to the researcher may represent developments over a longer time-span than the period used in the formulation of his economic models. In the cases given below, we consider the discrete approximation of other discrete models. A typical example would be the use of annual data and the appropriate modifications suggested for a quarterly model of investment expenditures in this situation. Our cases of 'temporal aggregation' differ markedly from the other models described in this Chapter in one important sense. They assume the existence of a single micro-relation, based on a 'natural' time period, and many alternative macro-relations based on time periods with durations given by integral multiples of this natural time unit.

Our first two cases illustrate how aggregation may reduce autocorrelation in errors between two alternative models. The other cases provide a framework for showing how aggregation can also introduce very substantial difficulties. Throughout these cases we assume that available data for the dependent variables in final empirical fits are non-overlapping in the sense that successive aggregate observations do not contain any common constituent parts. Overlapping (such as occurs when the aggregate variable is an annual flow of investment but is recorded at quarterly intervals) raises more difficulties and will not be discussed here.

In our cases, y_t and ε_t will denote the dependent micro-variable and the error associated with it in the micro-equations. The symbol η_t will be used to indicate a member of a white-noise sequence. That is, the sequence $\{\eta_t\}$ have zero means, are mutually uncorrelated and have constant variances σ^2. The dependent macro-variable $Y_{h,t}$ is always an unweighted sum of h successive dependent micro-variables. Macro-errors $\varepsilon_{h,t}$ are defined similarly:

$$Y_{h,t} = \sum_{j=0}^{h-1} y_{t-j}, \ \varepsilon_{h,t} \equiv \sum_{j=0}^{h-1} \varepsilon_{t-j} \tag{22}$$

In some of the later cases, this definition for $\varepsilon_{h,t}$ is modified. Other symbols represent unknown parameters except for r which is used to denote an arbitrary positive integer.

Case A: Reduction of autocorrelation—moving average micro-errors

Suppose the micro-equation is

$$y_t = \mu + \varepsilon_t, \qquad \text{where } \varepsilon_t = \eta_t + \lambda\eta_{t-1}. \tag{23}$$

Then, by simple addition, we obtain

$$(y_t + y_{t-1}) = 2\mu + (\varepsilon_t + \varepsilon_{t-1})$$

or

$$Y_{2,t} = 2\mu + \varepsilon_{2,t}, \tag{24}$$

where

$$\varepsilon_{2,t} = \eta_t + (1 + \lambda)\eta_{t-1} + \lambda\eta_{t-2}. \tag{25}$$

Thus

$$E(\varepsilon_{2,t}^2) = [1 + (1 + \lambda)^2 + \lambda^2]\sigma^2 \tag{26}$$

and

$$E(\varepsilon_{2,t}\varepsilon_{2,t-2r}) = \lambda\sigma^2 \tag{27}$$

if r has a unit value and zero otherwise. Thus, with sampling occurring at two-period intervals, the macro-errors $\{\varepsilon_{2,t} \text{ for } t = 0, 2, 4,...\}$ have a dispersion matrix with the same pattern as a first-order moving-average process. (We return to this feature in Case C.)

Consider the alternative four-period aggregates such that

$$Y_{4,t} = 4\mu + \varepsilon_{4,t}, \tag{28}$$

where

$$\varepsilon_{4,t} = \eta_t + (1 + \lambda)\eta_{t-1} + (1 + \lambda)\eta_{t-2} + (1 + \lambda)\eta_{t-3} + \lambda\eta_{t-4}. \tag{29}$$

Thus

$$E(\varepsilon_{4,t}^2) = [1 + 3(1 + \lambda)^2 + \lambda^2]\sigma^2 \tag{30}$$

and

$$E(\varepsilon_{4,t}\varepsilon_{4,t-4r}) = \lambda\sigma^2 \tag{31}$$

if r has a unit value and zero otherwise. Again, sampling at four-period intervals, the macro-errors $\{\varepsilon_{4,t} \text{ for } t = 0, 4, 8,...\}$ have a dispersion matrix with the same pattern as a first-order moving-average process.

These results should be compared with those for the micro-errors where $E(\varepsilon_t^2)$ is $(1 + \lambda^2)\sigma^2$,

$$E(\varepsilon_t\varepsilon_{t-r}) = \lambda\sigma^2$$

if r has a unit value and zero otherwise. Suppose we define autocorrelations for the various errors by

$$p_r \equiv \frac{E(\varepsilon_t\varepsilon_{t-r})}{E(\varepsilon_t^2)}$$

and

$$p_{h,r} \equiv \frac{E(\varepsilon_{h,t}\varepsilon_{h,t-hr})}{E(\varepsilon_{h,t}^2)} \qquad \text{for } h = 2, 4.$$

Then it is clear from (26), (27), (30) and (31) that

$$p_{4,1} < p_{2,1} < p_1. \tag{32}$$

This result might be said to illustrate the 'reduction' of autocorrelation due to aggregation. It provides an analytical basis for some comments often found in econometric literature whereby researchers suggest that quarterly time-series are associated with 'more autocorrelation' than annual time-series. Notice, however, that both $p_{4,1}$ and $p_{2,1}$ would be zero if λ were zero and the micro-errors free from autocorrelation.

Case B: Reduction of autocorrelation—autoregressive micro-errors

Consider the micro-equation (23) where micro-errors are generated by an alternative first-order autoregressive process

$$\varepsilon_t = \lambda \varepsilon_{t-1} + \eta_t, \quad 0 < \lambda < 1. \tag{33}$$

Then

$$\varepsilon_t = \sum_{t=0}^{\infty} \lambda^j \eta_{t-j} \tag{34}$$

by repeated substitution in (33). Then

$$Y_{2,t} = 2\mu + \varepsilon_{2,t}$$

as before but $\varepsilon_{2,t}$ is now given by

$$\varepsilon_{2,t} = \eta_t + (1+\lambda) \sum_{j=0}^{\infty} \lambda^j \eta_{t-j-1} \tag{35}$$

instead of (25). Further

$$E(\varepsilon_{2,t}^2) = \left[1 + \frac{(1+\lambda)^2}{1-\lambda^2}\right]\sigma^2 = \frac{2\sigma^2}{1-\lambda} \tag{36}$$

and

$$E(\varepsilon_{2,t}\varepsilon_{2,t-2r}) = [\lambda^{2r-1}(1+\lambda) + \lambda^{2r}(1+\lambda)^2 + \lambda^{2r+2}(1+\lambda)^2 + \ldots]\sigma^2$$

$$= \lambda^{2r-1}\frac{1+\lambda}{1-\lambda}\sigma^2. \tag{37}$$

Notice

$$p_{2,r} = \tfrac{1}{2}\lambda^{2r-1}(1+\lambda) \qquad \text{for } r = 1, 2, \ldots, \tag{38}$$

whereas

$$p_r = \lambda^r. \tag{39}$$

Thus

$$p_{2,r} < p_r \qquad \text{for all } r. \tag{40}$$

Consider now the four-period aggregates

$$Y_{4,t} = 4\mu + \varepsilon_{4,t},$$

where

$$\varepsilon_{4,t} = \eta_t + (1 + \lambda)n_{t-1} + (1 + \lambda + \lambda^2)\eta_{t-2} + (1 + \lambda + \lambda^2 + \lambda^3)\sum_{j=0}^{\infty}\lambda^j\eta_{t-3-j}, \quad (41)$$

$$E(\varepsilon_{4,t}^2) = \left[1 + (1 + \lambda)^2 + (1 + \lambda + \lambda^2)^2 + \frac{(1 + \lambda + \lambda^2 + \lambda^3)^2}{1 - \lambda^2}\right]\sigma^2$$

$$= \frac{2(2 + \lambda + \lambda^2)\sigma^2}{1 - \lambda}, \tag{42}$$

$$E(\varepsilon_{4,t}\varepsilon_{4,t-4r}) = \frac{\lambda^{4r-3}(1 - \lambda^4)(1 + \lambda^2)\sigma^2}{(1 - \lambda)^2}. \tag{43}$$

Thus

$$p_{4,r} = \lambda^{4r-3}\left[\frac{1 + \lambda + \lambda^2 + \lambda^3}{2 + \lambda + \lambda^2}\right]\left[\frac{1 + \lambda^2}{2}\right], \tag{44}$$

which is less than λ^{4r-3} since each of the two square-bracketed expressions are less than unity for the given range of λ. In both of the aggregate representations considered for this case, the macro-error processes cannot be associated with first-order autoregressive processes since the sequences $\{1, p_{h,1}, p_{h,2},...\}$ are not wholly geometric progressions. In each case, the first term is inappropriate. Autocorrelation is reduced in the particular sense defined in terms of the relative magnitudes of autocorrelations but at what expense? One obvious loss is the elimination of the simple autoregressive transformations from their popular roles moderating the effects of autocorrelation. For example, if micro-data were available, a researcher might adjust (23) to obtain

$$y_t = \lambda y_{t-1} + \mu(1 - \lambda) + \eta_t, \tag{45}$$

which form is free from autocorrelated errors. A similar adjustment cannot be used with either $Y_{2,t}$ or $Y_{4,t}$ because of the 'reduction in autocorrelation' mentioned above.

Case C: Lagged dependent variable—independent micro-errors

At the end of our description in Case B, we saw that aggregation might be a cause of difficulties in estimation. This point can be more easily demonstrated using the alternative specification

$$y_t = \alpha y_{t-1} + \mu + \varepsilon_t, \qquad 0 < \alpha < 1, \tag{46}$$

where the micro-errors are mutually independent. Set ε_t equal to η_t and substitute repeatedly for the lagged dependent variables. This yields

$$y_t = \frac{\mu}{1 - \alpha} + \sum_{j=0}^{\infty}\alpha^j\eta_{t-j}, \tag{47}$$

so that $E(y_{t-1}\varepsilon_t)$ is zero. This property is the basis for desirable asymptotic properties of least-squares estimates of α based on (46). We shall find that its analogue does not hold for the macro-equations based on temporal aggregates.

From (46), it is clear that

$$y_t = \alpha(\alpha y_{t-2} + \mu + \varepsilon_{t-1}) + \mu + \varepsilon_t$$

or

$$y_t = \alpha^2 y_{t-2} + \mu(1 + \alpha) + \varepsilon_t + \alpha\varepsilon_{t-1}. \tag{48}$$

Thus, with a slight adjustment to the definition of $\varepsilon_{2,t}$,

$$Y_{2,t} = \alpha^2 Y_{2,t-2} + 2\mu(1 + \alpha) + \varepsilon_{2,t} \tag{49}$$

and

$$\varepsilon_{2,t} = (\varepsilon_t + \alpha\varepsilon_{t-1}) + (\varepsilon_{t-1} + \alpha\varepsilon_{t-2}) = \eta_t + (1 + \alpha)\eta_{t-1} + \alpha\eta_{t-2}. \tag{50}$$

But

$$Y_{2,t} \equiv y_t + y_{t-1} = \frac{2\mu}{(1-\alpha)} + \eta_t + (1 + \alpha) \sum_{j=0}^{\infty} \alpha^j \eta_{t-j-1} \tag{51}$$

so $E(Y_{2,t-2}\varepsilon_{2,t})$ is σ^2. This contemporaneous correlation of the explanatory macro-variable and macro-error in (49) means that least-squares estimates of α^2 based on this equation will be biased even asymptotically.

$$E(\varepsilon_{2,t}^2) = [1 + (1 + \alpha)^2 + \alpha^2]\sigma^2$$

and $E(\varepsilon_{2,t}\varepsilon_{2,t-2r})$ is $\alpha\sigma^2$ for unit r and zero otherwise. Notice that the macro-errors again have a dispersion matrix that one might associate with a first-order moving-average process. (See Rowley (1973, Ch. 2).)

Consider the process

$$\varepsilon_{2,t}^* \equiv c_0\eta_t^* + c_1\eta_{t-2}^*, \tag{52}$$

where $\{\eta_t^*\}$ is another white-noise sequence such that $\{\eta_t\}$ and $\{\eta_t^*\}$ have common variances. The role of parameters c_0 and c_1 will soon be apparent. Then,

$$E(\varepsilon_{2,r}^*) = (c_0^2 + c_1^2)\sigma^2,$$

$$E(\varepsilon_{2,t}^*\varepsilon_{2,t-2r}^*) = c_0 c_1 \sigma^2$$

for unit r and zero otherwise. Suppose we set

$$c_0^2 + c_1^2 = 1 + (1 + \alpha)^2 + \alpha^2$$

and

$$c_0 c_1 = \alpha.$$

Then c_0 may take either of the values

$$c_0 = (1 + \alpha + \alpha^2) \pm (1 + \alpha)\sqrt{1 + \alpha^2}. \tag{53}$$

With either of these choices (and the corresponding ones implied for c_1), we can act as if

$$\varepsilon_{2,t} = c_0 \eta_t^* + c_1 \eta_{t-2}^* \qquad \text{for } t = 0, 2, 4, \ldots, \tag{54}$$

at least insofar as the dispersion matrix is concerned.

Consider the h-period aggregate as associated by

$$Y_{h,t} = \alpha^h Y_{h,t-h} + h\mu(1 + \alpha + \alpha^2 + \ldots + \alpha^{h-1}) + \varepsilon_{h,t}, \tag{55}$$

where

$$\varepsilon_{h,t} = \sum_{j=0}^{h-1} \sum_{i=0}^{h-1} \alpha^j \varepsilon_{t-j-i}. \tag{56}$$

It may readily be established that $E(Y_{h,t-h} \varepsilon_{h,t})$ is not zero and that, for sampling at h-period intervals, the macro-errors' dispersion matrix has a first-order moving-average pattern.

Engle and Liu (1972), who present a detailed investigation of the model used here, illustrate a further difficulty for determining 'mean lags' in patterns of temporal response. If a and A are the least-squares estimates (or other estimates) of α and α^h that might be derived from the micro-equation and the macro-equation (55) respectively, then estimated mean lags of response for this model would be $a/(1-a)$ and $hA/(1-A)$ in terms of the natural time-units. The difference between these expressions can be substantial as Engle and Liu show.

Case D: Exogenous variables

Suppose that, in addition to a lagged dependent variable, the micro-equation contains an exogenous explanatory variable, denoted by x_t, so that

$$y_t = \alpha y_{t-1} + \beta x_t + \varepsilon_t, \qquad 0 < \alpha < 1, \tag{57}$$

where the micro-errors are mutually independent. Then substitution yields

$$y_t = \alpha^2 y_{t-2} + \beta(x_t + \alpha x_{t-1}) + \varepsilon_t + \alpha \varepsilon_{t-1}.$$

$$Y_{2,t} = \alpha^2 Y_{2,t-2} + \beta[x_t + (1 + \alpha)x_{t-1} + \alpha x_{t-2}] + \varepsilon_{2,t}. \tag{58}$$

This equation cannot be fitted since α must be known in advance if the explanatory variable $[x_t + (1 + \alpha)x_{t-1} + \alpha x_{t-2}]$ is to be calculated. When this variable is mis-specified, it provides an additional source of bias. Clearly this problem may not arise if the x_t are sampled at natural intervals since the equation can then be written in the form.

$$Y_{2,t} = \alpha^2 Y_{2,t-2} + \beta(x_t + x_{t-1}) + \alpha\beta(x_{t-1} + x_{t-2}) + \varepsilon_{2,t}.$$

Unfortunately this form (and its extensions for longer-period aggregates) has been rarely used in empirical studies of investment and we must, therefore, accept that estimates have been affected by measurement errors especially after the widespread adoption of Koyck's specification for distributed-lag models.

Some concluding comments

Our four cases are indicative of the considerations that arise when only aggregate data are used or when these data are deliberately chosen even though micro-data are available. We have not pointed out the important distinction for temporal aggregation between stocks and flows. This is clarified by Moriguchi (1970). Further, we did not indicate how several authors have explored the respecification of macro-equations so that they fall within the frameworks of some familiar models with mixtures of autoregressive and moving-average elements. Our deficiencies can be partially eliminated by contact with the papers by Amemiya and Wu (1972) and Brewer (1973) as well as by Moriguchi.

5.5   ASSETS AND SECTORS

In Section 5.1, we introduce a model with p constituent micro-equations given by

$$\mathbf{y}_i = \mathbf{X}_i \boldsymbol{\beta}_i + \mathbf{u}_i \qquad \text{for } i = 1, 2, ..., p, \tag{1}$$

which represent the behaviour of distinct agents, assets, industrial sectors or regions. $\mathbf{y}_i$, $\mathbf{X}_i$ and $\mathbf{u}_i$ signify T observations for a dependent variable, K explanatory variables and an error. The explanatory variables are assumed to be non-stochastic and T exceeds K. In Section 5.2, further notation was defined for the situation where the vectors of parameters $\{\boldsymbol{\beta}_i\}$ were equal (to $\boldsymbol{\beta}$ say). Thus $\mathbf{Y}'$ and $\mathbf{Z}'$ were used to denote the long vector $[\mathbf{y}'_1, ..., \mathbf{y}'_p]$ and matrix $[\mathbf{X}'_1, \mathbf{X}'_2, ..., \mathbf{X}'_p]$. For this restricted case, the p micro-equations can be combined in a single matrix specification

$$\mathbf{y} = \mathbf{Z}\boldsymbol{\beta} + \mathbf{u}, \tag{10}$$

where $\mathbf{u}'$ is $[\mathbf{u}'_1, ..., \mathbf{u}'_p]$. For the unrestricted case, we can write

$$\begin{bmatrix} \mathbf{y}_1 \\ \mathbf{y}_2 \\ . \\ . \\ . \\ \mathbf{y}_p \end{bmatrix} = \begin{bmatrix} \mathbf{X}_1 & 0 & ... & 0 \\ 0 & \mathbf{X}_2 & ... & 0 \\ . & . & & . \\ . & . & & . \\ . & . & . & . \\ 0 & 0 & & \mathbf{X}_p \end{bmatrix} \begin{bmatrix} \boldsymbol{\beta}_1 \\ . \\ . \\ . \\ \boldsymbol{\beta}_p \end{bmatrix} + \begin{bmatrix} \mathbf{u}_1 \\ \mathbf{u}_2 \\ . \\ . \\ . \\ \mathbf{u}_p \end{bmatrix} \tag{59}$$

or

$$\mathbf{Y} = \mathbf{Z}_0 \boldsymbol{\beta}_0 + \mathbf{u} \tag{60}$$

with appropriately chosen notation. Least-squares estimators for the elements of $\boldsymbol{\beta}_0$ from (59) are identical with those obtainable from (1).

Zellner (1961) considered a 'feasible Aitken estimation' procedure based upon (59), which has often been described as a model with 'seemingly-unrelated equations' since, in the absence of additional constraints, they are related only through potential correlation between the errors of different constituent micro-equations. His approach can be used when the number of non-zero parameters in the dispersion matrix of the long vector of errors $\mathcal{D}(u)$ is small relative to pT. In particular, it has usually been considered when this matrix has the assumed form

$$\mathbf{E(uu')} = \begin{bmatrix} \sigma_{11}\mathbf{I} & \sigma_{12}\mathbf{I} & \dots & \sigma_{1p}\mathbf{I} \\ \sigma_{21}\mathbf{I} & \sigma_{22}\mathbf{I} & \dots & \sigma_{2p}\mathbf{I} \\ . & . & & . \\ . & . & & . \\ . & . & & . \\ \sigma_{p1}\mathbf{I} & \sigma_{p2}\mathbf{I} & \dots & \sigma_{pp}\mathbf{I} \end{bmatrix},$$

where the identity matrices $\mathbf{I}$ have order T by T. The parameters $\{\sigma_{mn}\}$ can be arranged in a symmetric matrix $\mathbf{\Sigma}$ so that we can abbreviate $\mathbf{E(uu')}$ in this case by the symbols $(\mathbf{\Sigma} \times \mathbf{I})$. A 'feasible' approach is used since $\mathbf{\Sigma}$ is generally unknown. This is defined for any particular estimator of $\mathbf{\Sigma}$, $\tilde{\mathbf{\Sigma}}$, by

$$\hat{\beta}_0 = [\mathbf{Z}'(\tilde{\mathbf{\Sigma}}^{-1} \times \mathbf{I})\mathbf{Z}]^{-1}\mathbf{Z}'(\tilde{\mathbf{\Sigma}}^{-1} \times \mathbf{I})\mathbf{Y}. \tag{61}$$

Zellner recommended the use of least-squares residuals from separate fits to the equations in (1) as basic components in the estimator $\tilde{\mathbf{\Sigma}}$. Its diagonal elements for this choice are residual sums of squares and non-diagonal elements are cross-products of residuals; all of these elements being divided by the scale factor $(T - K)$.

Two illustrations of the use of this approach in investment studies are provided by Jorgenson and Stephenson (1967a) and Guccione and Gillen (1972). The former considered subsectors for U.S. manufacturing industries and suggested that their evidence revealed 'a significant gain in efficiency for the equation estimates when the investment equation for total manufacturing was disaggregated into durable and nondurable manufacturing' and that 'significant efficiency gains can be obtained by further disaggregating the investment equation for durable and nondurable manufacturing'. Here the term efficiency applies to the relative variances of estimators as based upon formulae which only have asymptotic validity as the estimator $\tilde{\mathbf{\Sigma}}$ approaches the true matrix $\mathbf{\Sigma}$. (Recall the superiority of Aitken's estimator by comparison with other linear estimators, such as those given by the least-squares procedure.) Guccione and Gillen investigate an alternative classification of distinct total investment functions for the five traditional Canadian regions.

This approach also permits the approximate testing of the hypothesis that all β_i equal β ('perfect aggregation') since this can be easily introduced into (59) and yields (10). A simple comparison of the sums of squared residuals from two feasible Aitken fits for these two equations can be arranged as an approximate F statistic for testing the hypothesis. This is, apart from the use of $\tilde{\mathbf{\Sigma}}$, a standard test for structural change. (See Rowley (1973, Ch. 1).)

Often this inferential framework is not used and differences in parametric estimators are assessed by simple inspections of the results for different fits. On this basis, Hickman (1965) found values for output parameters' estimates which 'imply that aggregate investment can be significantly affected by shifts in the industrial composition of investment demand'. There are also some other sources of information which indicate possible parametric differences. For example, if a parameter in each of the constituent micro-equations can be associated with the elasticity of substitution for production functions at the sectoral or regional levels, then extraneous estimates of these elasticities might suggest such differences. Empirical evidence presented by Mayer (1971) might be used in this way. Clearly another example is provided by the different replacement parameters to be expected for different types of assets. Available evidence in this context does support such prior expectations and casts further doubt upon the acceptability of the popular proportionality hypothesis for replacement. A final example is provided by the simulative study of Aaron, Russek and Singer (1972).

5.6 POSTSCRIPT: SPATIAL AUTOCORRELATION

Cross-sectional data seldom have a 'natural' ordering. Thus researchers have difficulty in modelling different patterns of autocorrelation for such data. The popular specifications for time-series data, such as autoregressive and moving-average error processes, are obviously inappropriate in this context. Unfortunately past cross-sectional studies of investment have given little attention to this problem. We must look elsewhere for hints as to potentially desirable approaches for adoption in future studies. One particular source is the treatment of spatial autocorrelation by geographers. Here the papers of Cliff and Ord (1969, 1971, 1972) provide a suitable illustration. They discuss the use of a diagnostic statistic, based on least-squares residuals, for a first-order process of the form

$$u_t = \rho \sum_{t=1}^{T} c(s,t)u_s + \eta_t \qquad \text{for } t = 1, 2, ..., T. \qquad (62)$$

The weighting function $c(s,t)$ has a unit value if s and t are 'contiguous' in some sense and a zero one if they are not. ρ is an arbitrary parameter and $\{\eta_t\}$ is a white-noise sequence. Clearly two regions might be contiguous if they are spatially adjacent. Similarly assets and industries might be grouped for contiguity by Standard Industrial Classes or by other characteristics; for example, by period of fabrication, capital-intensity of production, growth-rates, joint dependence on particular sources of inputs, or patterns of ownership.

With an obvious change to matrix notation, (62) may be written as

$$\mathbf{u} = \rho \mathbf{Cu} + \eta, \qquad (63)$$

or

$$\mathbf{u} = (\mathbf{I} - \rho \mathbf{C})^{-1}\eta$$

if the inverse exists. The dispersion matrix of the errors is

$$\mathbf{E(uu')} = \sigma^2[\mathbf{I} - \rho(\mathbf{C} + \mathbf{C'}) + \rho^2\mathbf{C'C}]^{-1}. \tag{64}$$

Since $\mathbf{C}$ is usually fixed in advance, this matrix can be dependent upon 2 unknown parameters at most. Suppose the full model under consideration is given by (63) and

$$\mathbf{y} = \mathbf{X}\beta + \mathbf{u} \tag{65}$$

with familiar notation. Then, for known ρ, the Aitken estimator of β has a simple form. If ρ is unknown, the model might be transformed to yield

$$\mathbf{y} = \mathbf{C}\mathbf{y}(\rho) + \mathbf{X}\beta - \mathbf{CX}(\beta\rho) + \eta. \tag{66}$$

Least-squares estimators of β can then be calculated from this equation.

Cliff and Ord (1972) indicate various approaches to tests of autocorrelation based upon quadratic forms in residuals from least-squares fits to (65) and weights based upon $\mathbf{C}$. They are clearly influenced by the Durbin–Watson statistic and the later theoretical developments that it encouraged. Perhaps, in turn, future investment studies will apply and extend the spatial approaches to autocorrelation suggested by these authors.

Some final comments

In this chapter, we have indicated the diverse ways in which aggregation and pooling of data impinge upon the specification and estimation of models. One important conclusion should emerge from our account; namely, that the interaction between data, choice of models and choice of estimators is a critical area of concern in research. It should always be considered as a fundamental part of experimental design since it imposes severe constraints upon valid actions. The theoretical relationships suggested by economic theories may have mathematical representations but these may have to be substantially altered before estimation if data are not available at appropriately disaggregated levels. Further, the form of these data may indicate the desirability of prior adjustments to eliminate known sources of bias in inferential statistics or, in some cases of anticipated parametric variability over different micro-relations, the limited scope of empirical investigations. Neglect of aggregation problems does not eliminate them whereas recognition of their existence can suggest appropriate approaches to be adopted.

CHAPTER 6

Econometric Evidence on Inventories

This chapter is concerned with the following questions of direct and immediate relevance to econometric work: choice of dependent and explanatory variables, interdependence between two or more decision variables and the heterogeneity in behaviour of inventory components. To deal with various questions in an exhaustive manner, while at the same time maintaining clarity, it is essential to keep in mind the two-way classification of type-of-industry, Production-to-Order (PTO) or Production-for-Stock (PFS), and the three-way stage-of-fabrication classification. For each of six cases, we examine both the specification and determinants of inventory changes and the relevance of broad working hypotheses such as the acceleration principle. In each case, we survey the available empirical evidence. This material is organized in the next two distinct sections, but it should be clear that they are closely connected. Section Three deals with behaviour of inventories within distributive trades and the concluding section explores the role of inventories in the dynamics of a developed economy using, in an illustrative manner, a large quarterly aggregative model of Canada, RDX2, developed by the research staff of the Bank of Canada.

6.1 PTO–PFS DISTINCTION, PRODUCTION AND FINISHED GOODS INVENTORY

The PTO–PFS distinction was introduced and elaborated in Chapter 2. In econometric work, an essential question is whether it is meaningful to regard the level of finished goods inventories as an appropriate decision variable in each broad category. This leads to consideration of backlogs as a decision variable. Furthermore, one has to tackle the question of specifying decision rules (or behavioural relations) in industries where both modes of production coexist. This provides the appropriate background against which to assess the available empirical evidence on role of sales and orders, production-smoothing and costs of adjustment in determining finished goods inventories and unfilled orders, as well as the interrelation between the last two.

PTO and PFS categories occupy polar positions in a spectrum, and it is convenient to ignore intermediate groups until later. We assume that the conceptual distinction between them can be made operational by measurement of orders, or, for instance, by using a ratio such as that between finished goods inventory and unfilled orders, as suggested by Zarnowitz (1962). The larger the value of this ratio, the smaller the importance of pure PTO, and vice versa. In an extreme case of pure PTO, no finished goods stocks are held at all, except due to lags between completion and shipment. We next consider the question of choosing the dependent variable in the PFS category. For convenience we list at the outset all the notation used in the next two sections.

Notation

Q : actual rate of production
Q^d : desired rate of production
$Q^p_{t,j}$: planned rate of production in jth quarter of tth year
I^* : desired level of finished goods inventory
I_t : actual level of finished goods inventory at the end of period t
$I_{t,j}$: actual level of finished goods inventory, jth quarter of tth year
$\hat{X}_t$: expected sales during period t
$\hat{X}_{t,j}$: expected sales in jth period of tth year
X : actual sales
U^* : unfilled orders, desired
U : unfilled orders, actual
$\hat{N}$: new orders, expected
N : new orders, actual
WIP : level of work in progress
R : level of raw materials inventory
M : withdrawals from raw materials inventory
A : addition to raw materials inventory
P : price of materials and fuels
R^p : planned level of materials stocks
$\hat{X}^L$: long-term anticipated sales
$\hat{X}^1$: short-term anticipated sales
I^p : short-term planned finished goods inventory level
D : deliveries or shipments
$\Delta I^u_t = I_t - I^p_t =$ unplanned inventory change.

PFS: Choice of the dependent variable

The empirical literature shows a dichotomy between the view that it is the production decision which is basic and the view that the inventory decision is basic with production being merely the sum of inventory investment and sales. It is proposed to examine the relation between the two.

Suppose, for simplicity, that there is no other purpose served by holding inventories than to help smooth production. That is, the main cost involved in changing inventories is the cost of changing the level of production. The larger the absolute change, the greater the associated costs. Given these costs, a firm attempting to minimize them will not attempt to move to a new desired level of production Q_t^d, immediately but would rather partially adjust to that level. Define Q_t^d as follows:

$$Q_t^d = (I_t^* - I_{t-1}) + \hat{X}_t, \tag{1}$$

where the parenthetic term on the right-hand side is the desired inventory investment and the second term denotes expected sales. Next assume the partial adjustment model for planned change on production:

$$Q_t^p - Q_{t-1} = \gamma(Q_t^d - Q_{t-1}), \qquad 0 < \gamma \leq 1. \tag{2}$$

Finally assume that

$$I_t^* = \alpha + \beta\hat{X}_t. \tag{3}$$

(It is probably better to replace $\hat{X}_t$ by $\hat{X}_{t+1}$, but here we follow the argument presented in the literature.) Combining the three equations we obtain the relation for planned production:

$$Q_t^p = \gamma\alpha + \gamma(1+\beta)\hat{X}_t + (1-\gamma)Q_{t-1} - \gamma I_{t-1}. \tag{4}$$

If γ has a unit value, planned production and desired production would coincide.

Now suppose that for certain reasons to be presently considered, one chooses to work in terms of a flexible-inventory-accelerator model which states that planned inventory change is a certain proportion δ of the discrepancy between desired inventory level I_t^* and initial level I_{t-1}. Thus

$$I_t^p - I_{t-1} = \delta(I_t^* - I_{t-1}), \qquad 0 < \delta \leq 1 \tag{5}$$

which, when combined with (3), yields

$$I_t^p = \delta\alpha + \delta\beta\hat{X}_t + (1-\delta)I_{t-1}. \tag{6}$$

A question then arises whether (4) is a more appropriate behavioural equation to study than (6). Or, to put it differently, is the partial-production-adjustment model more appropriate than the partial-inventory-adjustment model? What is the relation between the two? For purposes of exposition suppose that, for residual ξ_t,

$$Q_t^p = Q_t + \xi_t \tag{7}$$

and

$$I_t^p = I_t + \xi_t, \tag{8}$$

which, when combined with (4) and (6), yield

$$Q_t = \gamma\alpha + \gamma(1+\beta)\hat{X}_t + (1-\gamma)Q_{t-1} - \gamma I_{t-1} - \xi_t, \tag{9}$$

$$\Delta I_t = \delta\alpha + \delta\beta\hat{X}_t - \delta I_{t-1} - \xi_t. \tag{10}$$

Adding X_t to both sides of (9) we obtain an equivalent equation which, for purposes of comparison with (10), may be written as

$$\Delta I_t = \gamma\alpha + \gamma(1 + \beta)\hat{X}_t + X_t + (1 - \gamma)Q_{t-1} - \gamma I_{t-1} - \xi_t. \tag{11}$$

Note that the most conspicuous difference between (9) and (11) is the absence of the lagged production variable in the latter. It appears that the choice of (10) when (11) is the correct model involves a specification error of unknown magnitude. It is worthwhile, therefore, to investigate more closely the source of the difference between the two models.

Hay (1970b) has questioned whether there are any significant costs specifically associated with changing the level of inventories other than those associated with changes in the level of production which may (or may not) be required to bring about the necessary stock adjustment. He argues that, in fact, the most important factor which is associated with changing the inventory level is the cost of changing the level of production. That being the case, the model embodied in (9) is the more appropriate focus for our attention whereas any failure of inventories to achieve their desired level will be simply a by-product of the inventory–sales–production relationship.

Notice that there is no reference here to the time-period to which the production-smoothing model refers. The inflexibility of production schedules may be a matter of days or weeks, but not quarters or years. Thus, it is reasonable to suppose that abrupt changes of the production levels are to be avoided but there is still the question of what is 'abrupt'. If a large change occurs in a matter of days, it is obviously abrupt, but it is not so if the change is distributed over many weeks or months for production cannot be completely inflexible. Moreover, what may be regarded as an abrupt change in one industry may not be so abrupt in another. The reader may recall that Modigliani and Hohn (1955) (see Ch. 2) argued that, for goods with a seasonal pattern of demand, the plan horizon would not extend beyond a full seasonal cycle. That is, the usefulness of the production-smoothing hypothesis may lie entirely in the explanation that it provides for the divergence between the seasonal pattern of demand and that of production. If this is so, the complication arising out of production-smoothing considerations may be suppressed by employing seasonally corrected data. However, this is only a weaker form of the production-smoothing hypothesis. In its stronger version, the hypothesis suggests that the pattern of production will diverge from that of sales even after a seasonal correction has been made. Is this likely to be so? Of course, this is largely an empirical matter but there are at least two factors which will determine the accuracy with which the hypothesis can be tested in practice. The first is the extent of time aggregation in the data. We should expect production smoothing to be a more fruitful hypothesis if we are examining monthly data than, say, quarterly or annual data. When dealing with data for periods longer than the production-decision period, we have to consider the possibility of revision in plans within that period. And in so doing we introduce an internal contradiction in the model. But the greater the flexibility in production planning, the closer the inventory-accelerator model comes to the production-smoothing model. A second factor which complicates tests of the production-smoothing hypothesis is high level of aggregation in the data, but, since this problem also creates other difficulties, we shall not dwell on it here.

Later in this chapter, we consider more evidence on the production-smoothing hypothesis and the assistance it gives in choosing the appropriate dependent variable and further specification.

PTO: Choice of the dependent variable

Childs (1967) and Belsley (1969) have emphasized that unfilled orders, and not just finished goods inventories, is an endogenous (or decision) variable to be studied empirically. This is in contrast to earlier work where emphasis was placed on finished goods inventories; unfilled orders being treated as exogenous. Both authors indicate how decision rules may be derived from the quadratic costs–linear constraints framework. (See Chapter 2.) For example, beginning with the quadratic cost function in period t,

$$c_1(U_t - c_{13} - c_{14}Q_t)^2 + c_2(I_t - c_{21} - c_{23}N_t)^2 + 2c_{32}Q_t + c_3(Q_t - Q_{t-1})^2,$$
$$\text{for } t = 1, ..., T,$$

where the undefined symbols are parameters. Decisions are subject to the constraints

$$N_t - D_t = U_t - U_{t-1}$$

and

$$Q_t - D_t = I_t - I_{t-1},$$

for all t, so that minimization of the present value of costs over the horizon leads to the decision rules

$$U_t = A_0 + A_1 Q_{t-1} + A_2(I_{t-1} - U_{t-1}) + \sum_{i=0}^{T} A_{3+i}\hat{N}_{t+i}, \tag{12}$$

$$I_t = B_0 + B_1 Q_{t-1} + B_2(I_{t-1} - U_{t-1}) + \sum_{i=0}^{T} B_{3+i}\hat{N}_{t+i}, \tag{13}$$

where the coefficients A_i and B_i are functions of the parameters of the cost function. Note that the form of the two behavioural relations implies a constraint on the coefficients of I_{t-1} and U_{t-1}; that is, they are equal in size and opposite in sign. The constraint only applies in the highly restrictive conditions of the model, and cannot be expected to hold in the context of aggregated industry data. This is recognized explicitly by Childs. Second, note that the two relations constitute a pair of difference equations which jointly determine the time-paths of unfilled orders and inventories, given new orders. Third, note that the framework does not provide an alternative to the flexible accelerator model, but provides a rationale for it by associating partial adjustment with the associated costs. To the extent that new orders feature in both equations, through the link with I^*, an accelerator mechanism is clearly evident. Finally, specific forecasting assumptions and stochastic specification are needed before (12) and (13) can be estimated.

Childs does not explicitly consider integrating into his framework the firm which produces goods partly to order and partly for stocks. The essential resulting complication from considering such a case, as Belsley has argued, is that the two production activities are not independent. 'If, for example, there are capacity constraints in effect', suggests Belsley, '... increased production of one line could only occur at the expense of reduced production elsewhere. Likewise, if some salable items of multiproduct firm are also used by that firm in the production of other lines, production decisions for various items cannot be made independently'. To take interdependencies into account he specifies an appropriate cost function. Using superscripts O and s to denote the stock and order components, the following equations are suggested to describe the production behaviour of the hybrid firm:

$$Q_t^O = A_0 + A_1 Q_{t-1}^s + A_2 Q_{t-1}^O + A_3(I_{t-1}^s - U_{t-1}^s) + A_4(I_{t-1}^O - U_{t-1}^O)$$
$$+ \sum_{i=0}^{T} \lambda_i \hat{N}_{t+i}^s + \sum_{i=0}^{T} w_i \hat{N}_{t+i}^O, \tag{14}$$

$$Q_t^s = B_0 + B_1 Q_{t-1}^s + B_2 Q_{t-1}^O + B_3(I_{t-1}^s - U_{t-1}^s) + B_4(I_{t-1}^O - U_{t-1}^O)$$
$$+ \sum_{i=0}^{T} \mu_i \hat{N}_{t+i}^s + \sum_{i=0}^{T} v_i \hat{N}_{t+i}^O. \tag{15}$$

Note that when there are no significant interdependencies and A_1, A_3 and λ_i are equal to zero, then (14) reduces to pure-PTO behavioural relations similar to Child's; similarly, if B_2, B_4 and v_i are zero, (15) reduces to an equation for the pure-PFS group.

Both Belsley and Childs treat the production decision as the primary consideration, inventories being determined residually.

PTO–PFS distinction: Empirical evidence

It is convenient to summarize empirical evidence collected by the two authors mentioned above. There are some further related issues concerning the PFS sector which we shall return to later. It is not intended to present a digest of regression results, for which the interested reader may consult Bridge (1971). Childs' results relate to four U.S. durable goods industries; Belsley's cover nineteen different 2-digit level S.I.C. industry groups, of which six correspond to the pure-PFS group. Both employ autoregressive forecasting formulae as well as the assumption of perfect forecasts. Estimation is by the ordinary least-squares principle.

Child's results are not robust, but they lend some support to the hypothesis that unfilled orders and finished goods inventories have a joint buffer-stock role. Current orders, rather their than past or future values, and U_{t-1} have positive coefficients in estimates of (12) whereas Q_{t-1} and I_{t-1} have negative coefficients. The former confirms the practice of production smoothing, though its relative importance is not found to be great. The inventory equation (13) is very weak, and hardly any variable other than I_{t-1} has a coefficient significantly different from zero. Only for unfilled orders does Childs get reasonably strong empirical validation of his model.

Belsley's results for the six 'pure' PFS industries indicate that, although the coefficient of Q_{t-1} is frequently statistically significant, especially when seasonally unadjusted data are used, its role is small relative to that of expected sales. A similar conclusion for I_{t-1} also holds which suggests that, although the costs of carrying inventories and changing the rate of production are not negligible, neither are they of more than minor importance relative to expected sales which largely determine the rate of production. The same conclusion holds for the PFS component of hybrid industries which indicates that 'cross effects' are unimportant. Finally, the production-smoothing considerations are found to be much more important for the PTO component, and the role of expected new orders quantitatively less important than for the PTS group. This last result is quite important but is conditional on the quality of data (which for Belsley's study is not very high), the estimation procedure and so on.

PFS: Further evidence on finished goods inventory

In this section, we consider the results on finished goods inventory which directly use the flexible-accelerator framework without starting from cost functions. We also reconsider production-smoothing and the buffer-stock role played by inventories by reference to Lovell (1961), Hirsch and Lovell (1969), Johnston (1961) and Trivedi (1970c).

In the simplest version of the flexible accelerator model, we specify

$$\Delta I_t^p = \delta[(\alpha + \beta \hat{X}_t) - I_{t-1}] = \delta\alpha + \delta\beta\hat{X}_t - \delta I_{t-1}$$

and

$$\Delta I_t^u = \lambda(\hat{X}_t - X_t) \tag{16}$$

which, when added together, yield

$$\Delta I_t = \delta\alpha + (\delta\beta + \lambda)\hat{X}_t - \lambda X_t - \delta I_{t-1}. \tag{17}$$

Here λ may be interpreted as the 'coefficient of production flexibility' in the sense that a unit value implies that inventories bear the full brunt of errors in sales anticipation whereas a zero value implies full adjustment of production plans to such errors. A contentious issue has been the identification and estimation of λ given that, in absence of sales anticipatory data, $\hat{X}_t$ must be replaced by a proxy variable(s) in (17). For instance, Lovell (1961) estimated this equation on the assumption that the forecast is a weighted sum of current and past value; that is,

$$\hat{X}_t = \rho X_t + (1 - \rho)X_{t-1}. \tag{18}$$

Substitution in (17) yields

$$\Delta I_t = \delta\alpha + \delta\beta X_t - (\delta\beta + \lambda)\rho\Delta X_t - \delta I_{t-1}. \tag{19}$$

Clearly with four coefficients and five parameters λ can only be estimated conditional on a given value of ρ and vice versa. Thus it is not possible to distinguish between the case of inflexible production plans and accurate forecasts on one hand, and flexible production plans and inaccurate forecasts on the other. The ambiguity is troublesome since several empirical findings, Lovell (1961) and Trivedi (1970c), find ΔX_t to be an important explanatory variable. It may be noted that an unambiguous determination of λ would provide one way of measuring unplanned stocks.

It is useful to examine some evidence based on anticipatory data such as that given in Hirsch and Lovell (1969) which is based at the firm level. They were able to estimate the following version of equation (17):

$$I_t^p - I_{t-1}^p = \delta\beta_1 + \delta\beta_2 \hat{X}^L + \delta\beta_3 \hat{X}_{t+1}^s - \delta I_{t-1} + \varepsilon_t, \tag{20}$$

which differs from (17) in having two, rather than one, anticipatory variables. The sample data related to five industrial groups which varied in the number of firms included from 104 to 342. Separate estimates were obtained for 'large' and 'small' firms as well as for the pooled sample. Goodness-of-fit statistics did not reveal a particularly close fit for any one group, and in some cases the fit was distinctly poor. However, it was evident that whereas for some groups $\hat{X}^S$ has a higher explanatory power than $\hat{X}^L$, that is, β_2 is positive and β_3 is zero, yet for other groups β_3 is positive and β_2 is zero. Indeed in some cases β_2 was negative and significantly so, which suggests the firm's production schedule is so rigid that it plans on sufficing with a lower end-of-quarter inventory when current sales are expected to be higher. Another feature of the results is that δ is found to be larger for small firms than large firms in the same industry group which suggests that small firms adjust faster.

How satisfactory is the flexible accelerator model?

If the adequacy of the modified flexible accelerator model as embodied in, say, equation (17) is to be judged by its adoption in empirical econometric work, then it has proved to be an adequate working hypothesis. However, it is not a straightforward matter to assess how 'plausible' the estimates reported by different investigators are. Plausibility of estimates must depend largely on one's comprehension of the precise relationship between parameters of the theoretical model and its empirical counterpart. Carlson and Wehrs (1974) have argued that in case of the flexible accelerator model this interrelationship is too inadequately spelt out to permit a clear answer to the question: is the flexible accelerator model well supported by empirical investigations?

A starting point for this discussion is provided by Table 6.1 containing estimates of δ and λ (see equation (17)) obtained in several empirical studies.

Given these results some investigators have felt that the combination of small values of δ and λ is *a priori* implausible because the small value of δ implies a slow rate of adjustment (possibly because of adjustment costs) whereas a small value of λ implies great flexibility in production plans which in turn would suggest that the adjustment costs are rather unimportant. There is clearly a contradiction here.

Table 6.1.   Estimated Value of δ and λ

References	Total manufacturing		Durable manufacturing		Non-durable manufacturing	
	$\hat{\delta}$	$\hat{\lambda}$	$\hat{\delta}$	$\hat{\lambda}$	$\hat{\delta}$	$\hat{\lambda}$
Pashigian (1965)–Orr (1967)	0·29	−0·02	0·34	0·02	0·10	0·02
Lovell (1964)	0·24	0·05	0·31	0·03	0·12	0·07
Lovell (1967)			0·33	−0·03	0·46	0·02
Modigliani and Sauerlander (1955)					0·47	−0·06

Source: Carlson and Wehrs (1974).

Carlson and Wehrs (1974), impelled by the consideration that such an inconsistency could imply a major shortcoming of the flexible accelerator model, develop a model of a cost-minimizing firm explicitly incorporating a feature ignored in such simple models, i.e. the distinction between the firm's decision period and the econometrician's data period which may cover several decision periods. This model of expected cost minimization leads to a linear relationship between inventory changes and anticipated and actual sales, and initial inventory similar to equation (17). However, they are able to show that the size of the coefficients δ and λ will depend not only on the parameters of cost function, the sales anticipations function and the desired inventory sales ratio but *also* on the number of decision periods within the data period and the sensitivity of the production plans to changes in the length of plan horizon. A sensitivity analysis designed to suggest the combination of parameter values which could give rise to the kind of parameter values thrown up in empirical studies shows that the parametric restrictions required to make the theoretical model consistent with empirical estimates are unlikely to be satisfied by the data. Thus, they argue the flexible accelerator model in its simple form fails to withstand critical scrutiny and more complex models must be devised to furnish better explanations of the data.

The preceding discussion is an example of the difficulty (common in applied econometrics) of clearly interpreting the regression results based on highly aggregated data and rather simple theoretical models which, though they account for certain broad patterns of behaviour, fail to yield the detailed information and implications necessary to discriminate between competing hypotheses.

PFS: Production smoothing reconsidered

The question of production-smoothing is considered by Johnston (1961) where the problem is treated in a production-decision model where planned production in the jth quarter of the tth year depends upon expected sales in the current quarter and the following quarter, and previous quarter's inventory. Thus,

$$Q^{p}_{t,j} = \beta_{j+1}\hat{X}_{t,j+1} + (1 - \gamma\beta_j)\hat{X}_{t,j} - (1 - \gamma)I_{t,j-1}. \tag{21}$$

Observe that the coefficient of $\hat{X}_{t,j+1}$ depends upon the quarter to which the observation relates. He assumes that the difference between planned and actual inventory is a random variable and makes alternative assumptions with respect to the generation of expectations. The resulting equations are fitted to quarterly data for the period 1946–58 for eight U.S. industries. To allow for production-smoothing possibilities, quarterly dummy variables are introduced in the regression. This amounts to saying that production-smoothing takes the form of a systematic departure of the seasonal pattern in production from that of sales. Stocks may be built up in the 'slack' season to be used up in the peak demand period. Johnson produces evidence for this mode of behaviour.

If production-smoothing only took the form of divergences in seasonal patterns of production and sales, this complication could be suppressed in econometric studies by employing seasonally adjusted data. If, however, a much stronger form of production-smoothing prevails, the above approach will not suffice. One possibility is to introduce the previous level of production directly into a regression equation which uses seasonally adjusted data. If the lagged production variable is statistically significant, and has the correct positive sign, then this would be construed as evidence of production smoothing. Proceeding in this way Lovell (1964) finds production-smoothing a significant factor in only one out of the five U.S. industries which he studied. Using the same approach, Trivedi (1970c) found that two of the five U.K. industry groups showed some evidence of production-smoothing.

In another attempt to test the production-smoothing hypothesis using anticipatory data, Hirsch and Lovell (1969) reported that production smoothing was an important factor in explaining the realized investment in all but one of the five industries they looked at. Recall that the same study found no influence of production-smoothing considerations on planned inventory investment. They suggest that even though firms ignored the necessity to smooth production at the planning stage, they may have been forced to take it into account in their actual plant operations.

In summary, production-smoothing is not an easy hypothesis to test. Evidence suggests that the answer to the question of its importance depends on whether or not seasonally adjusted data are employed, on the appropriateness of procedures used to proxy anticipated sales and on the degrees of both industrial and temporal aggregation. Temporal aggregation is especially important, though often neglected, since production must respond to sales eventually and plans cannot always continue to remain inflexible. As a rather extreme case, consider whether we would expect production-smoothing to be a significant factor in analysing weekly data as opposed to annual data. It is clear that insofar as its importance arises from the operation of constraints which are essentially features of the short-run, we would expect weekly data to reveal production-smoothing to be a significant feature much more than annual data. Therefore, the buffer-stock motive would be more important in explaining data subject to considerable temporal aggregation.

In summary, the main motivation behind the PTO–PFS distinction is the idea that the cost-structures in the two groups are sufficiently different to give rise to differences in production and finished-goods inventory behaviour. Evidence adduced here suggests that this is so, but it is a complex matter to make inferences about differences in cost structures of two industries on basis of such evidence only. In the next section, we consider the usefulness of distinction in the specification of equations for work in progress and raw materials inventory.

6.2 WORK IN PROGRESS AND MATERIALS INVENTORY

Whereas some, for example Eisner and Strotz (1963), have questioned the usefulness of classification of inventories by stages of fabrication, other researchers, notably Mack (1967), Lovell (1961), Courchene (1967) and Trivedi (1970c), have usefully exploited the distinction in empirical work even though it is somewhat arbitrary. A key issue which arises in this context concerns the theoretical relevance of the flexible accelerator model in understanding the behaviour of work in progress and materials inventory. Another empirical issue is whether or not significant biases or loss of structural information are likely to result from aggregation of different types of inventory.

We first consider some arguments which show that in dealing with work in progress it is necessary to explicitly take into account the time-consuming nature of production. By definition the investment in work in progress is given by

$$\text{WIP}_t - \text{WIP}_{t-1} = V_t - F_t, \tag{22}$$

where

$$V_t = \sum_{i=0}^{p-1} v_i F_{t+i}; \tag{23}$$

V_t represents the value of inputs in the production process, F_t represents the value of completions, or withdrawals from the production process, the former being regarded simply as a weighted sum of finished goods, output in p periods, p being the longest production period. The sequence $\{v_i\}$ should not be treated as time invariant, though such a simplication may be helpful in some cases. Given a temporally invariant sequence $\{v_i\}$, the average production time is defined by

$$\bar{p} = \sum_{j=1}^{p-1} v_j \cdot j. \tag{24}$$

Furthermore if rate of production is constant at, say $\bar{F}$, work in progress inventory will be constant, that is,

$$\text{WIP}_t = \bar{p}\bar{F}. \tag{25}$$

If, however, an increase in the rate of consumption of inputs takes place such that no increase in output can take place for at least p periods, work in progress level will rise; the converse is true if consumption of inputs takes place at a decreasing rate. Thus, variations in the time-shape of production will lead to investment in work in progress. This tendency may reinforce, or nullify, any increase in work in progress resulting from an acceleration in the rate of production. Specific illustrations of this are provided by shortening of $\bar{p}$ by working overtime or by operating more machines; both possibilities retard the operation of the accelerator mechanism. $\bar{p}$ may vary cyclically and may be systematically related to capacity utilization. Not enough is known to us from theoretical models to suggest what factors underlie such variation. However, if it is present, it tends to vitiate the mechanical operation of the accelerator. Empirical research on the time shape of production processes throws some indirect light on this question.

Two other issues concern the validity of a stock adjustment type model and the importance of the buffer stock motive. In the case in which accelerator mechanism applies, investment in work in progress takes place at a rate determined by the rate of change of output, so it is quite usual to replace sales by an output variable, but to retain the flexible accelerator framework as in the case of finished goods inventories; but, empirical evidence has not always provided strong support for the lagged adjustment hypothesis. Abramovitz (1950; pp. 160–177, 380–388) reported that his findings for the continuous process industries in the U.S. showed work in progress investment to be related to the rate of change of output without a lag, and with slight lead in the discontinuous process industries. Stanback's study (1962), which is also not econometric, lends further support to these findings. Econometric investigation of the issue is hampered by unavailability of reliable disaggregated data. Although Lovell's (1961) results give some support to the flexible accelerator, these relate to the sum of work in progress and raw materials inventories, rather than to one component alone. Further results provided by Courchene (1967) and Trivedi (1969) provide at best only weak support for the lagged adjustment hypothesis, leaving open a distinct possibility that various other factors such as changes in composition of goods and time profile of production dominate the mechanical role of the accelerator. Lastly, mention must be made for the need to incorporate sales expectations in this context; for when we admit the possibility of accumulating work in progress between stages of production, it is possible that its behaviour is akin to that of finished goods, though its actual importance is an empirical matter.

Raw (or purchased) materials inventory

The appropriate decision variable to look at in this context is the purchases made by the firm, but published data usually relate to the observed change in materials inventories, $R_t - R_{t-1}$, which represents the difference between additions A_t and withdrawals from stocks, M_t. Beginning with the identity

$$R_t - R_{t-1} = A_t - M_t, \tag{26}$$

the variables A_t and M_t are often eliminated by use of auxiliary relations such as

$$A_t = \beta_0 + \beta_1 R_t^* + \beta_2 R_{t-1} + \beta_3 A_{t-1} \tag{27}$$

and

$$M_t = \beta_4 Q_t \tag{28}$$

or

$$M_t = \sum_{i=0}^{L} \delta_i N_{t-i}, \tag{28a}$$

where R_t^* represents the desired level of materials stocks. The logic behind (27) is simply the gradual adjustment of additions to stock to a desired level which is itself determined by either past commitments or future expectations. The choice of the appropriate variables determining R_t^* and M_t depends on the industry in question. Thus, for instance, where one is dealing with the PTO case, it seems realistic to substitute (28a) and (29) in (27);

$$R_t^* = \sum_{i=0}^{K} \alpha_i N_{t-i}, \tag{29}$$

where the integer K (like L) is unknown. Substitution into (27) and (26) yields

$$\Delta R_t = \beta_0 + \beta_1 \sum_{i=0}^{K} \alpha_i N_{t-i} - \beta_4 \sum_{i=0}^{L} \delta_i N_{t-i} + \beta_2 R_{t-1} + \beta_3 A_{t-1}. \tag{30}$$

When dealing with PFS industries modifications to (30) are needed, though not necessarily of a fundamental nature.

Some of the empirical estimates available in the literature are variants of (30). For instance, Lovell (1961) uses the level and the rate of change of output, the level of unfilled orders and the previous period's inventory level. Trivedi (1970c) uses a slightly different variant of (30) incorporating a slightly more general pattern of temporal response and a more elaborate stochastic specification, but omitting A_{t-1}. (In the specific context of (30) note that identification of α_i and δ_j ($i = 1, ..., K; j = 1, ..., L$) poses a problem since some of the terms such as $(\beta_1 \alpha_1 - \beta_4 \delta_1)$, $(\beta_1 \alpha_2 - \beta_4 \delta_2)$ could be close to zero, see Trivedi (1970c). Thus the terms with low-order lags might be wrongly thought as playing an insignificant role in the investment process).

Hirsch and Lovell (1969) is based on new OBE quarterly time series survey data at the *firm* level which include information on the following: *planned* accumulation of stocks, $R_t^P - R_{t-1}$, sales anticipations held at the beginning of quarter t concerning that quarter's sales volume, $\hat{X}^L$ sales anticipations held at the beginning of quarter $t-1$ concerning quarter's t's sales volume, $\hat{X}^s$ planned finished inventory at the end of quarter t, actual finished goods inventory at the end of period t. The availability of anticipatory data allow Hirsch and Lovell to formulate an equation in terms of variables which are usually unobserved. In their model of planned accumulation in raw material and work in progress inventories and finished goods inventories equilibrium stock is a function of anticipated sales. Thus

$$R_t^P - R_{t-1} = \beta_0 + \beta_1 \hat{X}_t^s + \beta_2(I_t^P - I_{t-1}) + \beta_3 \hat{X}_t^L + \beta_4 \hat{X}_{t+1}^L + \beta_4 R_{t-1}.$$

This model explains behaviour of small firms in the sample marginally better than that of large firms though the results as a whole are not very robust. The anticipatory variables appear to make a significant contribution to the total explanation.

To analyse realized inventory investment behaviour the authors put forward the model

$$R_t - R_{t-1} = \gamma_0 + \gamma_1 X_t + \gamma_2(I_t - I_{t-1}) + \gamma_3 \hat{X}_t^s + \gamma_4 R_{t-1} + \gamma_5 R_t^P.$$

This model is intended to test, *inter alia*, the role of plans *vis a vis* the actual outcome. Small values of γ_5, for example, indicate that departure from previously planned magnitudes is common. The results suggest that such a flexibility in plans is more common among small rather than large firms. It is also found that $\hat{X}_t^s$ is an important positive influence on realized inventory investment. But apart from these prominent uniformities the results are too mixed to make safe generalizations beyond that the accelerator model provides a slightly better explanation of realized rather than planned stocks.

In conclusion observe that there is very little econometric evidence of widespread speculation in raw materials inventories. This may be because of the simplistic formulation used to test that hypothesis, but it may also be a consequence of highly aggregated data on which empirical work is based. (Successful speculation may, for instance, take the form of changes in composition of stocks held in which case the aggregate data will obscure behaviour.) Another somewhat neglected factor is the role of supply constraints which may inhibit the realization of plans. Inclusion in the equation of a variable(s) purporting to measure the degree of capacity utilization is a step in this direction but is somewhat rudimentary in conception.

The preceding discussion utilizes a classification of stocks according to the use in the *holding* industry rather than in the *producing* industry. Insofar as the final output of one industry may be the intermediate output of another such a classification is arbitrary. Disaggregation along these lines follows the national income accounting scheme. In input–output tables which are compiled less frequently, the estimates of stock changes are by producing industry. Which of the two concepts is relevant depends upon the use to which the analysis is to be put. There is very little econometric work which utilizes the data classified by producing industry. (For some theoretical work which utilizes this concept see Kornai and Martos (1973).) Clearly the concept of the stock desired by a particular type of inventory-holder is in the latter case replaced by the concept of total desired stocks of a particular type of good. In such a framework a stock-signal to the producer can reach from any holder of that commodity and the use to which the commodity is put, intermediate or final, has no importance. Such a framework clearly has advantages over the holding industry classification.

6.3 INVENTORY BEHAVIOUR IN DISTRIBUTIVE TRADES

The basic motives underlying stockholding behaviour in retail and wholesale trade are not markedly different from those in manufacturing, so no great difference in analysis is called for. However, available econometric evidence on the distributive sector is fragmentary. (See Darling and Lovell (1965), Lovell (1968), Wallis (1965) and Trivedi (1973).) This suggests that in such cases analysis is made easier by the pronounced seasonal pattern of retail sales. Inventory investment also exhibits a pronounced seasonal pattern which 'leads' sales. Thus seasonal variation constitutes a large part of total variation of inventories, and buffer-stock models can successfully explain much of the total variation. Another feature of retailers' behaviour is the rapid response to changes in expectations which manifests itself both in the ordering policies of the retailers and probably in their pricing policies. To estimate this response accurately, it is necessary to take as finely spaced observations as possible. A third and obvious distinguishing feature is the absence of production-smoothing costs and the presence of ordering costs which is presumed to reduce the interrelatedness of inventory with other decisions.

Lovell (1968) and Trivedi (1973) provide two illustrations. The former allows for interaction between inventory and order backlogs and incorporates a clear connection between seasonal movements in inventories and the process generating sales anticipations. His empirical results relating to monthly models for seven department stores offer some 'micro' evidence in a context in which 'macro' studies predominate. Trivedi (1973), though similar to Lovell (1968), is based on more aggregated data and differs in methodological detail.

In the notation of 6.1, Lovell's model consists of two behavioural equations of the form

$$I_t = \beta_1 + \sum_{i=1}^{T} \beta_{1i}\hat{X}_{t,i} + \gamma_{11}I_{t-1} + \gamma_{12}U_{t-1} - \delta_{10}X_t - \lambda_1(X_t - \hat{X}_{t-1,1}) + \varepsilon_1,$$

$$U_t = \beta_2 + \sum_{i=1}^{T} \beta_{2i}\hat{X}_{t,i} + \gamma_{21}I_{t-1} + \gamma_{22}U_{t-1} + \lambda_2(X_t - \hat{X}_{t-1,1}) + \varepsilon_2.$$

The planned inventories at the end of period t depend upon a weighted sum of expected sales in T future periods and on initial stocks and initial unfilled orders; similarly for unfilled orders at the end of period t. To the extent that expectations are not fulfilled, actual inventory change will exceed or fall short of the planned change. Where λ_1 is unity, actual and planned changes differ by the full extent of the forecast error; where λ_1 is less than unity, the inventory change is kept (for example, by ordering on rush basis) to less than the forecast error. The same considerations underlie inclusion of the term $\lambda_2(X_t - \hat{X}_{t-1,1})$ in the unfilled orders equation. The sum of the two equations yields a relation explaining the sum of inventories unfilled orders, which Mack has called the 'ownership position'.

A noteworthy feature of this work is that the two behavioural relations in question may be interpreted as derived from cost-minimizing behaviour. The relevant cost function includes the cost of deviation from a target level of backlogs and inventories. This is reflected in the two derived equations which are interrelated in the sense that the changes in I_t and U_t are determined by the extent of disequilibrium in both I_t and U_t. The empirical results of Lovell provide support for this model of interrelated adjustment. He finds, for example, that γ_{12} and γ_{21} are approximately 0·2 and $-0·15$, respectively. If I_t and U_t were treated as adjusting independently when in fact they interact, that is, the restriction $\gamma_{12} = \gamma_{21} = 0$ is incorrect, the misspecification could lead to substantially biased estimates of speeds of adjustment. (This notion that adjustments interact is not, of course, limited to distributors' inventories. It arises in a broader context in the work of Miller (1971), Schramm (1970) and Nadiri and Rosen (1974). The ideas and their empirical implication are discussed later in this chapter.)

Lovell considers three alternative expectations-generating mechanisms

$$\hat{X}_t = w_i X_{t+i-12}, \tag{31}$$

$$\hat{X}_{t,1} = X_{t+1} + \varepsilon_t, \tag{32}$$

$$\hat{X}_{t,1} = s(t+i)X_{t,1} \quad \text{for } i > 1, \tag{33}$$

where $s(t)$ is a seasonal factor.

The first and the simplest is the 'same as corresponding period last year'; the second is the straightforward substitution of realized values for anticipated values by appeal to the rational-expectations hypothesis; the third is based on the idea that 'firms have reasonably precise notions about sales in the immediately following month, but that anticipations concerning sales volume in subsequent months are obtained by simply extrapolating on the basis of the customary seasonal pattern'.

With a constant seasonal pattern,

$$\Delta I_t = \beta_1 + \beta_1(m)X_{t+1} + (\gamma_{11} - 1)I_{t-1} + \gamma_{12}U_{t-1}$$
$$- \beta_1 X_t + \beta_1(m)\hat{\varepsilon}_t - \lambda_1\hat{\varepsilon}_{t-1} + \varepsilon_1, \tag{34}$$

$$\beta_1(m) = \beta_{11} + \sum_{i=2}^{T} \beta_{1i}s(t+i),$$

where m denotes the month of the year.

Lovell's empirical results indicate that the third forecasting scheme is perhaps the best. In the case of each store, the inventory model fits the data well and most of the estimated coefficients for (34) have expected signs and are generally significantly different from zero at 95 percent significance level. γ_{12} is found to be significantly different from zero for most stores which supports the hypothesis of interdependence between inventories and orders in the sense that inventory investment is influenced by initial level of inventories and of outstanding orders. Further, the use of an interactive dummy variable is justified by empirical results, indicating that, for each store, the monthly intercept terms are substantially different. He concludes that 'the accelerator principle provides an appropriate vehicle for describing behaviour at the level of the individual firm as well as the aggregate' (p. 36).

Despite similarities such as the use of buffer-stock principle, Trivedi (1973) contains some additional points of econometric interest. These concern the specification of expectations and seasonality in the model, the argument being that it is sensible to deal with them simultaneously. The specification which provides the centre of interest is

$$\Delta I_t = \beta_0 + \beta'_1 \hat{X}_{t+1} + \dots + \beta'_k \hat{X}_{t+k} + \beta_{k+1} I_{t-1}. \tag{35}$$

The equation has a straightforward interpretation that inventory investment depends upon a weighted sum of forecast sales in K future periods and the initial level of inventories. If (34) is 'correct', then (35) is 'misspecified'. This could be reflected partly in an inadequate fit if (35) is fitted using the available data. The extent of misspecification would depend of course on the size of γ_{12} in (34).

Substitution from Lovell's first mechanism for expectations generation in (35) yields

$$\Delta I_t = \beta_0 + \sum_{i=1}^{k} \beta_i X_{t-12+i} + \beta_{K+1} I_{t-1}, \tag{36}$$

where $\beta_i = \beta'_i w_i$.

If the seasonality in inventories is only a consequence of seasonality in sales, and has a constant temporal pattern, no seasonal shift variables need be included in (36).

Since retail sales data exhibit a fairly strong seasonal and trend variation, it is more likely that the forecasters employ a forecasting model which brings out the relationship between the same month in successive years and between successive months in the same year, for example,

$$(1 - \theta_1 B)(1 - \theta_{12} B^{12}) X_t = \xi_t \tag{37}$$

or

$$X_t = \theta_{12} X_{t-12} + \theta_1 (X_{t-1} - \theta_{12} X_{t-13}) + \xi_t,$$

where ξ_t is a random error. Here θ_{12} may be interpreted as the weight given to the corresponding month in the previous year and θ_1 the weight given to the deviation of the sales in the previous month from the value that would be obtained with a constant pattern of seasonality. The random error partly reflects the effects of cyclical forces on X_t so we should expect it to be serially correlated. Further improvements in forecasts of X_t would result from explicitly incorporating the effects of errors of forecasting in the previous periods, especially in the same 'season' of the preceding year on the grounds that there is error-learning at work. For example, we can assume

$$\xi_t = (1 - \theta_1 B)(1 - \theta_{12} B^{12})\varepsilon_t$$

$$= \varepsilon_t - \theta_1 \varepsilon_{t-1} - \theta_{12}\varepsilon_{t-12} + \theta_1\theta_{12}\varepsilon_{t-13},$$

where ε_t is (say) the Gaussian white noise process.

The suggestion that sales forecasts are generated by (37) has to be modified to take account of the fact that it is necessary to generate forecasts k periods ahead, conditional on information available at the beginning of period t; that is, conditional on X_{t-1}, X_{t-2}, ... and earlier values. Thus (ignoring ξ_t) the conditional sales forecast $\hat{X}_{t+i}$ is given by

$$\hat{X}_t = \theta_1 X_{t-1} + \theta_{12} X_{t-12} - \theta_1\theta_{12} X_{t-13},$$

$$\hat{X}_{t+i} = \theta_1 \hat{X}_{t+1-i} + \theta_{12} X_{t-12+i} - \theta_1\theta_{12} X_{t-13+i} \quad (1 \leq i \leq 11),$$

$$\hat{X}_{t+i} = \theta_1 \hat{X}_{t+1-i} + \theta_{12} \hat{X}_{t-12+i} - \theta_1\theta_{12} X_{t-13+i} \quad (i = 12),$$

$$\hat{X}_{t+i} = \theta_1 \hat{X}_{t+1-i} + \theta_{12} \hat{X}_{t-12+i} - \theta_1\theta_{12} \hat{X}_{t-13+i} \quad (i \geq 13).$$

Clearly the weighted sum of forecasts for k future periods, conditional on information at the time t, is

$$\sum_{i=1}^{k} \beta_i \hat{X}_{t+i} = \left(\sum_{i=1}^{k} \beta_i \theta_1^{i+1}\right) X_{t-1} - \theta_{12}\left(\sum_{i=1}^{k} \beta_i \theta_1^{i+1}\right) X_{t-13} \tag{38}$$

$$+ \beta_1 \theta_{12} X_{t-11} + \dots + \beta_k \theta_{12} X_{t-12+k}.$$

Substituting (38) in (35) and introducing a stochastic term we obtain

$$\Delta I_t = \beta_0 + \left(\sum_{i=1}^{k} \beta_i \theta_1^{i+1}\right) X_{t-1} - \theta_{12}\left(\sum_{i=1}^{k} \beta_i \theta_1^{i+1}\right) X_{t-13}$$

$$+ \beta_1 \theta_{12} X_{t-11} + \dots + \beta_k \theta_{12} X_{t-12+k} + \beta_{k+1} I_{t-1} + u_t. \tag{39}$$

Notice that, if greater weight were given to the forecast value for the adjacent periods than to periods in the more distant future, the coefficients of X_{t-11}, X_{t-10}, X_{t-9} and earlier values in (38) would form a decreasing sequence. Observe also that if both θ_1 and β_1 are less than unity, the coefficient of X_{t-1} should be roughly the same size as that of X_{t-13} since θ_{12} will be close to unity when the seasonal pattern of X is not evolving too rapidly. In absolute terms, we expect the coefficients of X_{t-1} and X_{t-13} to be small but not necessarily zero. But it is hardly a straightforward matter to identify θ_1, θ_{12} and β_i $(i = 1, \dots, k)$.

A methodological digression

An econometric point of some interest concerns the specification of equation (39) and equations like it which arise in studies of inventory as well as fixed investment. There are at least two aspects to it. First, whether the dynamic specification of the model is appropriately specified; second, whether the stochastic part of the equation is well specified and finally, what statistical tests are available to detect these shortcomings. The commonly applied Durbin–Watson test is just one such test and it tests only one particular parametric hypothesis concerning the stochastic specification, viz., the hypothesis of serially independent residuals against the alternative that they are generated by a first-order autoregressive process. However, there are other tests based on the autocorrelation coefficients of residuals, the cumulated periodogram of residuals, the cross-correlations between residuals and independent variables, all of which provide valuable information regarding the limitations of the model under consideration. (See Trivedi (1973) for some applications of these tests.) It is highly desirable that these should be applied where necessary. For illustrative purposes two tests due to Box and Jenkins (1970) and Pierce (1972) may be mentioned. Consider the following rational distributed lag model

$$y_t = \frac{\omega(B)}{\delta(B)} x_t + \frac{\theta(B)}{\phi(B)} e_t \qquad (t = 1, \dots, T),$$

where $\omega(B)$, $\delta(B)$, $\theta(B)$ and $\phi(B)$ are polynomials in the backward shift operator B, x_t is an endogenous variable and $\{e_t\}$ are disturbances. Equation (39) is a special case of this general model. After a particular model has been estimated the question will frequently arise whether the fit of the model is adequate. Two diagnostic tests of the goodness of fit based on estimates of residuals $\hat{e}_t$ calculated after estimating the coefficients of polynomials $\omega(B)$, $\delta(B)$, $\theta(B)$ and $\phi(B)$ are worth mentioning. They are based on the residual autocorrelation statistic

$$\hat{r}_k = \frac{\sum_{t=k+1}^{T} \hat{e}_t \hat{e}_{t+k}}{\sum_{t=1}^{T} \hat{e}_t^2}$$

and the cross-correlation statistic

$$\hat{R}_k = \frac{\sum_{t=k+1}^{T} \hat{e}_t x_{t-k}}{\left(\sum_{t=1}^{T} x_t^2 \sum_{t=1}^{T} \hat{e}_t^2 \right)^{1/2}}$$

Provided the true errors $\{e_t\}$ are serially uncorrelated, and assuming that $\{\hat{e}_t\}$ from a correctly specified model would also behave similarly, we might infer from large values of $\hat{r}_k$ that the stochastic part of the model is misspecified. Similarly large values of $\hat{R}_k$ would indicate that a better statistical fit would result from improving the dynamic specification of the model. Details of large sample tests and associated sampling theory which forms the basis of these tests is provided by Pierce (1972).

In conclusion, it is emphasized that the residuals from a fitted model should be carefully examined since they contain useful information regarding the limitation of the model. Lack of space does not permit elaboration of this point but an example conveys the essence of the argument. A model which incorporates an error-learning expectations hypothesis, such as the adaptive expectations model, leads us to expect autocorrelated errors on the equation. So it is natural to see if the residuals do in fact show serial dependence and if this were so, it would (under ideal circumstances) constitute additional evidence for the maintained hypothesis. Similarly, models incorporating (or inadvertently omitting) seasonal effects may also exhibit seasonality or periodic non-randomness in residuals which one should look out for. Previous econometric studies have unfortunately paid inadequate attention to these issues.

6.4 SPECIFICATION OF INVENTORY ADJUSTMENT EQUATIONS

A generalization of the flexible accelerator model that has recently attracted increasing attention is the multivariate flexible-accelerator model which has the form

$$(y_t - y_{t-1}) = B(y_t^* - y_{t-1}), \tag{40}$$

where $(y_t - y_{t-1})$ and $(y_t^* - y_{t-1})$ are $K \times 1$ vectors of changes in actual and desired stocks (or utilization rates of assets or inputs), B is a $(K \times K)$ matrix of adjustment rates (β_{ij}). B is not necessarily diagonal so that the adjustment rates of different inputs, say inventories and fixed investment, interact. Adjustment of y_i will depend upon differences $(y_{j,t}^* - y_{j,t-1})$ $(i \neq j, j = 1, 2, \ldots, K)$.

The matrix equation (40) is derived from minimization of total costs of adjustments of all K factors subject to a production function constraint, see for example Nadiri and Rosen (1969). The usefulness of the multivariate flexible accelerator model lies in the insight it provides into the hierarchy of adjustments. For example, the analysis suggests that if input i has high adjustment costs relative to input j, then the difference $(y_i^* - y_i)$ will have relatively more influence on the decision to change y_j, then the difference $(y_j^* - y_j)$ will have on the decision to change y_i. Thus if the costs of adjustment of fixed capital goods are high relative to cost of changing inventories, then the second decision is much lower in the hierarchy than the capital stock decision in the sense that the difference between desired and actual value of capital stock will affect changes in inventories but not vice versa.

Several authors have recently used the model of interrelated adjustments to establish a relationship between decisions concerning changes in labour and capital inputs as well as inventories, see Miller (1971), Schramm (1970) and Nadiri and Rosen (1974). Schramm's production function includes labour and capital inputs, and liquid capital which is defined to include inventories, cash, short-term securities, and receivables (net of payables) or approximately the accounting definition of working capital. He derives an investment function in which changes in investment are explained by relative prices and lagged values of capital, labour and liquid capital inputs. In a special sense, therefore, such a model integrates the role of fixed and liquid capital inputs. Nadiri and Rosen have an even more general specification of a cost function featuring seven inputs, including capital stock, capital utilization and inventories. Constrained cost minimization together with a generalized adjustment process yields a set of equations which are of the same general type as (40). However, the essential manner in which the adjustments of different inputs interact is as outlined earlier.

The notion of a generalized adjustment process is empirically useful. It has been argued that by avoiding the use of possibly arbitrary zero restrictions (e.g. $\beta_{ij} = 0$, $i \neq j$) it enables more precise estimation of the parameters of interest. Furthermore, the adjustment process embodied in such a model embraces many possibilities such as overshooting of equilibrium and feedbacks. By focusing attention on adjustments of individual inputs only, one may reach misleading conclusions regarding the speeds of response which play a very important role in efficiency of stabilization measures.

Though the notion of interrelated factor demand is suggestive, and hence useful in empirical work, strict adherence to the framework yields tractable estimating equations only when the assumed cost and production functions are mathematically convenient, for example quadratic and log–linear respectively. If, for instance, the CES form of production functions were used, the resultant factor demand equations would be quite difficult to estimate. Secondly, when only limited data of doubtful quality are available one is probably quite justified on pragmatic grounds to assume a certain hierarchy of adjustment patterns, that is, assume that some $\beta_{ij} = 0$ $(i \neq j)$, or that B is an almost decomposable matrix so that some, but not all, input adjustments are interrelated. This assumption is very common in macroeconometric models, which in general assume virtually no interaction between inventory adjustment on one hand, and fixed investment, labour demand or demand for hours on the other. At a lower level of disaggregation Miller (1971) and Nadiri and Rosen (1974) provide empirical evidence that such interactions between inventories and other inputs are significant.

A further limitation of the type of model under discussion is that it takes insufficient account of physical constraints on production. The possibility should be entertained that when capacity utilization is high, price adjustment rather than quantity adjustment is normal. Thus even if actual inventories and desired stocks diverge no adjustment could be made as long as a situation of full capacity continues. Similarly, in a situation of peak-capacity utilization of degree of interdependence between (say) demand for hours and inventories may be much smaller compared with the situation in which the employed labour force is underutilized so that carrying additional inventories is not necessary since any unforeseen increase in sales may be met by utilizing the employed labour force more intensively. We do not appear to have a sufficiently general model which would encompass these various possibilities.

6.5 INVENTORIES AND SHORT-RUN BEHAVIOUR OF THE ECONOMY

Given that one is often interested in the interactions between aggregate inventories, or a component thereof, and other expenditure and output decisions, it is useful to consider how an economy-wide econometric model provides an appropriate vehicle for investigating the short-run dynamics. In this context a number of pertinent questions to investigate are suggested in the theoretical literature. For instance, Metzler's work suggests investigations of the sensitivity of the economy to changes in lag structures of the inventory equation; Lovell's work suggests investigations into the stability of the economy when inventory investment reacts to changes in its determinants at a faster rate; Bergstrom's models (see Chapter 1) suggest an enquiry into the role of the buffer-stock mechanism in ameliorating or aggrevating fluctuations in aggregate national income; Pearce's model motivates one to examine the interrelatedness of supply decisions and unplanned inventories. Even when an aggregate econometric model is available, it is not a straightforward matter to look into these questions for several reasons. First there are the usual computational problems associated with solving large systems of dynamic non-linear equations, see Klein and Fromm (1969). Second, whereas the most widely available and used computer programmes facilitate the carrying out of dynamic simulations in a historical context, such a framework is not the most suitable for looking into questions we raised above. An alternative approach based on the notion of a steady-state simulation is explained below. Third, the inventory equation in a given econometric model may not be specified in sufficient detail to make it possible to consider all the questions mentioned above. Typically the constraints operating on builders of large models dictate a simple equation which rules out the kind of interesting simulation work we have in mind.

Suppose we have a linear structural dynamic model of the form

$$\mathbf{A}\mathbf{y}_t = \mathbf{B}\mathbf{y}_{t-1} + \mathbf{C}\mathbf{x}_t + \mathbf{D}\mathbf{x}_{t-1} + \mathbf{u}_t \qquad (t = 1, \dots, T),$$

where $\mathbf{A}, \mathbf{B}, \mathbf{C}, \mathbf{D}$ are matrices of coefficients of appropriate order, $\mathbf{y}_t$ is the vector of endogenous variables and $\mathbf{x}_t$ the vector of exogenous variables. One approach to assessing the dynamic properties of such a model is dynamic simulation which is based on calculating the time path of $\mathbf{y}_t$ by recursively solving for a sequence of time periods.

$$\mathbf{y}_t = \mathbf{A}^{-1}(\mathbf{B}\mathbf{y}_{t-1} + \mathbf{C}\mathbf{x}_t + \mathbf{D}\mathbf{x}_{t-1})$$

for a given vector of exogenous variables and lagged values of y. (An alternative analytical approach is based on calculation of all real and complex roots of the matrix $\mathbf{A}^{-1}\mathbf{B}$.) A major limitation of the method of dynamic simulation is that the actual timepath of the system is determined jointly by exogenous variables and the lag structure of the model, so that the role of the latter feature alone is often obscured. An alternative approach is to examine the response of a dynamic model to 'shocks' of various types after that model has attained its stationary or steady state. This may be done by setting $\mathbf{X}_t = \mathbf{X}_t^*$, where the latter is a vector of constants, and solving the model for a number of periods sufficiently large to reach a state in which endogenous variables attain their steady-state values. (This assumes that the model does have a steady state to which it converges. A certain amount of tinkering with the model may be necessary to ensure this, though care must be exercised so that such tinkering does not alter the essential dynamic properties one is investigating.) The steady-state solution provides us with a bench-mark with which to compare a particular 'perturbed' or 'shocked' solution; hence the use of the control solution for the former case. It is not necessary, of course, to use only one bench-mark; the particular choice simply depends on what one wants to compare. When the model is subjected to some 'shock', such as an increase in the value of the equilibrium inventory–sales ratio, the simulations will have to extend far enough into the subsequent periods to obtain reliable information about the dynamic characteristics of the economy. For a non-linear model this has the disadvantage of being computationally very expensive. Furthermore, the resulting information is no more than just one case history conditional on a given set of initial conditions.

Some illustrative steady-state simulations with RDX2

Below we report on a limited number of steady-state simulations using RDX2, a large quarterly aggregative econometric model of the Canadian economy constructed by Helliwell and associates (1971). The choice of this model was a matter of convenience resulting from the willingness of Professor Helliwell to give considerable assistance in translating our ideas into practice. However, it should be clear that RDX2 has an elaborate inventory equation which captures significant interactions between inventories and output. The model itself has been validated in many different ways, see Helliwell *et al.* (1971). The inventory equation is of the flexible accelerator type, modified by the presence of lag distributions on three expenditure series expending over current and seven previous quarters, see below. Of special interest is the buffer stock variable [UGPPS – (UGPP – IIB)] which measures the difference between aggregate supply and final demand, (UGPP – IIB), as determined within the model. The coefficient attached to this variable measures the extent to which the discrepancy between the two is met from inventories; when aggregate supply exceeds final demand, there is an addition to inventories and when final sales exceed available supply, there is a reduction in inventories. If production plans were completely flexible such that output plans could be altered to meet any potential discrepancy between supply and demand, inventories will not display marked fluctuations. In the opposite case of inflexible production plans inventories will fluctuate more.

Simulations

In our simulations of the model the initial conditions chosen were those of 1965(4), i.e. the values of all exogenous variables were fixed at this level and the model was solved repeatedly for 50 periods. The time paths of four selected variables resulting from this simulation are displayed in Figure 3 below. A perusal of these time paths indicates that 50 periods is not a sufficiently long span for the model to assume its steady-state path, assuming it exists. After about thirty-five periods it appears that the rate of change of these variables at least is 'small'. Taking into account the constraints prevailing at the time this work was done it was decided to proceed with shock control experiments from the 51st period onwards. Clearly since it should be possible to improve on this, the path traced out by the model is not the true steady-state path.

For convenience the steady-state simulations were confined to about 85 periods. Thus, when studying the response of the system to external stimuli, the system of equations was solved for 50 periods to 'start it up', before introducing a particular shock, and for about 35 periods thereafter. This aspect is also not entirely satisfactory. It would be best, therefore to treat subsequent results in this section as illustrating a method rather than providing grounds for firm conclusions.

The basic method used was the following. Fifty periods after 'starting-up' the system, the value of one of the components of demand, (XNMV12 in the original model), the exports of goods (excluding uranium, aircraft and parts, and motor vehicles and parts) to the U.S., was increased by \$25,000,000 at 1961 prices. The model was then solved for 35 periods. This is the control solution. In each subsequent experiment, the same shock was introduced at the same stage, but in addition some feature of the inventory equation was suppressed or modified; the model was then solved, and the resulting solution, termed the 'perturbed solution', compared with the control solution. A brief account of a selection of such experiments is given below.

Experiment A (Figure 4)

This is simply the control solution in which we observe the dynamic response of the system to a once for all change in the value of one component of export demand. The immediate effect of this on inventories is for the rate of investment to fall to about 50 percent of the level prevailing immediately prior to the shock. Here inventories are simply performing their function as a buffer.

The increase in aggregate demand, resulting from the initial injection of export demand, leads after three periods to increases in the rate of inventory investment through the flexible accelerator mechanism. The rate of investment reaches its maximum after thirteen periods, and then it begins to decline, reaching the minimum after twenty-six periods; then, once again it begins to increase. Note, however, that the three major components of aggregate demand enter the inventory equation with different lag structures; furthermore,

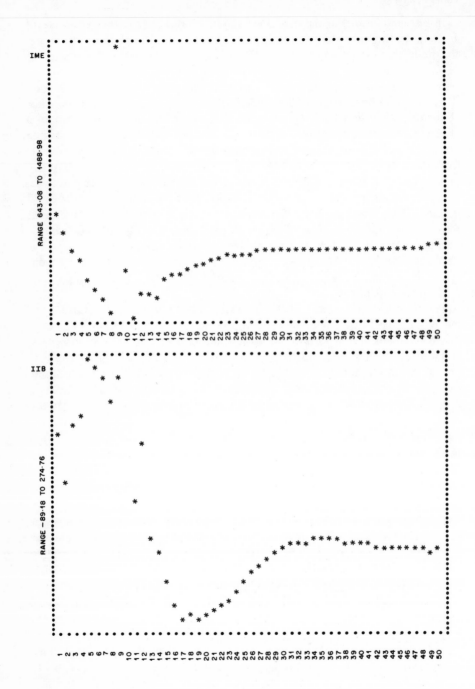

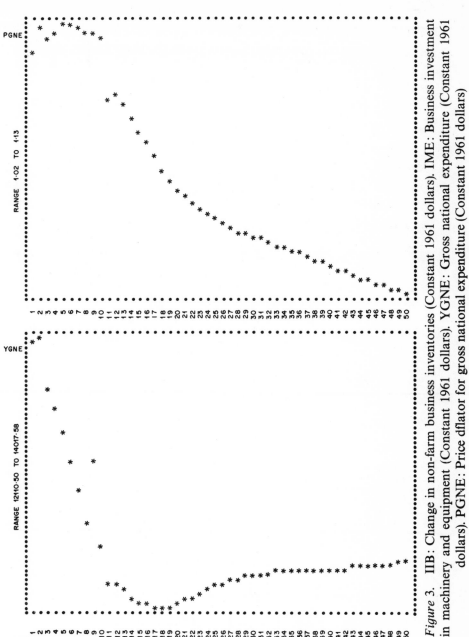

Figure 3. IIB: Change in non-farm business inventories (Constant 1961 dollars). IME: Business investment in machinery and equipment (Constant 1961 dollars). YGNE: Gross national expenditure (Constant 1961 dollars). PGNE: Price dflator for gross national expenditure (Constant 1961 dollars)

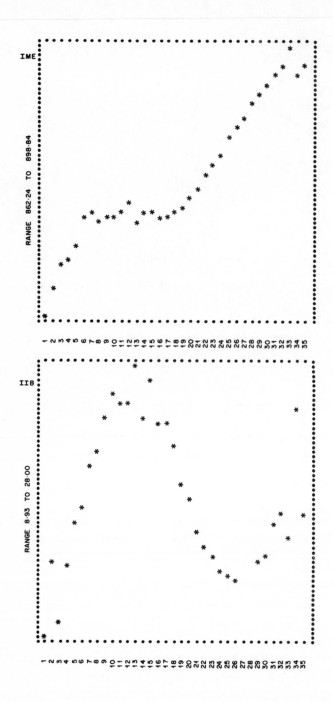

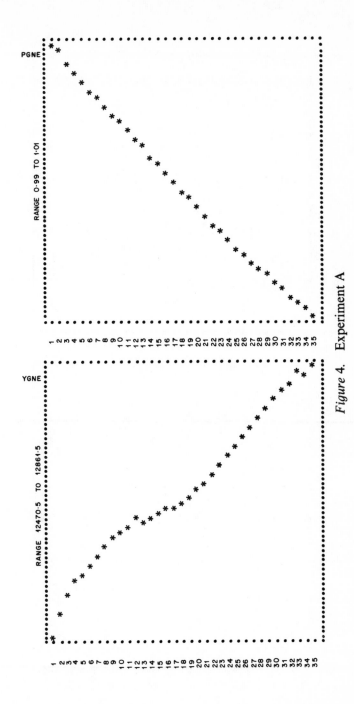

Figure 4. Experiment A

178

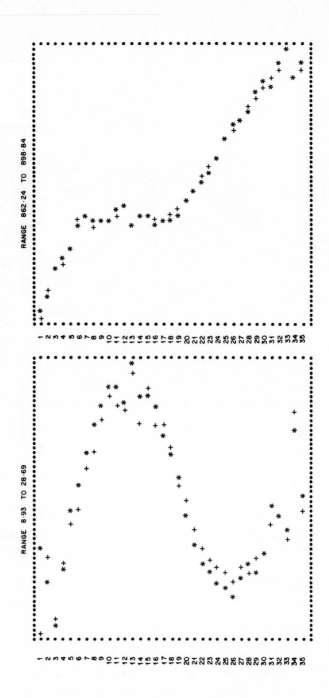

179

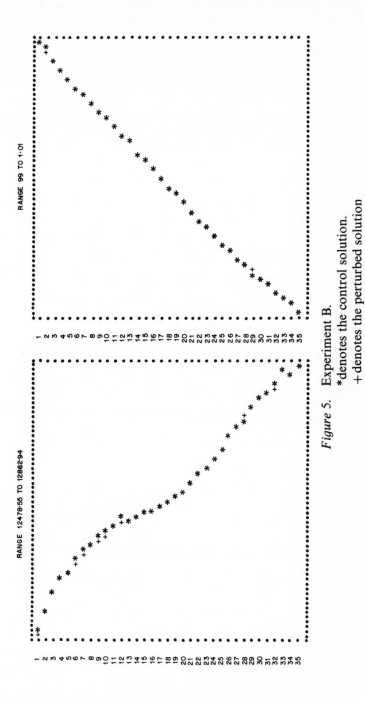

Figure 5. Experiment B.
*denotes the control solution.
+denotes the perturbed solution

the subcomponents of each of these components themselves have widely varying time paths. Thus, for example, IME changes very little from the sixth to the severnteenth period, whereas CDO and CNDSD maintain a relatively steady rate of growth in that period. A detailed examination of the timepaths of the expenditure variables suggests that the oscillations in inventory investment are closely related to the rate of change of expenditure variables. However, the pattern of interaction is fairly complex given the differences in the distributed lag response for each major expenditure variable. The main feature of interest in this case is the oscillatory time path of inventories, raising the interesting question of what factors determine the cyclicity and amplitude of this response.

Experiment B (Figure 5)

This experiment is a slight modification of experiment A. The model is subjected to the same shock as previously, but the coefficients of the distributed lag on each of the three principal expenditure variables are changed so that

$$\omega_1(0) = 0.24769, \ \omega_2(0) = -0.25542, \text{ and } \omega_3(0) = 0.06077;$$

that is, the new assigned value of the coefficient in the current period, for each variable, is the sum of the eight distributed lag coefficients. This modification simplifies the temporal response pattern implying a faster rate of response. The equilibrium sales–inventory ratio is not affected. The result of the simulation is compared, for the four selected variables, with the control solution, shown by * in Figure 5. This shows that whereas the timepaths are not radically altered, at least over the first thirty-five periods, the perturbed solution is less damped than the control solution. The effect on YGNE and UGPP is negligible, except in the very short run.

Experiment C

Experiment B was repeated with the coefficient of lagged inventories changed from -0.1609 to -0.5000, which implies a faster rate of response still but a lower marginal equilibrium inventory–sales ratio. This experiment failed in that the solution could not be computed except for the first period. The safest conclusion here is that the model is quite sensitive to such changes and such a faster rate of response of inventories may even imply dynamic instability.

RDX2 inventory equation

IIB$_t$: $373.96 + 0.00823 \text{QCK1}_t + 0.00281 \text{QCK2}_t - 0.00859 \text{QCK3}_t$
$- 0.1609 \text{KIB}_{t-1} + 0.46104 [\text{UGPPS} - (\text{UGPP} - \text{IIB})]$

$$+ \sum_{i=1}^{7} w(1,i)x_{1,i} + \sum_{i,1}^{7} w(2,i)x_{2,i} + \sum_{i,1}^{7} w(3,i)x_{3,i}$$

IIB   : Change in non-farm business inventory

QCK1 : First seasonal dummy variable multiplied by KIB_{t-1}
QCK2 : Second seasonal dummy variable multiplied by KIB_{t-1}
QCK3 : Third seasonal dummy variable multiplied by KIB_{t-1}
KIB : Stock of non-farm business inventories
UGPPS: Aggregate supply based on production function with actual factor inputs
UGPP : Gross private business product (excluding agriculture and non-commercial services)
x_1, x_2, x_3 : Three components of aggregate demand

	0	1	2	3	4	5	6	7
$w(1,i)$	0·02842	0·03485	0·03843	0·03916	0·03703	0·03205	0·02422	0·01354
$w(2,i)$	0·13186	0·04464	−0·02236	−0·06916	−0·09574	−0·10212	−0·08829	−0·05425
$w(3,i)$	0·1622	0·0862	0·0261	0·0181	−0·04634	−0·05865	−0·05503	−0·03548

6.6. CONCLUDING REMARKS

The earlier part of this chapter was concerned with assessing the empirical evidence for several alternative specifications of inventory equations which are found in the empirical literature. Later on in the chapter the basis of analysis was broadened to highlight the interconnectedness of inventories, fixed investment, demand for labour services and so on. This suggested that there may be a danger of taking a very narrow view in studying individual equations alone. Finally in Section 6.5 we illustrated the method of dynamic simulation as a way of understanding the implications of alternative specifications of an individual equation or a group of equations for the economy as a whole. This method appears to be a major available alternative to the usual method of comparison based mainly on single equation criteria. Since a major part of our interest in choosing between available alternatives arises from the possibility that their implications for the dynamic behaviour of the economy may be substantially different, then it seems appropriate to use a method of discriminating between rival specifications which uses much more information about the interaction between the individual variable one is interested in and the rest of the economy. Although dynamic simulations, such as those illustrated in 6.5, use such information and are potentially very useful, in practice they suffer from the limitation that the results of such exercises cannot be given unambiguous interpretations since there always remain in such large models non-trivial misspecifications whose effects on model simulations are difficult to evaluate. Nevertheless, with improvements in specification and estimation of large models, it should be possible to make greater use of them for understanding the detailed implications of rival specifications.

CONCLUSION

Though the subject matter of this book is the econometric work in fixed and inventory investment, many of the topics dealt with have considerable general relevance to applied econometrics. Throughout we have stressed the limitations of applied econometric work as an amalgam of economic theory, statistical estimation and inference in the presence of complex *a priori* restrictions. In surveying the 'relevant' body of economic theory we have looked for some guidance with respect to improved specification of functional form of relationships embodying all important prior information, the measurement of variables which play a significant role in the relationship(s) to be quantified, and unambiguous interpretation of the numerical results obtained. We have provided many illustrations of the failure of theoretical models to provide such guidance or to suggest econometrically relevant alternatives. If our notions about what is relevant are vague, we cannot expect to quantify them satisfactorily. The practical significance of this point is even greater if we recognize that many of the important factors such as expectational variables are unobservable. On the econometric side we have emphasized the limitations placed by imprecision of statistical methods adopted in estimation and inference, the inadequacy of many commonly used variables to reflect the influence of theoretically relevant concepts and the tentative and exploratory nature of the modelling process itself, not to mention the poor quality of data one sometimes works with. These features are in practice often so important that pragmatic and judgemental methods are applied which, though often intuitively appealing, lack a firm theoretical grounding. As a consequence applied econometrics has some in for a good deal of criticism, for example see Brunner (1972, 1973). Only further theoretical analysis will reveal the full implications of what one commonly does in applied work.

References

Aaron, H. J., K. S. Russek, Jr. and N. M. Singer (1972). 'Tax changes and the composition of fixed investment', *National Tax Journal*, **25**, 1, 1–13.

Abramovitz, M. (1939). *An Approach to a Price Theory for a Changing Economy*, Columbia University Press, New York.

Abramovitz, M. (1950). *Inventories and Business Cycles*, National Bureau of Economic Research, New York.

Agarwala, R., T. Burns and M. Duffy (1969). 'Forecasting gross private fixed investment using intentions survey data', *The Manchester School of Economic and Social Studies*, **37**, 4, 279–293.

Aigner, D. J. (1971). 'A compendium on estimation of the autoregressive–moving average model from time series data', *International Economic Review*, **12**, 3, 348–371.

Allen, R. G. D. (1966). *Mathematical Economics*, Second Edition, Macmillan, London.

Allen, R. G. D. (1967). *Macro-Economic Theory*, Macmillan, London.

Almon, S. (1965). 'The distributed lag between capital appropriations and expenditures', *Econometrica*, **33**, 178–196.

Almon, S. (1968). 'Lags between investment decisions and their causes', *Review of Economics and Statistics*, **50**, 2, 193–206.

Amemiya, T., and R. Y. Wu (1972). 'The effect of aggregation on prediction in the autoregressive model', *Journal of the American Statistical Association*, **67**, 339, 628–632.

Anderson, W. H. L. (1964). *Corporate Finance and Fixed Investment*, Division of Research, Harvard Graduate School of Business Administration, Boston.

Anderson, W. H. L. (1967). 'Business fixed investment: A marriage of fact and fancy', in R. Ferber (Ed.), *Determinants of Investment Behaviour*, Columbia University Press, New York.

Ando, A. K., F. Modigliani, R. Rasche and S. J. Turnovsky (1974). 'On the role of expectations of price and technological change in an investment function', *International Economic Review*, **15**, 2, 384–414.

Anscombe, F. J. (1960). 'Rejection of outliers', *Technometrics*, **2**, 2, 123–147.

Anscombe, F. J. (1967). 'Topics in the investigation of linear relations fitted by the method of least squares', *Journal of the Royal Statistical Society*, Series B, **29**, 1–59.

Archer, S. H., and C. A. D'Ambrosio (1967). *The Theory of Business Finance: A Book of Readings*, Macmillan, London.

Arrow, K. J. (1964). 'Optimal capital policy, the cost of capital, and myopic decision Rules', *Annals of the Institute of Statistical Mathematics*, **16**, 21–30.

Arrow, K. J., S. Karlin and H. Scarf (1958). *Studies in the Mathematical Theory of Inventory and Production*, The University Press, Stanford.

Arrow, K. J., and M. Kurz (1970). *Public Investment, the Rate of Return, and Optimal Fiscal Policy*, The Johns Hopkins Press, Baltimore.

Ashar, V. G., and T. D. Wallace (1963). 'A sampling study of minimum absolute deviations estimators', *Operations Research*, **11**, 747–758.

Astrom, V. G. (1970). *Introduction to Stochastic Control Theory*, Academic Press, New York.

Astrom, V. G., and P. Eykhoff (1971). 'System identification—A survey', *Automatica*, **7**, 123–162.

Atkinson, A. C. (1970). 'A method of discriminating between models', *Journal of the Royal Statistical Society*, Series B, **32**, 3, 323–353.

Bacon, R. W. (1972). 'On the game of miximizing $\bar{R}^2$: A comment', *Australian Economic Papers*, **11**, 19, 222–223.

Ball, R. J., and P. S. Drake (1963). 'Stock adjustment inventory models of the United Kingdom Economy', *Manchester School of Economic and Social Studies*, **31**, 87–102.

Ball, R. J., and P. S. Drake (1964). 'Investment intentions and the prediction of private gross fixed capital formation', *Economica*, **31**, 229–246.

Bancroft, T. A. (1944). 'On biases in estimation due to the use of preliminary tests of significance', *Annals of Mathematical Statistics*, **15**, 190–204.

Bancroft, T. A. (1972). 'Some recent advances in inference procedures using preliminary tests of significance', in T. A. Bancroft (Ed.), *Statistical Papers in Honor of George W. Snedecor*, Iowa State University Press, Ames.

Barna, T. (1962). *Investment and Growth Policies in British Industrial Firms*, The University Press, Cambridge.

Bartlett, M. S. (1946). 'On the theoretical specification and sampling properties of auto-correlated time series', *Journal of the Royal Statistical Society (Supplement)*, **7**, 27–41.

Baumol, W. J. (1970). *Economic Dynamics*, Third Edition, Collier-Macmillan, New York.

Beale, E. M. L. (1970). 'Selecting an optimal subset' in J. Abadie (Ed.), *Integer and Non-linear Programming*, North-Holland, Amsterdam.

Beale, E. M. L., M. G. Kendall and D. W. Mann (1967). 'The discarding of variables in multivariate analysis', *Biometrika*, **54**, 3 and 4, 357–366.

Belsley, D. A. (1969). *Industry Production Behaviour: The Order-Stock Distinction*, North-Holland, Amsterdam.

Belsley, D. A. (1972). 'Specification with deflated variables and specious spurious correlation', *Econometrica*, **40**, 5, 923–927.

Bergstrom, A. R. (1966). 'Nonrecursive models as discrete approximations to systems of stochastic differential equations', *Econometrica*, **34**, 1, 173–182.

Bergstrom, A. R. (1967). *The Construction and Use of Economic Models*, English Universities Press, New York.

Bierwag, G. O., and M. A. Grove (1966). 'Aggregate Koyck functions', *Econometrica*, **34**, 4, 828–832.

Bischoff, C. W. (1969). 'Hypothesis testing and the demand for capital goods', *Review of Economics and Statistics*, **51**, 3, 354–368.

Bischoff, C. W. (1971a). 'The effect of alternative lag distributions', in G. Fromm (Ed.), *Tax Incentives and Capital Spending*, The Brookings Institution, Washington.

Bischoff, C. W. (1971b). 'Business investment in the 1970s: A comparison of models', *Brookings Papers in Economic Activity*, 1, 13–63.

Blattberg, R., and T. Sargent (1971). 'Regression with non-Gaussian stable disturbances: Some sampling results', *Econometrica*, **39**, 3, 501–510.

Bock, M. E., G. G. Judge and T. A. Yancey (1973a). 'Some comments on estimation in regression after preliminary tests of significance', *Journal of Econometrics*, **1**, 2, 191–200.

Bock, M. E., G. G. Judge and T. A. Yancey (1973b). 'The statistical consequences of preliminary test estimators in regression', *Journal of the American Statistical Association*, **68**, 341, 109–116.

Bock, M. E., G. G. Judge and T. A. Yancey (1974). 'Post data model evaluation', *Review of Economics and Statistics*, **56**, 2, 245–253.

Boot, J. C. G., and G. M. De Wit (1960). 'Investment demand: An empirical contribution to the aggregation problem', *International Economic Review*, **1**, 1, 3–30.

Borch, K. (1973). 'The place of uncertainty in the theories of the Austrian School', in J. R. Hicks and W. Weber (Eds.), *Carl Menger and the Austrian School of Economics*, The Clarendon Press, Oxford.

Bossons, J., and F. Modigliani (1960). 'The source of regressiveness in surveys of businessmen's short-term expectations', in Hart *et al.* (Eds.), pp. 239–259.

Box, G. E. P., and G. M. Jenkins (1970). *Time Series Analysis, Forecasting and Control*, Holden-Day, San Francisco.

Brannon, G. M. (1972). 'The effects of tax incentives for business investment: A survey of economic evidence', in *The Economics of Federal Subsidy Programs, Part 3—Tax Subsidies*, Joint Economic Committee, U.S. Government Printing Office, Washington.

Brechling, F. (1973). *Investment and Employment Decisions*, The University Press, Manchester.

Brewer, K. R. W. (1973). 'Some consequences of temporal aggregation and symmetric sampling for ARMA and ARMAX models', *Journal of Econometrics*, **1**, 2, 133–154.

Bridge, J. L. (1971). *Applied Econometrics*, North-Holland, Amsterdam.

Brown, B. M. (1965). *The Mathematical Theory of Linear Systems*, Chapman and Hall, London.

Brunner, K. (Ed.) (1972). *Problems and Issues in Current Econometric Practice*, Ohio State University, Columbus, Ohio.

Brunner, K. (Ed.) (1973). Review of *Econometric Models of Cyclical Behaviour*, B. G. Hickman (Ed.), *Journal of Economic Literature*, **XI**, 3, 926–933.

Campagna, A. S. (1968). 'Capital appropriations and the investment decision', *Review of Economics and Statistics*, **50**, 2, 207–214.

Carlson, J. A. (1967). 'Forecasting errors and business cycles', *American Economic Review*, **57**, 3, 462–481.

Carlson, J. A. (1973). 'The production lag', *American Economic Review*, **63**, 1, 73–86.

Carlson, J. A., and T. B. O'Keefe (1969). 'Buffer stocks and reaction coefficients: An experiment with decision making under risk', *Review of Economic Studies*, **37 (4)**, 467–484.

Carlson, J. A., and W. E. Wehrs (1974). 'Aggregate inventory behaviour', in George Horwich and P. A. Samuelson (Eds.), *Trade, Stability and Macroeconomics: Essays in Honour of L. A. Metzler*, Academic Press, New York and London.

Chenery, H. (1952). 'Overcapacity and the acceleration principle', *Econometrica*, **20**, 1–28.

Chetty, V. K. (1971). 'Estimation of Solow's distributed lag models', *Econometrica*, **20**, 1–28.

Childs, G. C. (1967). *Inventories and Unfilled Orders*, North-Holland, Amsterdam.

Christenson, L. R., and D. W. Jorgenson (1969). 'The measurement of U.S. real capital input, 1929–1967', *Review of Income and Wealth*, **15**, 4, 293–320.

Clark, J. M. (1917). 'Business acceleration and the law of demand: A technical factor in economic cycles', *Journal of Political Economy*, **25**, March, 217–235.

Cliff, A. D., and J. K. Ord (1969). 'The problem of spatial autocorrelation', in A. J. Scott (Ed.), *London Papers in Regional Science*, Pion, London, pp. 25–55.

Cliff, A. D., and J. K. Ord (1971). 'Evaluating the percentage points of a spatial autocorrelation coefficient', *Geographical Analysis*, **3**, 1, 51–62.

Cliff, A. D., and J. K. Ord (1972). 'Testing the spatial autocorrelation among regression residuals', *Geographical Analysis*, **4**, 3, 267–284.

Clower, R. W. (1954a). 'An investigation into the dynamics of investment', *American Economic Review*, **44**, 64–81.

Clower, R. W. (1954b). 'Productivity, thrift and the rate of interest', *Economic Journal*, **64**, 107–115.

Coen, R. M. (1968). 'Effects of tax policy on investment in manufacturing', *American Economic Review*, **58**, 200–211.

Coen, R. M., and B. G. Hickman (1970). 'Constrained joint estimation of factor demand and production functions', *Review of Economics and Statistics*, **52**, 3, 287–300.

Cohen, M. (1960). 'The National Industrial Conference Board Survey of Capital Appropriations', in A. G. Hart *et al.* (Eds.), *The Quality and Economic Significance of Anticipations Data*, Princeton University Press, Princeton, for National Bureau of Economic Research, pp. 299–320.

Cohen, M., R. Gillingham and D. Heien (1973). 'A Monte Carlo study of complex finite distributed lag structures', *Annals of Economic and Social Measurement*, **2**, 1, 53–63.

Corner, D. C., and A. Williams (1965). 'The sensitivity of businesses to initial and investment allowances', *Economica*, **32**.

Courchene, T. J. (1967). 'Inventory behaviour and the stock-order distinction. An analysis by industry and stage of fabrication with empirical application to Canadian manufacturing sector', *Canadian Journal of Economics and Political Science*, **33**, 325–357.

Courchene, T. J. (1969). 'An analysis of the price–inventory nexus with empirical application to the Canadian manufacturing sector', *International Economic Review*, **10**, 3, 315–326.

Couts, D., D. Grether and M. Nerlove (1966). 'Forecasting non-stationary economic time series', *Management Science*, **13**, 1, 1–21.

Cox, D. R. (1961). 'Tests of separate families of hypotheses', in J. Neyman (Ed.), *Proceedings of the Fourth Berkeley Symposium on Mathematical Statistics and Probability; Vol. 1, Contributions to the Theory of Statistics*, University of California Press, Berkeley.

Cox, D. R. (1962). 'Further results on tests of separate families of hypotheses', *Journal of the Royal Statistical Society*, Series B, **24**, 2, 406–424.

Craine, R. (1971). 'Optimal distributed lag responses and expectations', *American Economic Review*, **61**, 5, 1–9.

Daniel, C., and F. S. Wood (1971). *Fitting Equations to Data*, Wiley, New York.

Darling, P. G., and M. C. Lovell (1965). 'Factors influencing investment in inventories', in J. S. Duesenberry *et al.* (Eds.), *The Bookings Quarterly Econometric Model of the United States*, North-Holland, Amsterdam.

De Leeuw, F., and E. M. Gramlich (1969). 'The channels of monetary policy', *Federal Reserve Bulletin*, June, 472–491.

Denison, E. F. (1969). 'Some major issues in productivity analysis: An explanation of estimates by Jorgenson and Griliches', *Survey of Current Business*, **49**(5), Part I, 1–28.

Dhrymes, P. J. (1970). 'On the game of maximizing $\bar{R}^2$', *Australian Economic Papers*, **9**, 15, 177–185.

Dhrymes, P. J. (1971). *Distributed Lags: Problems of Estimation and Formulation*, Holden-Day, San Francisco.

Dhrymes, P. J., E. P. Howrey, S. H. Hymans, J. Kmenta, E. E. Leamer, R. E. Quandt, J. B. Ramsey, H. T. Shapiro and V. Zarnowitz (1972). 'Criteria for evaluation of econometric models', *Annals of Economic and Social Measurement*, **1**, 3, 291–323.

Dhrymes, P. J., and M. Kurz (1967). 'Investment, dividend, and external finance behaviour of firms', in R. Ferber (Ed.), *Determinants of Investment Behavior*, Columbia University Press, New York.

Dow, J. C. R. (1964). *The Management of the British Economy, 1945–1960*, The University Press, Cambridge.

Draper, N. R., and H. Smith (1966). *Applied Regression Analysis*, Wiley, London.

Duesenberry, J. S., G. Fromm, L. R. Klein and E. Kuh (1965). *The Brookings Quarterly Econometric Model of the United States*, North-Holland, Amsterdam.

Durbin, J. (1961). 'Efficient fitting of continuous stationary time series from discrete data', *Bulletin of the International Statistical Institute*, **38**, 273–282.

Duris, C. S., and V. P. Sreedharan (1968). 'Chebyshev and L'—Solutions of linear equations using least squares solutions', *SIAM Journal of Numerical Analysis*, **5**, 3, 491–505.

Edwards, J. B., and G. H. Orcutt (1969). 'Should aggregation prior to estimation be the rule', *The Review of Economics and Statistics*, **51**, 4, 409–420.

Efroymson, M. A. (1960). 'Multiple regression analysis', in A. Ralston and H. S. Wilf (Eds.), *Mathematical Methods for Digital Computers*, Wiley, New York, pp. 191–203.

Einarsen, J. (1938). 'Pure and secondary reinvestment cycles', *The Review of Economic Statistics*, **20**, 1, 1–10.

Eisner, R. (1956). *Determinants of Capital Expenditures: An Interview Study*, Studies in Business Expectations and Planning No. 2, University of Illinois, Urbana.

Eisner, R. (1960). 'A distributed lag investment function', *Econometrica*, **28**, 1, 1–29.

Eisner, R. (1962). 'Investment plans and realizations', *American Economic Review*, **52**, 190–203.

Eisner, R. (1963). 'Investment: Fact and fancy', *American Economic Review*, **53**, 2, 237–246.

Eisner, R. (1964). 'Capital expenditures, profits and the acceleration principle', in *Models of Income Distribution*, NBER Studies in Income and Wealth, Princeton University Press, Princeton, pp. 137–176.

Eisner, R. (1965). 'Realization of investment anticipations', in J. S. Duesenberry *et al.* (Eds.), *The Brookings Quarterly Econometric Model of the United States*, North-Holland, Amsterdam, pp. 95–128.

Eisner, R. (1967). 'A permanent income theory for investment: Some empirical explorations', *American Economic Review*, **57**, 3, 363–390.

Eisner, R. (1969). 'Investment and the frustrations of econometricians', *American Economic Review*, **59**, 2, 50–64.

Eisner, R. (1972). 'Components of capital expenditures: Replacement and modernization versus expansion', *Review of Economics and Statistics*, **54**, 3, 297–305.

Eisner, R., and M. I. Nadiri (1968). 'Investment behavior and neoclassical theory', *Review of Economics and Statistics*, **50**, 3, 369–382.

Eisner, R., and M. I. Nadiri (1970). 'Neoclassical theory of investment behavior: A comment', *Review of Economics and Statistics*, **52**, 2, 216–222.

Eisner, R., and R. H. Strotz (1963). 'Determinants of business investment', in *Impacts of Monetary Policy*, Commission on Money and Credit, Prentice-Hall, Englewood Cliffs, pp. 60–338.

Ellison, A. P., and E. M. Stafford (1973). 'The order–delivery lag in the world's civil aircraft industry', *Applied Economics*, **5**, 19–34.

Engle, R. F., and T. C. Liu (1972). 'Effects of aggregation over time on dynamic characteristics of an econometric model', in B. G. Hickman (Ed.), *Econometric Models of Cyclical Behaviour*, Columbia University Press, New York.

Evans, G. C. (1924). 'The dynamics of monopoly', *The American Mathematical Monthly*, **31**, 77–83.

Evans, M. K., and E. W. Green (1966). 'The relative efficacy of investment anticipations', *Journal of the American Statistical Association*, **61**, 313, 104–116.

Feige, E. L., and H. W. Watts (1972). 'An investigation of the consequences of partial aggregation of micro-economic data', *Econometrica*, **40**, 2, 343–360.

Feldstein, M. S. (1973). 'Tax incentives, corporate saving, and capital accumulation in the United States', *Journal of Public Economics*, **2**, 159–171.

Feldstein, M. S. (1974). 'Tax incentives, stabilization policy and the proportional replacement hypothesis: Some negative conclusions', *Southern Economic Journal*, **40**, 4, 544–552.

Feldstein, M. S., and D. Foot (1971). 'The other half of gross investment: Replacement and modernization expenditures', *Review of Economics and Statistics*, **53**, 1, 49–58.

Feldstein, M. S., and M. Rothschild (1974). 'Towards an economic theory of replacement investment', *Econometrica* (forthcoming).

Feller, W. (1965). *An Introduction to Probability Theory and its Applications, Vol. I*, Third Edition, Wiley, New York, pp. 275–277.

Feller, W. (1971). *An Introduction to Probability Theory and its Applications, Vol. II*, Second Edition, Wiley, New York.

Ferber, R. (1953). *The Railroad Shippers' Forecasts*, University of Illinois, Bureau of Economic and Business Research, Urbana.

Ferber, R. (1960). 'The Railroad Shippers' Forecasts and the Illinois employers' labour force anticipations: A study in comparative expectations', in A. G. Hart *et al.* (Eds.), *The Quality and Economic Significance of Anticipations Data*, Princeton University Press, Princeton, for National Bureau of Economic Research, pp. 181–199.

Ferber, R. (Ed.) (1967). *Determinants of Investment Behavior*, Columbia University Press, New York.

Fisher, F. M. (1962). *A Priori Information and Time Series Analysis*, North-Holland, Amsterdam.

Fisher, W. D. (1961). 'A note on curve fitting with minimum deviations by linear programming', *Journal of the American Statistical Association*, **56**, 359–362.

Flemming, J. S., and M. S. Feldstein (1971). 'Tax policy, corporate saving and investment in Britain', *Review of Economic Studies*, 415–434.

Foot, D. K. (1970). *The Interactive Components of Gross Investment: An Industry Analysis*, Working Paper No. 7207, Institute for the Quantitative Analysis of Social and Economic Policy, Toronto.

Foss, M. F. (1963). 'The utilization of capital equipment', *Survey of Current Business*, **43**, 8–16.

Foss, M. F., and V. Natrella (1957). 'Ten years' experience with business investment anticipations', *Survey of Current Business*, **37**, 1, 16–24.

Foster, E. (1963). 'Sales forecasts and the inventory cycle', *Econometrica*, **31**, 3, 400–421.

Froehlich, B. R. (1973). 'Some estimators for a random coefficient regression model', *Journal of the American Statistical Association*, **68**, 342, 329–335.

Gabor, A., and I. F. Pearce (1952). 'A new approach to the theory of the firm', *Oxford Economic Papers*, **4**, 252–265.

Gabor, A., and I. F. Pearce (1958). 'The place of money capital in the theory of production', *Quarterly Journal of Economics*, **72**, 537–557.

Garside, M. J. (1965). 'The best subset in multiple regression analysis', *Applied Statistics*, **14**, 196–200.

Garside, M. J. (1971). 'Some computational procedures for the best subset problem', *Applied Statistics*, **20**, 1, 8–15.

Georgescu-Roegen, N. (1970). 'The economics of production', *American Economic Review*, **60**, 2, 1–9.

Glynn, D. R. (1969). 'The CBI industrial trends survey', *Applied Economics*, **1**, 183–196.

Goodwin, R. M. (1948). 'Secular and cyclical aspects of the multiplier and accelerator', in L. A. Metzler *et al.* (Ed.), *Income, Employment and Public Policy*, Norton, New York.

Gordon, M. J. (1962). *The Investment, Financing and Valuation of the Corporation*, Irwin, Homewood, Illinois.

Gordon, R. J. (1971). 'Measurement bias in price indices for capital goods', *Review of Income and Wealth*, Series 17, 2.

Gordon, R. J. (1973). 'The use of unit values to measure deviations of transaction prices from list prices', *Review of Income and Wealth*, Series 19, 3, 267–269.

Gorman, W. M. (1968). 'Measuring the quantities of fixed factors', in J. N. Wolfe (Ed.), *Value, Capital, and Growth: Papers in Honour of Sir John Hicks*, University Press, Edinburgh.

Gort, M. (1962). 'Systematic errors in budgeting capital outlays', *Review of Economics and Statistics*, **44**, 72–75.

Gould, J. P. (1968). 'Adjustment costs in the theory of investment of the firm', *Review of Economic Studies*, **35(1)**, 101, 47–55.

Gould, J. P., and R. N. Waud (1973). 'The neoclassical model of investment behaviour: Another view', *International Economic Review*, **14**, 1, 33–48.

Graybill, F. A. (1969). *Introduction to Matrices with Applications in Statistics*, Wadsworth, Belmont.

Green, H. A. J. (1964). *Aggregation in Economic Analysis*, The University Press, Princeton.

Greenberg, E. (1964). 'A stock adjustment investment model', *Econometrica*, **32**, 3, 339–357.

Greenberg, E. (1965). 'Appropriations data and the investment decision', *Journal of the American Statistical Association*, **60**, 310, 503–515.

Grether, D. M., and G. S. Maddala (1973). 'Errors in variables and serially correlated disturbances in distributed lag models', *Econometrica*, **41**, 2, 255–262.

Griliches, Z. (1967). 'Distributed lags: A survey', *Econometrica*, **35**, 1, 16–49.

Griliches, Z. (1968). 'The Brookings model volume: A review article', *Review of Economics and Statistics*, **50**, 2, 215–234.

Griliches, Z, and N. Wallace (1965). 'The determinants of investment revisited', *International Economic Review*, **6**, 3, 311–329.

Grossman, S. D. (1973). 'A test of speed of adjustment in manufacturing inventory investment', *The Quarterly Review of Economics and Business*, **13**, 3, 21–32.

Grunfeld, Y., and Z. Griliches (1960). 'Its aggregation necessarily bad?', *Review of Economics and Statistics*, **42**, 1–13.

Guccione, A., and W. J. Gillen (1972). 'A single disaggregation of a neoclassical investment function', *Journal of Regional Science*, **12**, 2, 279–294.

Hadley, G., and M. C. Kemp (1971). *Variational Methods in Economics*, North-Holland, Amsterdam.

Haley, C. W. (1971). 'Taxes, the cost of capital, and the firm's investment decisions', *The Journal of Finance*, **26**, 4, 901–917.

Hall, R. E., and D. W. Jorgenson (1967). 'Tax policy and investment behavior', *American Economic Review*, **57**, 3, 391–414.

Hall, R. E., and D. W. Jorgenson (1969). 'Tax policy and investment behavior: Further results', *American Economic Review*, **59**, 388–401.

Hall, R. E., and D. W. Jorgenson (1971). 'Application of the theory of optimal capital accumulation', in G. Fromm (Ed.), *Tax Incentives and Capital Spending*, The Brookings Institution, Washington.

Hamermesh, D. S. (1973). 'On adjustment in factor markets', *Western Economic Journal*, **11**, 1, 118–125.

Harkins, E. P., and F. J. Walsh (1968). 'Current corporate debt practices', *The Conference Board Record*, **5**, 6, 36–42.

Hart, A. G. (1942). *Anticipations, Uncertainty, and Dynamic Planning*, The University of Chicago Press, Chicago.

Hart, A. G. (1960). 'Quantitative evidence for the interwar period on the course of business expectations: A revaluation of the shippers' forecasts', in A. G. Hart *et al.* (Eds.), *The Quality and Economic Significance of Anticipations Data*, Princeton University Press, Princeton, for National Bureau of Economic Research, pp. 205–234.

Hart, A. G. (1965). 'Capital appropriations and the accelerator', *The Review of Economics and Statistics*, **47**, 2, 123–136.

Hart, A. G., F. Modigliani and G. H. Orcutt (Eds.) (1960). *The Quality and Economic Significance of Anticipations Data*, Princeton University Press, Princeton, for National Bureau of Economic Research.

Hartman, R. (1972). 'The effects of price and cost uncertainty in investment', *Journal of Economic Theory*, **5**, 2, 258–266.

Hay, G. A. (1970a). 'Adjustment costs and the flexible accelerator', *Quarterly Journal of Economics*, **84**, 1, 140–143.

Hay, G. A. (1970b). 'Production, price and inventory theory', *American Economic Review*, **60**, 4, 531–545.

Hay, G. A. (1972). 'The dynamics of firm behaviour under alternative cost structures', *American Economic Review*, **62**, 3, 403–414.

Helliwell, J., and G. Glorieux (1970). 'Forward-looking investment behaviour', *Review of Economic Studies*, **37(4)**, 112, 499–516.

Helliwell, J. F., H. T. Shapiro, G. R. Sparks, I. A. Stewart, F. W. Gorbet and D. R. Stephenson (1971). *The Structure of RDX2*, Staff Research Study No. 7. Bank of Canada, Ottawa.

Hendry, D. F., and P. K. Trivedi (1972). 'Maximum likelihood estimation of difference equations with moving average errors: a simulation study', *Review of Economic Studies*, **39**, 117–145.

Hickman, B. G. (1965). *Investment Demand and U.S. Economic Growth*, The Brookings Institution, Washington.

Hirsch, A. A., and M. C. Lovell (1969). *Sales Anticipations and Inventory Behavior*, Wiley, New York.

Hirshleifer, J. (1970). *Investment, Interest and Capital*, Prentice-Hall, Englewood Cliffs, New Jersey.

Hochman, E., O. Hochman and A. Razin (1973). 'Demand for investment in productive and financial capital', *European Economic Review*, **4**, 1, 67–83.

Hodgins, C. D., and J. E. Tanner (1973). 'Forecasting non-residential building construction', *Canadian Journal of Economics*, **6**, 1, 79–89.

Holt, C. C., and F. Modigliani (1961). 'Firm cost structures and the dynamic response of inventories, production, workforce and order to sales fluctuations', in *Inventory Fluctuations and Economic Stabilization*, Joint Economic Committee of the U.S. Congress, Washington.

Holt, C. C., F. Modigliani, J. Muth and H. Simon (1960). *Planning Production, Inventories and Work Force*, Prentice-Hall, Englewood Cliffs.

Horvat, B. (1958). 'The depreciation multiplier and a generalized theory of fixed capital costs', *The Manchester School of Economics and Social Studies*.

Houthakker, H. S., and L. D. Taylor (1966). *Consumer Demand in the United States, 1929–1970*, Harvard University Press, Cambridge.

Howrey, P. (1965). 'A note on the dampening of pure replacement cycles', *Review of Economics and Statistics*, **47**, 3, 334–337.

Ijiri, Y. (1971). 'Fundamental queries in aggregation theory', *Journal of the American Statistical Association*, **66**, 336, 766–782.

Intriligator, M. D. (1971). *Mathematical Optimization and Economic Theory*, Prentice-Hall, Englewood Cliffs.

Jack, A. B. (1966). 'The capital expenditure decision', *The Manchester School of Economic and Social Studies*, **34**, 2, 133–158.

Johnston, J. (1961). 'An econometric study of the production decision', *Quarterly Journal of Economics*, **75**, 234–261.

Jorgenson, D. W. (1963). 'Capital theory and investment behavior', *American Economic Review*, **53**, 2, 247–259.

Jorgenson, D. W. (1965). 'Anticipations and investment behavior', in J. S. Duesenberry *et al.* (Eds.), *The Brookings Quarterly Econometric Model of the United States*, North-Holland, Amsterdam, pp. 35–92.

Jorgenson, D. W. (1966). 'Rational distributed lag functions', *Econometrica*, **32**, 1, 135–148.

Jorgenson, D. W. (1967). 'The theory of investment behavior', in R. Ferber (Ed.), *Determinants of Investment Behavior*, Columbia University Press, New York, pp. 129–156.

Jorgenson, D. W. (1969). 'The demand for capital services', in K. A. Fox, J. K. Sengupta and G. V. L. Narasimham (Eds.), *Economic Models, Estimation and Risk Programming: Essays in Honor of Gerhard Tintner*, Springer-Verlag, New York.

Jorgenson, D. W. (1971). 'Econometric studies of investment behavior: A survey', *Journal of Economic Literature*, **9**, 4, 1111–1147.

Jorgenson, D. W. (1972). 'Investment behavior', *The Bell Journal of Economics and Management Science*, **3**, 1, 220–251.

Jorgenson, D. W. (1974). 'The economic theory of replacement and depreciation', in W. Sellekaerts (Ed.), *Essays in Honor of Jan Tinbergen*, North-Holland, Amsterdam.

Jorgenson, D. W., and Z. Griliches (1967). 'The explanation of productivity change', *Review of Economic Studies*, **34**, 249–283.

Jorgenson, D. W., J. Hunter and M. I. Nadiri (1970a). 'A comparison of alternative econometric models', *Econometrica*, **38**, 2, 187–212.

Jorgenson, D. W., J. Hunter and M. I. Nadiri (1970b). 'The predictive performance of econometric models of quarterly investment behavior', *Econometrica*, **38**, 2, 213–224.

Jorgenson, D. W., and C. D. Siebert (1968a). 'Optimal capital accumulation and corporate investment behavior', *Journal of Political Economy*, **76**, 6, 1123–1151.

Jorgenson, D. W., and C. D. Siebert (1968b). 'A comparison of alternative theories of corporate investment behavior', *American Economic Review*, **58**, 4, 681–712.

Jorgenson, D. W., and J. A. Stephenson (1967a). 'Investment behavior in U.S. manufacturing 1947–1960', *Econometrica*, **35**, 2, 169–220.

Jorgenson, D. W., and J. A. Stephenson (1967b). 'The time structure of investment behavior in U.S. manufacturing, 1947–1960', *Review of Economics and Statistics*, **49**, 16–27.

Jorgenson, D. W., and J. A. Stephenson (1969). 'Issues in the development of the neoclassical theory of investment behavior', *Review of Economics and Statistics*, **51**, 3, 346–353.

Kaldor, N. (1939). 'Speculation and economic stability', *Review of Economic Studies*, **7**, 1, 1–27.

Kalecki, M. (1937). 'The principle of increasing risk', *Economica*, **4**, 440–447.

Kamien, M. I., and N. L. Schwartz (1972). 'Uncertain entry and excess capacity', *American Economic Review*, **62**, 5, 918–927.

Keezer, D. M., R. P. Ulin, D. Greenwald and M. Matulis (1960). 'Observations on the predictive quality of McGraw-Hill surveys of business', in A. G. Hart *et al.* (Eds.), *The Quality and Significance of Anticipations Data*, Princeton University Press, Princeton, for National Bureau of Economic Research, pp. 369–385.

Keynes, J. M. (1936). *The General Theory of Employment, Interest and Money*, Macmillan, London.

King, M. A. (1972). 'Taxation and investment incentives in a vintage investment model', *Journal of Public Economics*, **1**, 1, 121–147.

Kiountouzis, E. A. (1973). 'Linear programming techniques in regression analysis', *Applied Statistics*, **22**, 69–73.

Kisselgoff, A., and F. Modigliani (1957). 'Private investment in the electric power industry and the acceleration principle', *Review of Economics and Statistics*, **39**, 4, 363–380.

Klein, L. R., and G. Fromm (1969). 'Solutions of the complete system', Chapter 11 in J. S. Duesenberry *et al.* (Eds.), *The Brookings Model: Some Further Results*, North-Holland Publishing Co., Amsterdam.

Klein, L. R., and R. S. Preston (1967). 'Some new results in the measurement of capacity utilization', *American Economic Review*, **57(1)**, 34–58.

Kloek, T. (1961). 'Notes on convenient matrix notation in multivariate analysis and in the theory of linear aggregation', *International Economic Review*, **1**, 351–360.

Knox, A. D. (1952). 'The acceleration principle and the theory of investment: A survey', *Economica*, **19**, 269–297.

Koerts, J., and A. P. J. Abrahamse (1970). 'The correlation coefficient in the general linear model', *European Economic Review*, **1**, 3, 401–427.

Koopmans, T. C. (1950). 'Models involving a continuous time variable', in T. C. Koopmans (Ed.), *Statistical Inference in Dynamic Economic Models*, Wiley, New York, pp. 384–392.

Kornai, J., and B. Mattos (1973). 'Autonomous control of the economic system', *Econometrica*, **41(3)**, 509–528.

Koyck, L. M. (1954). *Distributed Lags and Investment Analysis*, North-Holland, Amsterdam.

Kruskal, W. H. (1960). 'Some remarks on wild observations', *Technometrics*, **2**, 1, 1–3.

Kuh, E. (1963). *Capital Stock Growth: A Micro-Econometric Approach*, North-Holland, Amsterdam.

Lachman, L. M. (1956). *Capital and its Structure*, Bell, London.

Lange, O. (1936). 'The place of interest in the theory of production', *The Review of Economic Studies*, **3**, 159–192.

Leland, H. E. (1974). 'Production theory and the stock market', *The Bell Journal of Economics and Management Science*, **5**, 1, 125–144.

Lianos, T. P., and G. C. Rausser (1972). 'Approximate distribution of parameters in a distributed lag model', *Journal of the American Statistical Association*, **67**, 337, 64–67.

Lindley, D. V. (1968). 'The choice of variables in multiple regression', *Journal of the Royal Statistical Society*, Series B, **30**, 31–66.

Lindley, D. V., and A. F. M. Smith (1972). 'Bayes estimates for the linear model', *Journal of the Royal Statistical Society*, Series B, **34**, 1–41.

Lovell, M. C. (1961). 'Manufacturers' inventories, sales expectations and the acceleration principle', *Econometrica*, **29**, 3, 267–296.

Lovell, M. C. (1962). 'Buffer stocks, sales expectations, and the acceleration principle', *Econometrica*, **30**, 2, 267–296.

Lovell, M. C. (1963). 'Seasonal adjustment of economic time-services and multiple regression', *Journal of American Statistical Association*, **58**, 304, 993–1010.

Lovell, M. C. (1964). 'Determinants of inventory investment', in *Models of Income Distribution*, NBER Studies in Income and Wealth, Princeton University Press, Princeton, pp. 193–195.

Lovell, M. C. (1967). 'Sales anticipations, planned inventory investment, and realizations', in R. Ferber (Ed.), *Determinants of Investment Behavior*, Columbia University Press, New York.

Lovell, M. C. (1968). 'Department store inventory, sales, order relationships', in Duesenberry, Fromm, Klein and Kuh (Eds.), *The Brookings Model: Some Further Results*, North-Holland Publishing Co., Amsterdam.

Lovell, M. C., and E. Prescott (1970). 'Multiple regression with inequality constraints: Pretesting bias, hypothesis testing and efficiency', *Journal of the American Statistical Association*, **65**, 330, 913–925.

Lucas, R. E. (1967a). 'Optimal investment policy and the flexible accelerator', *International Economic Review*, **8**, 78–85.

Lucas, R. E. (1967b). 'Adjustment costs and the theory of supply', *Journal of Political Economy*, **75**, 4, 321–334.

Lundberg, E. (1968). *Instability and Economic Growth*, Yale University Press, New Haven.

Maccini, L. J. (1973a). 'On optimal delivery lags', *Journal of Economic Theory*, **6**, 107–125.

Maccini, L. J. (1973b). 'Delivery lags and the demand for investment', *Review of Economic Studies*, **40(2)**, 122, 269–281.

Mack, R. P. (1957). 'Business reasons for holding inventories and their macro-economic implications', in *Problems of Capital Formation: Concepts, Measurement and Controlling Factors*, NBER Studies in Income and Wealth, Princeton University Press, Princeton.

Mack, R. P. (1967). *Information, Expectation and Inventory Fluctuations*, Columbia University Press, New York.

Maddala, G. S., and T. D. Mount (1973). 'A comparative study of alternative estimators for variance components models used in econometric applications', *Journal of the American Statistical Association*, **68**, 342, 324–328.

Marquardt, D. W. (1970). 'Generalized inverses, ridge regression, biased linear estimation, and non-linear estimation', *Technometrics*, **12**, 3, 591–613.

Matthews, R. C. O. (1959). *The Trade Cycle*, The University Press, Cambridge.

Maurice, R. (Ed.) (1968). *National Accounts Statistics, Sources and Methods*, Her Majesty's Stationary Office, London.

Mayer, T. (1960). 'Plant and equipment lead times', *Journal of Business*, **33**, 127–132.

Mayer, T. (1971). 'Equipment expenditures by input–output industries', *Review of Economics and Statistics*, **53**, 1, 26–48.

Mayne, D. Q. (1971). 'The identification of industrial processes', *1971 IEEE Conference on Decision and Control*, Paper No. F6-1.

Merriwether, J. D. (1973). 'Small sample properties of distributed lag estimators with mis-specified lag structure', *Journal of the American Statistical Association*, **68**, 343, 568–574.

Metzler, L. A. (1941). 'The nature and stability of inventory cycles', *Review of Economics and Statistics*, **23**, 113–129.

Meyer, J. R., and R. R. Glauber (1964). *Investment Decisions, Economic Forecasting and Public Policy*, Division of Research, Graduate School of Business Administration, Harvard University, Boston.

Meyer, J. R., and E. Kuh (1957). *The Investment Decision: An Empirical Inquiry*, Harvard University Press, Cambridge.

Meyer, J. R., and E. Kuh (1963). 'Investment, liquidity, and monetary policy', in *Impacts of Monetary Policy*, Commission on Money and Credit, Prentice-Hall, Englewood Cliffs.

Miller, R. L. (1971). 'A short-term econometric model of textile industries', *American Economic Review*, **61**, 279–289.

Mills, E. S. (1957). 'The theory of inventory decisions', *Econometrica*, **25**, 2, 222–238.

Mills, E. S. (1962). *Price, Output and Inventory Policy*, John Wiley, New York.

Modigliani, F. (1957). 'Business reasons for holding inventories and their macro-economic implications', in *Problems of Capital Formation: Concepts, Measurement and Controlling Factors*, NBER Studies in Income and Wealth, The University Press, Princeton.

Modigliani, F., and K. J. Cohen (1961). *The Role of Anticipations and Plans in Economic Behavior and Their Use in Economic Analysis and Forecasting*, University of Illinois, Bureau of Economic and Business Research, Urbana.

Modigliani, F., and F. M. Hohn (1955). 'Production planning over time and the nature of the expectation and planning horizon', *Econometrica*, **23**, 1, 46–66.

Modigliani, F., and M. H. Miller (1958). 'The cost of capital, corporation finance, and the theory of investment', *The American Economic Review*, **48**, 3, 261–297.

Modigliani, F., and O. Sauerlander (1955). 'Economic expectations and plans of firms in relation to short-term forecasting', in *Short-Term Economic Forecasting*, NBER Studies in Income and Wealth, Princeton University Press, Princeton.

Modigliani, F., and R. J. Shiller (1973). 'Inflation, rational expectations and the term structure of interest rates', *Economica*, **40**, 157, 12–43.

Modigliani, F., and H. M. Weingartner (1958). 'Forecasting uses of anticipatory data for investment and sales', *Quarterly Journal of Economics*, **72**, 23–54.

Moriguchi, C. (1967). *Business, Cycles and Manufacturers' Short-Term Production Decisions*, North-Holland Publishing Co., Amsterdam.

Moriguchi, C. (1970). 'Aggregation over time in macroeconomic relations', *International Economic Review*, **II**, 3, 427–440.

Moroney, J. R. (1972). 'The current state of money and production theory', *The American Economic Review*, **62**, 2, 335–343.

Morrison, J. L. (1970). 'Small sample properties of selected distributed lag estimators', *International Economic Review*, **11**, 1, 13–23.

Muth, J. F. (1960). 'Optimal properties of exponentially weighted forecasts', *Journal of the American Statistical Association*, **55**, 290, 299–306.

Muth, J. F. (1961). 'Rational expectations and the theory of price movements', *Econometrica*, **29**, 3, 315–335.

Nadiri, M. I. (1970). 'Some approaches to the theory and measurement of total factor productivity', *Journal of Economic Literature*, **8**, 4, 1137–1177.

Nadiri, M. I., and S. Rosen (1969). 'Interrelated factor demand functions', *American Economic Review*, **59**, 4, 457–471.

Nadiri, M. I., and S. Rosen (1974). 'A disequilibrium model of demand for factors of production', *Papers and Proceedings of the American Economic Association*, May 1974, 264–270.

Neild, R. (1964). 'Replacement policy', *National Institute Economic Review*, No. 30.

Nerlove, M. (1964). 'Spectral analysis of seasonal adjustment procedures', *Econometrica*, **32**, 3, 241–286.

Nerlove, M. (1967). 'Distributed lags and unobserved components in economic time series', in W. Fellner *et al.* (Eds.), *Ten Economic Studies in the Tradition of Irving Fisher*, Wiley, New York.

Nerlove, M. (1972). 'Lags in economic behavior', *Econometrica*, **40**, 2, 221–251.

Nerlove, M., and S. Wage (1964). 'On the optimality of adaptive forecasting', *Management Science*, **10**, 2, 207–223.

Nickell, S. J. (1974a). 'On the role of expectations in the pure theory of investment', *The Review of Economic Studies*, **XLI(1)**, 125, 1–20.

Nickell, S. J. (1974b). 'On expectations, government policy and the rate of investment', forthcoming *Economica*.

Nickell, S. J. (1974c). 'A closer look at replacement investment', forthcoming *Journal of Economic Theory*.

O'Neill, R., and G. B. Wetherill (1971). 'The present state of multiple comparison methods', *Journal of the Royal Statistical Society*, Series B, **33**, 2, 218–241.

Orcutt, G. H. (1965). 'Data needs for computer simulation of large-scale social systems', in J. M. Beshers (Ed.), *Computer Methods in the Analysis of Large-Scale Social Systems*, MIT–Harvard Joint Centre of Urban Studies, Cambridge, 189–198.

Orcutt, G. H. (1968). 'Research strategy on modelling economic systems', in D. G. Watts (Ed.), *The Future of Statistics*, Academic Press, New York.

Orr, L. D. (1967). 'A comment on sales anticipation and inventory investment', *International Economic Review*, **8**, 3, 368–373.

Pashigian, B. P. (1965). 'The relevance of sales anticipatory data in explaining inventory investment', *International Economic Review*, **6**, 1, 65–91.

Pearce, I. F. (1970a). *International Trade*, Macmillan, London.

Pearce, I. F. (1970b). 'The Southampton econometric model of the U.K. and Trading partners', in K. Hilton and D. F. Heathfield (Eds.), *Econometric Research in the United Kingdom*, Macmillan, London.

Penrose, E. T. (1966). *The Theory of the Growth of the Firm*, Basil Blackwell, Oxford.

Pesando, J. E. (1972). 'Seasonal variation in distributed lag models', *Journal of the American Statistical Association*, **67**, 338, 311–312.

Pesaran, M. H. (1974). 'On the general problem of model selection', *Review of Economic Studies*, **XLI(2)**, 126, 153–172.

Phillips, A. W. (1956). 'Some notes on the estimation of time-forms of reactions in interdependent dynamic systems', *Economica*, **23**, 99–113.

Phillips, A. W. (1959). 'The estimation of parameters in systems of stochastic differential equations', *Biometrika*, **46**, 67–76.

Phillips, A. W. (1966). *Estimation of Systems of Difference Equations with Moving Average Disturbances*, Paper read to Meeting of Econometric Society in San Francisco.

Phillips, P. C. B. (1972). 'The structural estimation of a stochastic differential equation system', *Econometrica*, **40**, 1021–1041.

Pierce, D. A. (1972). 'Residual correlations and diagnostic checking in dynamic–disturbance time series models, *Journal of the American Statistical Association*, **67**, 339, 636–640.

Popkin, J. (1966). 'Comment on the distributed lag between capital appropriations and expenditures', *Econometrica*, **34**, 719–723.

Prais, S. J., and J. Aitchison (1954). 'The grouping of observations in regression analysis', *Review of the International Statistical Institute*, **1**, 1–22.

Price Statistics Review Committee (1961). *The Price Statistics of the Federal Government*, National Bureau of Economic Research, New York.

Quandt, R. E. (1974). 'A comparison of methods for testing non-nested hypotheses', *Review of Economics and Statistics*, **56**, 1, 92–99.

Quirk, J. P. (1961). 'The capital structure of firms and the risk of failure', *International Economic Review*, **2**, 2, 210–228.

Rao, M. M. (1961). 'Consistency and limit distributions of estimates of parameters in explosive stochastic difference equations', *Annals of Mathematical Statistics*, **32**, 195–218.

Resek, R. (1966). 'Investment by manufacturing firms', *Review of Economics and Statistics*, **48**, 3, 322–333.

Rothschild, M. (1971). 'On the cost of adjustment', *Quarterly Journal of Economics*, **85**, 4, 605–622.

Rowley, J. C. R. (1969). 'An econometric study of fixed capital formation in the British economy, 1956–1965', Ph.D. dissertation, University of London.

Rowley, J. C. R. (1970). 'Investment functions: Which production function?', *American Economic Review*, **60**, 5, 1008–1012.

Rowley, J. C. R. (1972a). 'Fixed capital formation in the British economy, 1956–1965', *Economica*, **39**, 154, 183–195.

Rowley, J. C. R. (1972b). 'Investment and neoclassical production functions', *Canadian Journal of Economics*, **5**, 3, 430–435.

Rowley, J. C. R. (1973). *Econometric Estimation*, Weidenfeld and Nicolson, London.

Sachs, R., and A. G. Hart (1967). 'Anticipations and investment behavior: An econometric study of quarterly time series for large firms in durable goods manufacturing', in Ferber (Ed.), *Determinants of Investment Behavior*, Columbia University Press, New York, pp. 489–536.

Sargan, J. D. (1974). 'Some discrete approximations to continuous time stochastic models', *Journal of the Royal Statistical Society*, Series B, **36**, 1, 74–90.

Sayers, R. S. (1967). 'The timing of tax payments by companies', *The Three Banks Review*, 75, 24–32.

Schatzoff, M., R. Tsao, and S. Fienberg (1968). 'Efficient calculation of all possible regressions', *Technometrics*, **10**, 4, 769–779.

Scheffé, H. (1970). 'Multiple testing versus multiple estimation, improper confidence sets, estimation of directions and ratios', *Annals of Mathematical Statistics*, **41**, 1, 1–29.

Schmidt, P. (1973). 'Calculating the power of the minimum standard error choice criterion', *International Economic Review*, **14**, 1, 253–255.

Schramm, R. (1970). 'The influence of relative prices, production conditions and adjustment costs of investment behaviour', *Review of Economic Studies*, **37(3)**, 111, 361–376.

Schramm, R. (1972). 'Neoclassical investment models and French private manufacturing investment', *American Economic Review*, **62**, 4, 553–563.

Seber, G. A. F. (1966). *The Linear Hypothesis: A General Theory*, Griffin, London.

Shaw, E. S. (1940). 'Elements of a theory of inventory', *Journal of Political Economy*, **18**, 465–485.

Shiller, R. J. (1973). 'A distributed lag estimator derived from smoothness priors', *Econometrica*, **41**, 4, 775–788.

Silbertson, A. (1970). 'Price behaviour of firms', *Economic Journal*, **80**, 319, 511–562.

Silvey, S. D. (1969). 'Multicollinearity and imprecise estimation', *Journal of the Royal Statistical Society*, Series B, **31**, 3, 539–552.

Silvey, S. D. (1970). *Statistical Inference*, Penguin Books, Harmondsworth, England.

Simon, M. (1956). 'Dynamic programming under uncertainty with a quadratic criterion function', *Econometrica*, **23**, 74–81.

Sims, C. A. (1971a). 'Approximate specification in distributed lag models', *Bulletin of the International Statistical Institute*, **44**, Part 1, 285–294.

Sims, C. A. (1971b). 'Discrete approximations to continuous time distributed lags in econometrics', *Econometrica*, **39**, 545–564.

Sims, C. A. (1972). 'Are there exogenous variables in short-run production relations', *Annals of Economic and Social Measurement*, **1**, 1, 17–35.

Sinai, A., and H. H. Stokes (1972). 'Real money balances: An omitted variable from the production function?', *The Review of Economics and Statistics*, **54**, 3, 290–296.

Smith, K. R. (1969). 'The effects of uncertainty on monopoly price, capital stock, and utilization of capital', *Journal of Economic Theory*, **1**, 1, 48–59.

Smith, K. R. (1970). 'Risk and the optimal utilization of capital', *Review of Economic Studies*, **37(2)**, 110, 253–259.

Smith, V. K. (1973). 'Least squares regression with Cauchy errors', *Oxford Bulletin of Economics and Statistics*, **35**, 3, 223–231.

Smith, V. K., and T. W. Hall (1972). 'A comparison of maximum likelihood versus blue estimators', *Review of Economics and Statistics*, **54**, 2, 186–190.

Smith, V. L. (1961). *Investment and Production*, Harvard University Press, Cambridge.

Smithies, A. (1935). 'The Austrian theory of capital in relation to partial equilibrium theory', *Quarterly Journal of Economics*, **50**, 1, 117–150.

Solomon, E. (1963). *The Theory of Financial Management*, Columbia University Press, New York.

Solow, R. M. (1960). 'On a family of lag distributions', *Econometrica*, **28**, 2, 393–406.

Stanback, T. J. (1962). *Postwar Cycles in Manufacturer's Inventories*, National Bureau of Economic Research, New York.

Steuer, M. D., and A. Budd (1968). 'Price and output decisions of firms—A critique of E. S. Mills' theory', *The Manchester School of Economic and Social Studies*, **36**, 1, 1–25.

Stevenson, F. W. (1965a). 'Tax depreciation and business resources, Part I: Background on federal tax reform, and review of the board's research', *The Conference Board Record*, **2**, 7, 6–10.

Stevenson, F. W. (1965b). 'Tax depreciation and business resources, Part II: The structure of depreciation', *The Conference Board Record*, **2**, 9, 17–22.

Stevenson, F. W. (1966). 'Tax depreciation and business resources, Part III: The guide-lines—Benefits and consequences', *The Conference Board Record*, **3**, 3, 27–34.

Sumner, M. T. (1973). 'Announcement effects of profits taxation', in M. Parkin (Ed.), *Essays in Modern Economics*, pp. 17–32.

Swamy, P. A. V. B. (1971). *Statistical Inference in Random Coefficent Models*, Springer-Verlag, New York.

Takayama, A. (1972). *The Neoclassical Theory of Investment and Adjustment Costs*, Discussion Paper No. 349, Herman C. Krannert Graduate School of Industrial Adminis-tration, Purdue University.

Tanner, J. E. (1972). 'The relative efficiency of investment anticipations and commitments as short-term forecasting devices', *Southern Economic Journal*, **39**, 2, 228–236.

Taubman, P., and M. Wilkinson (1970a). 'User cost, capital utilization, and investment theory', *International Economic Review*, **11**, 2, 209–215.

Taubman, P., and M. Wilkinson (1970b). 'User cost, output, and unexpected price changes', in E. S. Phelps *et al.* (Eds.), *Microeconomic Foundations of Employment and Inflation Theory*, Norton, New York, pp. 411–420.

Taylor, L. (1970). 'The existence of optimal distributed lags', *Review of Economic Studies*, **37**, 95–106.

Teekens, R., and J. Koerts (1972). 'Some statistical implications of the log transformation of multiplicative models', *Econometrica*, **40**, 5, 793–819.

Telser, L. G., and R. L. Graves (1972). *Functional Analysis in Mathematical Economics*, The University Press, Chicago.

Theil, H. (1954). *Linear Aggregation of Economic Relations*, North-Holland, Amsterdam.

Theil, H. (1957). 'A note on certainty equivalence in dynamic planning', *Econometrica*, **25**, 2, 346–349.

Theil, H. (1959). 'The aggregation implications of identifiable structural macrorelations', *Econometrica*, **27**, 14–29.

Theil, H. (1962). 'Alternative approaches to the aggregation problem', in E. Nagel *et al.* (Eds.), *Logic, Methodology, and Philosophy of Science*, The University Press, Stanford.

Theil, H. (1964). *Optimal Decision Rules for Government and Industry*, North-Holland, Amsterdam.

Thomas, J. J., and K. F. Wallis (1971). 'Seasonal variation in regression analysis', *Journal of the Royal Statistical Society*, Series A, 134, 54–72.

Thurow, L. C. (1969). 'A disequilibrium neoclassical investment function', *Review of Economics and Statistics*, **51**, 4, 431–435.

Tinsley, P. A. (1967). 'An application of variable weight distributed lags', *Journal of the American Statistical Association*, **62**, 320, 1272–1289.

Tinsley, P. A. (1969). 'On optimal dynamic adjustment of quasi-fixed factors', *Federal Reserve Board Special Studies*, No. 9.

Tinsley, P. A. (1970). 'On ramps, turnpikes and distributed lag approximations of optimal intertemporal adjustment', *Western Economic Journal*, **8**, 4, 397–411.

Tintner, G. (1941). 'The Theory of Choice Under Subjective Risk and Uncertainty', *Econometrica*, **9**, 298–304.

Tobin, J. (1961). 'Money, capital and other stores of value', *American Economic Review*, **51**, 26–37.

Tobin, J. (1969). 'A general equilibrium approach to monetary theory', *Journal of Money, Credit and Banking*, **1**, 15–29.

Treadway, A. B. (1969). 'On rational entrepreneurial behaviour and the demand for investment', *Review of Economic Studies*, **36(2)**, 106, 227–239.

Treadway, A. B. (1970). 'Adjustment costs and variable inputs in the theory of the competitive firm', *Journal of Economic Theory*, **2**, 4, 329–347.

Treadway, A. B. (1971). 'The rational multivariate flexible accelerator', *Econometrica*, **39**, 5, 845–855.

Trivedi, P. K. (1969). 'An econometric study of inventory behaviour in the U.K. manufacturing sector', Unpublished Ph.D. Thesis, University of London.

Trivedi, P. K. (1970a). 'The relation between the order–delivery lag and the rate of capacity utilization in the engineering industry in the United Kingdom, 1958–1967', *Economica*, **37**, 145, 54–67.

Trivedi, P. K. (1970b). 'A note on the application of Almon's method of calculating distributed lag coefficients', *Metroeconomica*, **22**, 3, 281–286.

Trivedi, P. K. (1970c). 'Inventory behaviour in U.K. manufacturing, 1956–1967', *Review of Economic Studies*, **XXXVII(4)**, 517–536.

Trivedi, P. K. (1973). 'Retail inventory investment behaviour', *Journal of Econometrics*, **1**, 1, 61–76.

Tsurumi, H. (1971). 'A note on gamma distributed lags', *International Economic Review*, **12**, 2, 317–324.

Ture, N. B. (1967). *Accelerated Depreciation in United States, 1954–1960*, Columbia University Press, New York.

Uzawa, H. (1968). 'The Penrose effect and optimum growth', *Economic Studies Quarterly* **19**.

Uzawa, H. (1969). 'Time preference and the Penrose effect in a two-class model of economic growth', *Journal of Political Economy*, **77**, 2, Part 2, 628–652.

Valentine, T. J. (1972). 'On the game of maximizing $\bar{R}^2$: A comment', *Australian Economic Papers*, **11**, 19, 220–221.

Vickers, D. (1968). *The Theory of the Firm: Production, Capital and Finance*, McGraw-Hill, New York.

Wagner, H. M. (1959). 'Linear programming techniques for regression analysis', *Journal of the American Statistical Association*, **54**, 285, 206–212.

Wallis, K. F. (1965). *Distributed Lag Relationships Between Retail Sales and Inventories*, Institute for Mathematical Studies in Social Sciences, Stanford, Technical Report 14.

Wallis, K. F. (1966).'Some Econometrics Problems in the Analysis of Inventory Cycles', Unpublished Ph.D. dissertation, Stanford University.

Wallis, K. F. (1969). 'Some recent developments in applied econometrics', *Journal of Economic Literature*, **7**, 3, 771–796.

Whitin, T. M. (1953). *The Theory of Inventory Management*, Princeton University Press, Princeton.

Witte, J. G. (1963). 'The microfoundations of the social investment function', *Journal of Political Economy*, **71**, 5, 441–456.

Wymer, C. R. (1972). 'Econometric estimation of stochastic differential equation systems', *Econometrica*, **40**, 565–577.

Yaglom, A. M. (1962). *An Introduction to the Theory of Stationary Random Functions*, Prentice-Hall, Englewood Cliffs.

Young, A. H. (1968a). 'Alternative estimates of corporate depreciation and profits: Part I', *Survey of Current Business*, **48**, 4, 17–28.

Young, A. H. (1968b), 'Alternative estimates of corporate depreciation and profits: Part II', *Survey of Current Business*, **48**, 5, 16–28.

Youngson, A. J. (1956). 'The disaggregation of investment in the study of economic growth', *Economic Journal*, **66**, 236–243.

Zarnowitz, V. (1962). 'Unfilled orders, price changes and business fluctuations', *Review of Economics and Statistics*, **44**, 367–394.

Zarnowitz, V. (1973). *Orders, Production and Investment. A Cyclical and Structural Analysis*, Columbia University Press for NBER, New York.

Zellner, A. (1961). 'Econometric estimation with temporally dependent disturbance terms', *International Economic Review*, **2**, 2, 164–178.

Zellner, A. (1969). 'On the aggregation problem: A new approach to a troublesome problem', in K. A. Fox, J. K. Sengupta and G. V. L. Narasimham (Eds.), *Economic Models, Estimation and Risk Programming: Essays in Honor of Gerhard Tintner*, Springer-Verlag, New York.

Author Index

Subject Index